Gadamer on Art and Aesthetic Experience

SUNY series in Contemporary Continental Philosophy
───────────
Dennis J. Schmidt, editor

Gadamer on Art and Aesthetic Experience

Rethinking Hermeneutical Aesthetics Today

Edited by

STEFANO MARINO and
ELENA ROMAGNOLI

Published by State University of New York Press, Albany

© 2025 State University of New York

All rights reserved

Printed in the United States of America

No part of this book may be used or reproduced in any manner whatsoever without written permission. No part of this book may be stored in a retrieval system or transmitted in any form or by any means including electronic, electrostatic, magnetic tape, mechanical, photocopying, recording, or otherwise without the prior permission in writing of the publisher.

Links to third-party websites are provided as a convenience and for informational purposes only. They do not constitute an endorsement or an approval of any of the products, services, or opinions of the organization, companies, or individuals. SUNY Press bears no responsibility for the accuracy, legality, or content of a URL, the external website, or for that of subsequent websites.

For information, contact State University of New York Press, Albany, NY
www.sunypress.edu

Library of Congress Cataloging-in-Publication Data

Names: Marino, Stefano, editor. | Romagnoli, Elena, editor.
Title: Gadamer on art and aesthetic experience : rethinking hermeneutical aesthetics today / edited by Stefano Marino and Elena Romagnoli.
Description: Albany : State University of New York Press, [2025] | Series: SUNY series, SUNY series in Contemporary Continental Philosophy | Includes bibliographical references and index.
Identifiers: ISBN 9798855800968 (hardcover : alk. paper) | ISBN 9798855800975 (ebook) | ISBN 9798855800951 (pbk. : alk. paper)
Further information is available at the Library of Congress.

Contents

Introduction. Gadamer on Art and Aesthetic Experience: Rethinking Hermeneutical Aesthetics Today — 1
Stefano Marino and Elena Romagnoli

1. Gadamer's Understanding of Art as Presentation: Study on a Key Concept of Gadamer's Philosophy — 13
Jean Grondin

2. Gadamer's Hermeneutical Aesthetics *as* Practical Philosophy — 33
Stefano Marino

3. The Aesthetics of the Invisible in Hans-Georg Gadamer — 61
Mariannina Failla

4. The "Unshapely Form" of the Work of Art: Parsing the Structure of an Irresolvable Paradox — 77
John Arthos

5. Critiquing Gadamer's Aesthetics: Hermeneutics and the Specificity of the Aesthetic — 93
Georg W. Bertram

6. Language without Sentences: The Rhythmic Nature of Art — 111
James Risser

7. Gadamer and Pareyson on Hermeneutics and Improvisation — 127
Alessandro Bertinetto

8 Playing and Reading: The Performative Paradigm in
   Gadamer's Aesthetics   147
   Elena Romagnoli

9 On the Challenge of Poetry to Thought: A Gadamerian
   Perspective   167
   Gert-Jan van der Heiden

10 Gadamerian Reflections on Celan and the Witness and
   Wounding of the Poetic Word   187
   Cynthia R. Nielsen

List of Contributors   205

Author Index   209

Introduction

Gadamer on Art and Aesthetic Experience: Rethinking Hermeneutical Aesthetics Today

STEFANO MARINO AND ELENA ROMAGNOLI

For Günter Figal (1949 to 2024),
in memoriam.

Hans-Georg Gadamer (1900 to 2002) has been undoubtedly one of the greatest figures in twentieth-century philosophy and "clearly one of the greatest exponents or interpreters of hermeneutics of our time" (Hahn 1997, XVII). Strongly influenced by the phenomenological and ontological orientation of hermeneutics that had been developed by his teacher Martin Heidegger in the 1920s, he was also capable to open new and fruitful avenues for philosophical reflection beyond Heidegger (especially thanks to his unsurpassed knowledge of Greek philosophy and his capacity to originally actualize Plato's and Aristotle's thinking, also due to his apprenticeship with the great philologist Paul Friedländer). With his groundbreaking work *Truth and Method* (1960) Gadamer established philosophical hermeneutics as one of the leading traditions of contemporary philosophy. In addition to *Truth and Method*, his major theoretical work, Gadamer also published many other works that undoubtedly established him as one of the twentieth-century thinkers who paid the most attention to some of the most demanding issues of our time, especially after what has been convincingly defined by Jean Grondin as Gadamer's "'political' or cosmopolitan broadening of his hermeneutics" from the 1970s onwards (Grondin 2003, 329). It can be said that Gadamer's fundamental philosophical task was always guided by the effort and the ambition to seek the experience of truth that transcends the domain of scientific method wherever that experience is to be found, and to inquire into its legitimacy. Hence the human sciences are connected to modes of experience that lie outside science: with the experiences of philosophy, of art, and of history itself. These are all modes of experience in which a truth is communicated that cannot be verified by the methodological means proper to science (Gadamer 2004, XXI).

In light of this ambitious task, it becomes clear that the many dimensions of Gadamer's thinking actually represent the different faces of a unitary philosophy, guided by a fundamental concept of understanding [*Verstehen*] as the quintessential feature of hermeneutical experience as such. In this general context, notwithstanding the stimulating and genuinely pluralist copresence of many different interests and concerns in Gadamer's hermeneutical conception, it can be said anyway that a special role in his thinking has always been played by the question concerning art and aesthetic experience. This importance emerges in a very clear way in the first part of *Truth and Method*, dedicated to the rediscovery of the humanist tradition for the human sciences, the critique of the subjectivization of aesthetics in modern philosophy and culture, the retrieval of the question of artistic truth, and finally the development of a hermeneutical ontology of the artwork. However, the importance of art and aesthetic experience in Gadamer's thinking is not limited to the first part of *Truth and Method* but is also testified in a clear and significant way by many subsequent writings that he devoted to the investigation of artistic phenomena (with a special focus on poetry) and that he later collected in two volumes of his *Gesammelte Werke* (GW) (see GW 8 and GW 9).

The important "history of effect [*Wirkungsgeschichte*]" of *Truth and Method* and its worldwide reception in the 1970s and 1980s (also favored by Gadamer's indefatigable activity of lecturer in many countries, including the United States), gradually led to a situation that was famously described later by the Italian hermeneutical thinker Gianni Vattimo with an emphatic and ambitious formula: hermeneutics as the new " 'koine' of philosophy and, more generally, of culture" (Vattimo 1988, 399). Of course, the widespread diffusion of philosophical hermeneutics in those decades was not only connected to the name and the work of Gadamer, but also to the perspectives disclosed and developed by other hermeneutical philosophers, including those belonging to the very relevant French and Italian traditions of hermeneutical thinking (let us simply think of Paul Ricoeur, Luigi Pareyson, and many others). However, it is also out of doubt that the role played by *Truth and Method* and Gadamer's subsequent works of the 1960s, 1970s, and 1980s was particularly relevant in order to arrive to the situation that Vattimo (perhaps too ambitiously, but not unreasonably) tried to describe with the formula of the new philosophical "koine." From the point of view of the secondary literature on Gadamer and hermeneutics, this is testified by the rich and intense publication, in those decades and also in the following years (more or less, until the year 2000, which was the year of the celebration of Gadamer's one hundredth birthday), of a great number of articles, essays, and books dedicated to the reconstruction and detailed interpretation of all aspects of Gadamer's hermeneutical thinking. Limiting ourselves to just a few publications that, in this context, it can be relevant to remind our readers of, we would like to cite, for example, the following collections of essays: *Festival of Interpretations* (Wright 1990), *Gadamer and Hermeneutics* (Silverman 1991), *Hermeneutics and Truth* (Wachterhauser 1994), *The Specter of Relativism* (Schmidt 1995), *Hermeneutische Wege* (Figal, Grondin and Schmidt 2000), *Language and Linguisticality in Gadamer's Hermeneutics* (Schmidt 2000), *Begegnungen mit Hans-Georg Gadamer* (Figal 2000), *"Sein, das verstanden werden kann, ist Sprache"* (2001), *Gadamer's Century* (Malpas, Arnswald, and Kertscher 2002), *Kunst, Hermeneutik, Philosophie* (Fehér 2003), *Gadamer verstehen / Understanding Gadamer* (Wischke and Hofer 2003), *Gadamer: bilanci e prospettive* (Gardini and Matteucci 2004), *Gadamer's Repercussions* (Krajewski 2004), *Hans Georg Gadamer: Wahrheit und Methode* (Figal 2007), and *Il cammino filosofico di Hans-Georg Gadamer* (Failla 2008). In the context of the collections of essays dedicated to Gadamer's philosophical hermeneutics, works such as *The Philosophy of Hans-Georg Gadamer* (Hahn 1997) and *The Cambridge Companion to Gadamer* (Dostal 2002) must be surely mentioned and, in a sense, probably stand out because of the excellent scientific level of the authors involved and because of the prestigious series in which these edited volumes on Gadamer were included: respectively, the Library of Living Philosophers and the Cambridge Companions dedicated to the greatest figures in Western philosophy. Finally, the year 2010 (eight years after Gadamer's death) was the year of the fiftieth anniversary of the first publication of *Truth and Method* and also this anniversary was celebrated with conferences and some edited volumes or special issues of journals dedicated to Gadamer (limiting ourselves to three examples, see Vattimo and Chiurazzi 2009; Malpas and Zabala 2010; Cattaneo, Gentili and Marino 2011).

However, by the time when Gadamer's one hundredth birthday and *Truth and Method*'s fiftieth anniversary were celebrated with conferences, events, and *Festschriften* in various countries, the age of hermeneutics as the new koine of contemporary philosophy and culture had already started to decline. In fact, different philosophical paradigms and trends had started to gain (or sometimes regain) ground, so to speak, in the contemporary philosophical scene, sometimes simply as alternatives to hermeneutical thinking and sometimes instead with an attitude of veritable opposition against it. In general, we can say that, more or less in the last twenty years, despite its being one of the most relevant voices of twentieth-century philosophy, Gadamer's hermeneutics has often seemed to be overlooked, or at least other philosophical voices have been prioritized in contemporary debates.

At a certain level, this might not represent a big problem in itself for a genuine Gadamerian approach to philosophizing: by saying this, what we mean is simply that one of Gadamer's fundamental teachings has always been that philosophical wisdom invites us "to leave questions open and to keep them open"—on the basis of the idea that "[this] is not skepticism but originates from the spiritual need for freedom"—and also that "language has its true reality only in dialogue" (Gadamer 1997, 274). So, entering in dialogue with other philosophical approaches—or, as we said, with other voices—does not represent, in principle, a problem for Gadamer's hermeneutics; after all, it was Gadamer himself, at the end of a long and important conversation with Grondin about his *Gesammelte Werke* in ten volumes, who "designated as a central point of hermeneutical procedures that one is never supposed to have the last word" (Gadamer 2007, 417), thus implicitly claiming that keeping oneself open to the dialogue with the other (both in academic philosophy and in everyday life) can be probably considered as the hermeneutical virtue par excellence. At another level, however, in the last decades it has not been simply the case of sometimes prioritizing other philosophical voices in comparison to hermeneutics, but rather the case of often forgetting and canceling Gadamer's legacy, as if the *season* of philosophical hermeneutics were now over.

There are undoubtedly several reasons for this process. On the one hand, what we can observe is the development of other philosophical currents that, although moving in certain respects from hermeneutics—that is, assuming hermeneutics as their (positive or negative) starting point gradually acquired the status of independent theories, such as Gianni Vattimo's "weak thought" or Maurizio Ferraris's "new realism." Despite their evident diversity and, to some extent, also their contraposition, both these approaches have paid a particular attention to certain aspects that were already present in Gadamer's hermeneutics, such as the relation between being and language, in order to arrive at different and, as we said, sometimes opposite conclusions, thus revealing their status of autonomous theories that—in particular with Vattimo's "weak thought"—have been retrospectively overlapped with hermeneutics. This has been pointed out by, among others, an expert scholar of Gadamer and hermeneutics, Donatella Di Cesare (2013, 189ff), who has attempted instead to reestablish the philosophical distance of hermeneutics from nihilism, while holding firm at the same time to its anti-foundationalist value.

On the other hand, the strong emergence of analytic philosophy even in countries and cultural contexts that had been previously characterized by the primacy of so-called continental philosophical approaches has certainly had a certain weight, which has led to a renewed awareness of methodological and stylistic aspects, with a strong emphasis on the relevance of the component of method also in philosophical research. Moreover, still on the continental front, perhaps as a response to the growth of analytic philosophy and also as a consequence of Habermas's famous intepretation of Gadamer's philosophy as a sort of "urbanization" of Heidegger's thought, it was possible to observe in recent times a greater centrality of French theory, often understood as more capable of proposing critical and political investigations, as in the case of Foucault's philosophy and its legacy until today, not to mention more radical approaches such as decolonial and postcolonial studies, or the complex galaxy of gender studies.

It is therefore a matter of historical and cultural reasons, a *history of the effects* of hermeneutics itself, whereby a certain philosophical trend appears to respond more adequately to some crucial questions and challenges of its time, in comparison to other approaches. Beside this, we would also like to suggest that to all these reasons it can be probably added another aspect, which—although in a slightly different way—is also central to philosophical reflection: namely, that of *seasons*. It is clearly a term, the latter, that may easily remind us of a concept like that of fashion seasons, and thus of the notion of fashion as such. In a sense, our impression is that in the last decades it often seemed that a philosophical approach like Gadamer's was not trendy or "in" anymore.

To precise, it is *not* our thesis that philosophical changes, in terms of paradigms and models, are *just* a matter of fashions, and hence that the primacy once conferred to hermeneutics was later given to other philosophical approaches on the basis of caprices or superficial and irrational motives (as we often think that it actually happens in fashion, indeed).[1] Rather, we believe that, if we want to take seriously certain processes that are apparently at the basis of the very existence of the phenomenon of fashions in human existence in general (like the dialectics between our simultaneous needs for imitation and for differentiation, following Georg Simmel's seminal insights),[2] then we must accept that perhaps, at least to some extent, those processes may play a role also in intellectual life, including philosophy and other sciences. As has been thought-provokingly (but not unreasonably) noted by the Norwegian philosopher Lars Svendsen (2006, 15–16),

> [f]ashions naturally also exist among academics and intellectuals. They have to do with which subjects are "in" and which are "out," which approaches are "sexy" and which are not. It would be naïve to believe that all this is governed by completely rational considerations, since it is just as much a question of constantly shifting taste. . . . The idea that philosophy, among other things, is a fashion-controlled process can seem somewhat objectionable to philosophers, who like to believe that exclusively rational choices underlie what themes and approaches they employ. . . . To say that philosophy does not change solely for rational reasons, but quite often for the sake of change itself, is to concede that philosophy too, at least partially, is subject to fashion. This, though, is a description that challenges the ambition of modern philosophy to attain an absolutely rational self-determination.

Anyway, even if hermeneutics, in today's philosophical landscape, sometimes seems to be considered an outdated or old-fashioned philosophy that is not capable of providing satisfactory answers to contemporary challenges, and even if Gadamer's name sometimes seems to be considered démodé today (as if he were now discounting the notoriety acquired in the previous decades, so to speak),[3] it is our firm conviction that, notwithstanding these adventures and sometimes misadventures in the reception of Gadamer's hermeneutics in the last decades, his thinking is still relevant today, especially with regard to aesthetic questions and the role of art in contemporary society.

Some relevant examples, in this context, can be represented by Gadamer's original reinterpretation of the post-Hegelian question concerning the "past character of art"—with potential stimulating comparisons with other contemporary aestheticians who have similarly developed their views of the "end of art" (Gehlen, Danto, Baudrillard)—or his hermeneutical understanding of hermetic poetry, and particularly of Paul Celan's poems in the age of "the shadow of nihilism." In a similar way, also Gadamer's hermeneutical conception of a unique "truth of the work of art" that is not accessible to scientific methodologies but is rather connected to the event of human intersubjective understanding in tradition and dialogue, or his original reflections on art and aesthetic experience based on the concepts of play, symbol, and festival, still appear important and of great interest for current aesthetic debates. In contrast to the claim that Gadamer's philosophy is anti-modern or allegedly out of date in comparison to other philosophical approaches to aesthetic questions, it is rather our conviction that a renewed and critical confrontation with his main writings on this topic can offer stimulating and penetrating insights to understand the role of art in the present age in all its transformations and challenging manifestations.

By critically questioning certain readings of hermeneutics that seemingly reduce it to a mere form of ethical and political conservatorism or, in the specific case of Gadamer's philosophy of art, to an understanding of the aesthetic phenomenon that is merely based on the model of religious images, it becomes possible, in our view, to rethink Gadamer's thought in new directions: for example, in the direction of a sort of anthropological orientation, as it emerges in various writings of Gadamer after *Truth and Method*, or also in the direction of a rehabilitation and rediscovery of *minor* aesthetic phenomena, as testified by the Gadamerian recovery of the decorative arts. Gadamer's aesthetics, in fact, is a theory that, differently from other philosophical theories, has always proved to be extremely open to the positive influence of external stimuli. And we can add that this openness has been especially shown by Gadamer, among the various fields of his philosophical reflection, precisely in his hermeneutics of the fine arts, but also in his observations on other artistic forms or other aesthetic experiences.

From this point of view, we consider it as a very encouraging sign the fact that in the last years something like a recovery of Gadamer's philosophy has been taking place, as evidenced by the recent publication of the important edited volume *The Gadamerian Mind* (George and van der Heiden 2022) and, in the particular field of aesthetics, of Cynthia R. Nielsen's monograph *Gadamer's Hermeneutical Aesthetics* that fascinatingly applies the main concepts of Gadamer's philosophy of art to the understanding of contemporary phenomena such as Banksy's street art or free jazz (see Nielsen 2023, 94–155). Furthermore, a Hans-Georg Gadamer Society has been recently founded at the University of Heidelberg, with Professor Carsten

Dutt as its current president. In the current Italian philosophical scene, we also tried to offer a small contribution by editing a new edition of the Italian translation of Gadamer's *Scritti di estetica* (2022) and by publishing the monographs *Ermeneutica filosofica e crisi della modernità* (Marino 2009), *Fusioni di orizzonti* (Marino 2012), *Ermeneutica e decostruzione* (Romagnoli 2021), and *Oltre l'opera d'arte* (Romagnoli 2023).

The aim of the present edited volume, entitled *Gadamer on Art and Aesthetic Experience: Rethinking Hermeneutical Aesthetics Today*, is thus to further contribute to this reopening of the discussion on, and the interpretation of, Gadamer's hermeneutical conception of art and aesthetic experience, with a focus not only on *Truth and Method* but also on his other works collected in the eighth and ninth volumes of his *Gesammelte Werke*, which testify the breadth and complexity of his thought. The present collection of essays certainly does not aim, in what would be an exaggeratedly ambitious way, to exhaust the whole realm of all the potential updatings of Gadamer's aesthetics. As a matter of fact, many other paths are certainly possible and indeed stimulating, including, for example, the rethinking of the concept of the *classical*, the philosophical interest in architecture, the possible role of hermeneutics in current debates in environmental aesthetics and everyday aesthetics, etc. Rather, in the context of the recent recovery of Gadamer's philosophy, it is our aim with the present volume to simply highlight some of the many possible paths that this rethinking can follow.

Our volume includes essays written by expert scholars of aesthetics and hermeneutics such as Jean Grondin (University of Montréal), Mariannina Failla (University of Roma Tre), John Arthos (Indiana University Bloomington), Georg W. Bertram (Freie University Berlin), James Risser (Seattle University), Alessandro Bertinetto (University of Torino), Gert-Jan van der Heiden (Radboud University), and Cynthia R. Nielsen (University of Dallas). It is important for us to specify that the aim of our volume is *not* to simply repropose in an integral sense Gadamer's conception today, let alone to publish a book guided by an apologetic intent. Rather, ever since we started working on the present volume it has always been our aim to try to offer a useful contribution to a reconsideration and also a rethinking of Gadamer's hermeneutical conception of art and aesthetic experience, not sparing to highlight its limitations, criticalities, or potential weak points (as our readers will clearly see, especially in some of the essays collected here), but anyway attempting to offer detailed investigations of its main concepts, to clarify some delicate aspects in order to prevent (or sometimes correct) misunderstandings and wrong interpretations, and finally to imagine some possible developments of Gadamer's theory in the direction of stimulating topics such as improvisation, rhythm, and performativity.

Notes

1. According to Elizabeth Wilson (2003, 3, 6), fashion is "rapid and continual changing of styles. Fashion, in a sense *is* change . . . Yet despite its apparent irrationality, fashion cements social solidarity and imposes group norms." For Lars Svendsen (2006, 24, 28), "[f]ashion is irrational. It consists of change for the sake of change . . . A fashion object does not *in principle* need any particular qualities apart from being new. The principle of fashion is to create an ever-increasing velocity, to make an object superfluous as fast as possible, in order to let a new one have a chance . . . Fashion is irrational in the sense that it seeks change for the sake of change, not in order to 'improve' the object."

2. As is well-known, according to Simmel fashion, understood as "a universal phenomenon in the history of our species," must be contextualized in the totality of "the phenomena of life," *all* resting on the interplay of "a multiplicity of elements," on the intertwinement of deep forces and "unresolved tensions" that confer to every phenomenon in "its visible expression" a dualistic character. From Simmel's point of view, *all* human experiences and practices must be dualistically understood as "unique way[s] of unifying the interest in duration, unity and equality, and similarity," on the one hand, "with that in change, particularity and uniqueness," on the other hand. In this context, fashion appears as a social form characterized by a dialectic between two fundamental drives: the tendency towards imitation, that "satisfies the need for social adaptation," and "at the same time, and to no less a degree, . . . the need for distinction, . . . differentiation, change and individual contrast" (Simmel 1997, 187–89).

3. In particular, as is well-known, Gadamer's hermeneutics has been sometimes reduced to a mere methodology of the interpretation of texts, and has been accused to merely bear a sharp and naïf critique of modern science, as well as to endorse politically conservative instances. Moreover, Gadamer's hermeneutics has been often regarded as a mere "epigonal" philosophy, when it has been interpreted only in light of Heidegger's thinking and reductively understood as a kind of "urbanization" of the latter, following the famous expression coined by Habermas. Precisely the wide dissemination of hermeneutics and its pervasive capacity, which, on the one hand, led to its definition as new philosophical and cultural koine, on the other hand also entailed undoubted drawbacks and misunderstandings that for a long time have affected its reception. For example, a classical reading of Gadamer's hermeneutics that emerged above all after his famous debate with Habermas has been focused, in particular, on Gadamer's rehabilitation of the concept of tradition and reappraisal of prejudice. According to this reading, Gadamer's hermeneutics was to be blamed for

proposing a conciliatory view of the reality, as opposed to the tendency to unmask power relations that is characteristic of the critique of ideology. This reading—which, according to us, has interpreted in a reductive and partial way those parts of *Truth and Method*—has long conditioned the interpretation and reception of Gadamer's thinking in certain philosophical and cultural contexts, leading some authors to consider it as a conservative philosophy, rooted on a monolithic conception of tradition. Contrary to this reading, authors such as Figal and Grondin, and more recently American interpreters such as Risser and George, have convincingly shown the prejudicial nature of the aforementioned understanding of Gadamer's philosophy, emphasizing the real meaning of his concepts of tradition and prejudice and also his relation to the Enlightenment.

Bibliography

2001. *"Sein, das verstanden werden kann, ist Sprache." Hommage an Hans-Georg Gadamer.* Frankfurt a.M.: Suhrkamp.

Cattaneo, Francesco, Carlo Gentili, and Stefano Marino, eds. *Domandare con Gadamer. Cinquant'anni di* Verità e metodo. Milano–Udine: Mimesis, 2011.

Di Cesare, Donatella. *Gadamer: A Philosophical Portrait.* Translated by N. Keane. Bloomington–Indianapolis: Indiana University Press, 2013.

Dostal, Robert J., ed. *The Cambridge Companion to Gadamer.* Cambridge, MA: Cambridge University Press, 2002.

Failla, Mariannina, ed. *Il cammino filosofico di Hans-Georg Gadamer.* Special issue of *Paradigmi. Rivista di critica filosofica* 26, no. 3 (2008).

Fehér, István M., ed. *Kunst, Hermeneutik, Philosophie. Das Denken Hans-Georg Gadamers im Zusammenhang des 20. Jahrhunderts.* Heidelberg: Winter 2003.

Figal, Günter, ed. *Begegnungen mit Hans-Georg Gadamer.* Stuttgart: Reclam, 2000.

———. *Hans Georg Gadamer: Wahrheit und Methode.* Berlin: Akademie Verlag, 2007.

Figal, Günter, Jean Grondin, and Dennis J. Schmidt, eds. *Hermeneutische Wege. Hans-Georg Gadamer zum Hundertsten.* Tübingen: Mohr Siebeck, 2000.

Gadamer, Hans-Georg. *Gesammelte Werke* [GW]. 10 vols. Tübingen: Mohr Siebeck, 1985–1995.

———. 1997. "Reply to Frances J. Ambrosio." In *The Philosophy of Hans-Georg Gadamer*, edited by Lewis E. Hahn, 274. Chicago–La Salle: Open Court, 1997.

———. *Scritti di estetica.* Translated by G. Bonanni. Edited by S. Marino and E. Romagnoli. Palermo: Aesthetica, 2022.

———. *The Gadamer Reader: A Bouquet of the Later Writings.* Translated and edited by R. E. Palmer. Evanston: Northwestern University Press, 2007.

———. *Truth and Method.* Revised ed. Translated by J. Weinsheimer and D. G. Marshall. New York: Bloomsbury, 2004.

Gardini, Michele, and Giovanni Matteucci, eds. *Gadamer: bilanci e prospettive*. Macerata: Quodlibet, 2004.
George, Theodore, and Gert-Jan van der Heiden, eds. *The Gadamerian Mind*. New York: Routledge, 2022.
Grondin, Jean. *Hans-Georg Gadamer: A Biography*. Translated by J. Weinsheimer. New Haven–London: Yale University Press, 2003.
Hahn, Lewis E., ed. *The Philosophy of Hans-Georg Gadamer*. Chicago–La Salle: Open Court, 1997.
Krajewski, Bruce, ed. *Gadamer's Repercussions*. Berkeley–Los Angeles–London: University of California Press, 2004.
Malpas, Jeff, Ulrich Arnswald, and Jens Kertscher, eds. *Gadamer's Century. Essays in Honor of Hans-Georg Gadamer*. Cambridge, MA: The MIT Press, 2002.
Malpas, Jeff, and Santiago Zabala, eds. *Consequences of Hermeneutics. Fifty Years after Gadamer's* Truth and Method. Evanston: Northwestern University Press, 2010.
Marino, Stefano. *Ermeneutica filosofica e crisi della modernità. Un itinerario nel pensiero di Hans-Georg Gadamer*. Milano–Udine: Mimesis, 2009.
———. *Fusioni di orizzonti. Saggi su estetica e linguaggio in Hans-Georg Gadamer*. Roma: Aracne, 2012.
Nielsen, Cynthia R. *Gadamer's Hermeneutical Aesthetics. Art as a Performative, Dynamic, Communal Event*. New York: Routledge, 2023.
Romagnoli, Elena. *Ermeneutica e decostruzione. Il dialogo ininterrotto tra Gadamer e Derrida*. Pisa: ETS, 2021.
———. *Oltre l'opera d'arte. L'estetica performativa di Gadamer tra idealismo e pragmatismo*. Pisa: ETS, 2023.
Schmidt, Lawrence K. *Language and Linguisticality in Gadamer's Hermeneutics*. Lanham–Boulder–New York–Oxford: Lexington Books, 2000.
———, ed. *The Specter of Relativism: Truth, Dialogue, and* Phronesis *in Philosophical Hermeneutics*. Evanston: Northwestern University Press, 1995.
Silverman, Hugh J., ed. *Gadamer and Hermeneutics. Science, Culture, Literature*. London–New York: Routledge, 1991.
Simmel, Georg. "The Philosophy of Fashion." Translated by M. Ritter and D. Frisby. In *Simmel on Culture: Selected Writings*. Edited by D. Frisby and M. Featherstone, 187–205. London–Thousand Oaks–New Delhi: Sage Publications, 1997.
Svendsen, Lars. *Fashion: A Philosophy*. London: Reaktion Books, 2006.
Vattimo, Gianni. "Hermeneutics as Koine." *Theory, Culture and Society* 5, no. 2–3 (1988): 399–408.
Vattimo, Gianni, and Gaetano Chiurazzi, eds. *Gadamer: 50 anni di* Verità e metodo. Special issue of *Trópos. Rivista di ermeneutica e critica filosofica* 2, no. 2 (2009).
Wachterhauser, Brice R., ed. *Hermeneutics and Truth*. Evanston: Northwestern University Press, 1994.
Wilson, Elizabeth. *Adorned in Dreams: Fashion and Modernity*. London–New York: Tauris & Co, 2003.

Wischke, Mirko and Michael Hofer, eds. *Gadamer Verstehen / Understanding Gadamer.* Darmstadt: Wissenschaftliche Buchgesellschaft, 2003.

Wright, Kathleen, ed. *Festival of Interpretations. Essays on Hans-Georg Gadamer's Work.* Albany: State University of New York Press, 1990.

1

Gadamer's Understanding of Art as Presentation
Study on a Key Concept of Gadamer's Philosophy

Jean Grondin

> Play is really limited to presenting itself. Thus its mode of being is self-presentation (*Selbstdarstellung*). Now, self-presentation is a universal ontological characteristic of nature (*Das Spiel ist wirklich darauf beschränkt, sich darzustellen. Seine Seinsweise ist also Selbstdarstellung. Nun ist Selbstdarstellung ein universaler Seinsaspekt der Natur*).
>
> —GW 1, 113; Gadamer 2013, 112

The idea that I would like to defend here is that the notion of presentation (*Darstellung*) one encounters in *Truth and Method* is one of the keys to the entire work, indeed to Gadamer's whole hermeneutics. It remains however a relatively discreet notion in the book, where no specific analysis or chapter is devoted to it, as is the case for instance for notions such as play or the guiding concepts of humanism (*Bildung*, common sense, judgment, and taste), all of which are the objects of elaborate specific chapters, devoted to their history and conceptual import. The notion was also scarcely studied in the secondary literature.[1] In what follows, I would like to highlight its meaning, indeed its many different levels of meaning, and importance in the work as a whole in order to show that it is one of its key concepts and one that helps to understand its unity.

I follow the (revised) translation of Joel Weinsheimer and Donald G. Marshall when I use the term *presentation* for *Darstellung*. I believe it is the best translation, but the English reader should know that the term has been translated differently in other languages. In French, Pierre Fruchon preferred the term *représentation*[2] (representation of course, a term, it should be noted, one *also* encounters, as we will see, in the English translation), because the artistic work, as Gadamer understands it, has to be viewed as a re-presentation, in at least two senses of the term: on the one hand, it is the renewed, and thus transformed (*verwandelt*) presentation of something or someone, hence a *re*-presentation, on the other, the artwork exerts for Gadamer a supplementing, replacement or substitutive function, when, say, the picture of a sovereign or the statue of a Greek god serves to stand in for what it represents and not without bestowing upon it accrued presence. The standard Spanish translation spoke, for its part, of "manifestation" (*manifestación*),[3] certainly in order to drive home the point that the artwork would present the true manifestation of things, but in some contexts it also used *representación*.[4] The Italian translator Gianni Vattimo also spoke here of *rappresentazione*,[5] while also venturing the term of *pro-duzione*[6] (pro-duction), to underscore the performative action of an artwork that brings to the fore and hence pro-duces ("brings forth") the being of things. In English, one can also speak of an artistic production, to name both the artistic creation and the process of creation itself. These notions of representation and production are important to keep in mind since they also retain key elements of the notion of *Darstellung* that we will point out shortly. However, neither the notions of presentation and representation nor that of production, which all follow the Latin language, correspond perfectly to the German idea of *Darstellung*, whose construction is different: it evokes something like a placing forward (*dar-stellen*), a laying forth, where the accent appears to lie on the activity of a *stellen*, that is, on the process of putting or placing something before us, in the manner of an offering (this is the meaning of the "*dar*" that one can also find in the *Dargabe*, the offering, the *Darreichen*, to present to someone, or the *Darbietung*, the performance for someone). Ultimately, one could hear in the "*dar*" of *Darstellung* something like a *Da-stellen*, a putting *there*, in the strong sense that both Heidegger and Gadamer give to the *da*: just as the *Da-sein* is the being that is there and actuates this *there* in the transitive sense, the artwork is *there* for Gadamer as something like an autonomous play that draws its spectators, better still, its participants, in its orbit, and thus presents (or represents) itself.

The grand idea of Gadamer throughout *Truth and Method* is indeed that it is such a manifestation emanating from the artwork itself that is at play in any interpretation worthy of this name. Indeed, one of the best translations of *Darstellung*, at least the most philosophically satisfying, would be that of *interpretation*: every interpretation is for Gadamer the unfolding of the meaning of the work and its truth, which always *presents* itself here and now, in front of us, while still flowing from the work itself. There are indeed many art forms where their presentation is identical to their interpretation. This happens most vividly in the performing arts, which will thus enjoy an exemplary function for Gadamer.

The crucial insight of Gadamer's aesthetics, if not his entire hermeneutics, is that this *Darstellung*, that is, this manifestation that presents itself, is indeed constitutive of *every* work of art and *every* true interpretation. It is thus no surprise that the most telling analyses of the notion of *Darstellung* are to be found in the aesthetics of the first part of *Truth and Method*. The insights gained in this first part regarding the notion of *Darstellung* can however help us understand the more far-reaching theses of the second and third parts on truth, understanding, history, language, and Being itself, which will all be understood as forms of self-presentation (*Selbstdarstellung*). However, in the context of the aesthetics of the first part (which is, of course, not an aesthetics per se, because the experience of the artwork is never merely aesthetic for Gadamer; one does not need to recall here this important and well-known critique of aesthetic consciousness), the notion of *Darstellung* comports many different dimensions, and layers, which are not always distinguished by Gadamer, but that can be sorted out if one is to gauge the full meaning of his understanding of the truth of the art experience. It is a clarification of these interrelated levels of meaning that I would like to provide in what follows.

One could certainly question whether all the elements that go into Gadamer's notion of *Darstellung* can cohabit under the aegis of a single concept, but it is important, I believe, to distinguish them clearly *before* one questions their fusion in a single concept. I will give these different elements (there will be four) specific names that are intentionally *profiling* since their aim is to put into relief the different facets of Gadamer's *Darstellung*. For reasons of space and time, I will limit myself here to the artistic sphere, but will conclude with a few words on the application of this notion of *Darstellung* to the broader activity of interpretation and the expression of meaning through the medium of language in the second and third parts of *Truth and Method*.

Darstellung as Performance

The notion of *Darstellung* first carries with it, most evidently, a dimension of performance or execution. Gadamer likes to illustrate his notion of *Darstellung* by focusing on what the English language calls the *performing arts* (they have other names in other languages, as we will point out). These are the arts that demand to be presented, executed, or performed by actors, dancers, singers that we call *interpreters*. This is what happens (or what pro-duces itself, if one recalls Vattimo's rendition of *Darstellung* as *pro-duzione*) in dance, ballet, theater, or music. A ballet that is not danced or a music that is not played out is not dance nor music. Here, it is essential to note that it is the work itself—the ballet, the song, the play, the symphony—that *requires* this interpretative performance. If this is paramount for Gadamer, it is because for him interpretation is not an activity that would be "added" to the work and its meaning, it describes its essential mode of being: a theater play must be "played" on stage (it is, of course, possible to read a play or the notes of a partition, but when one does so, one always visualizes the way they would be played out on stage). This will have far-reaching consequences for Gadamer's understanding of interpretation in the humanities. In his view, the interpretation put forward by a philologist or literary historian should not be understood as a reproductive activity, of second order, which would seek to reenact or reactivate a meaning that would be independent from this activity of interpretation, say, in the *mens auctoris* of the writer, a meaning, that would only be re-activated or re-created by the interpretation. No, interpretation has to be understood as the first and foremost actualization of the meaning of the work, without which it would not exist.

This appears most evidently in the performing arts, which are called in German the *transitorische Künste* (i.e., the arts that require a "transitive" function, e.g., interpreters) or *Darstellungskünste* (arts of presentation), which would be called in French, in a translation that is also powerful and illuminating, since it confirms Gadamer's thesis, the *arts d'interprétation* (the interpretative arts; they can also be called the *arts de la scène*, the arts played out on a stage). It is Gadamer's far-reaching thesis, as we will soon see, that there is no artwork without presentation or interpretation.

It is indeed Gadamer's strong contention that the notion of *Darstellung*, in the meaning of performance, not only defines the performing arts, but *all* forms of art also. One of the master strokes of the first part of *Truth and Method* resides in the argument that every work of art calls out for a specific performance or interpretation, which would be constitutive of its mode of being (*Seinsweise*) as such. Thus, in the literary arts, where there are no actual performers, this performance would be carried out by the act of reading (aloud or silently), understood as the interpretation or actualization of meaning by the reader. In the figurative arts, this performance of presentation would take place, first, in the exposition (*Ausstellung*) of these arts, and second, in their contemplation by those who gaze at a picture, a sculpture, or experience (in a host of different ways) a work of architecture. In both cases, argues Gadamer, the artwork has no other being than the one it receives through this performance or interpretation by the spectator or the reader.

Gadamer did not set up a system of all the different art forms, but one can say that his idea is that all the different arts are defined by a specific form of *Darstellung*, understood as the performance that is constitutive of them. This distinction is not meant to be authoritative, but one can distinguish broadly three different art forms, the performing arts, the literary arts, and the figurative arts, which are all characterized by a specific type of performance or presentation (see table 1.1).

The specific type of presentation (here in the meaning of performance) varies according to every art form. While the presentation understood as a performance exemplarily characterizes the interpretation of a play or of piece by actors, dancers, and musicians in the performing arts, it refers

Table 1.1. Three Different Forms of Art

Art forms	In German	Type of presentation
Performing arts (theater, music, dance, opera)	*Transitorische Künste, Darstellungskünste*	Interpretation, execution = *Darstellung*, often: *Vorstellung* (to name the entire event of the artistic presentation in front of a public)
Literary arts (poetry, literature)	*Literarische Künste, Wortkünste*	Reading mostly, listening also, possibly singing and dancing (as in the performing arts)
Figurative arts (painting, sculpture, architecture)	*Plastische Künste, Baukünste*	*Ausstellung*, Exposition geared toward a contemplation

mostly to the act of reading (in the broadest sense) and listening in the literary arts (an act of interpretation, it must be noted, that *also* takes place in the performing arts, since these must *also* be interpreted or read by spectators). This presentation also occurs in the figurative arts, but with the added dimension that these art forms are in most cases openly presented to a public or an audience, in what is generally called an "exposition" or an *Ausstellung* (a derivative, if one wants, of *Darstellung*): a painting or a sculpture is made to be exposed in a museum, in an open setting, a home, or a public edifice. These works of art, which are exposed (*ausgestellt*), are there to be contemplated and thus elicit reflection or interpretation.

One could certainly ask whether it is legitimate to conflate these different types of performance—most specifically (1) the performing interpretation by actors and musicians, (2) their reading and contemplation by spectators—in a single concept. For the time being, it is only important to single out this *performative* component of Gadamer's notion of *Darstellung*, which is exemplified by the performing arts, but which would be constitutive of all art forms.

Darstellung as Interpretation

When we spoke of the act of reading, we already alluded to the second decisive dimension of *Darstellung*, its *interpretative* component. It goes without saying that there is already an interpretive element in the execution carried out by the performers in the performing arts: to perform a musical piece, to direct it in a specific way, to embody a role in a play is also to interpret the work in a specific manner and thus to bring it to life (which is the point of the *Darstellung*). However, the second constitutive moment of *Darstellung*, that of interpretation, goes beyond the actual performance itself in that it mostly alludes to the interpretation of works of art by its spectators, listeners, and readers. For Gadamer, this is obvious because the *Darstellung* of a work of art is always a presentation *for someone* who interprets the work, consciously or not, in the way she understands it and is affected by it. Gadamer argues that there is no artistic presentation that is not a presentation, indeed even a present, *for* or *to* someone who is evoked in the dative of the gift to someone (in German, where there is a dative case, one would say: *jemandem stellt sich etwas dar, mir stellt es sich so dar*). *Darstellung* obviously implies here something else than the actual performance of a work by artists: it takes place in the interpretation of a work by a reader who listens to or reads a piece of art. Gadamer's point is that this is also a performance of sorts because it is *also* an interpretation that brings out the meaning of the work, just like the performance-interpretation by the artists. For Gadamer, this activity represents, of course, far less an action on the part of the interpreting subject than an action (*Wirkung*, which comes from the *Werk* in question) of the work on it. It is the artwork that draws one into its universe, its "higher reality," as Gadamer often says. This is quite an original thesis: the performance of the work (by interpreters) and its interpretation (by readers) are fused into one another. Gadamer draws an important lesson from this fusion: interpretation is not (or not primarily) some subjective coloring that an interpreter would add to a work, it describes the action of the work on the interpreter and it is in this actualization, and only in it, that the meaning of the work would come to fruition.

Thus, according to Gadamer, the meaning of the work only exists in this interpretation. It is, to be sure, a thesis one can call into question: can one identify without further ado the meaning of the artwork with the meaning it has for me? This fusion certainly appears essential to Gadamer's notion of *Darstellung* (and of course to the notion of fusion of horizons that goes hand in hand with it[7]), yet it seems difficult to sustain since it tends to equate the work, the artwork but also any work of the spirit, with its particular presentation. Can one claim, for example, that the Plato interpretations put forward by interpreters such as Natorp, Cherniss, and Krämer are all legitimate interpretations of Plato's work? This seems to me problematic. I believe one could only speak of such an equivalence of interpretation when one is dealing with high levels of artistic virtuosity, say, when one wishes to compare the manner in which a Beethoven symphony is directed by a Furtwängler, a Boehm, or a Karajan. Here, it is probably possible to say that the same artwork is more than adequately presented in different ways, different interpretations, but philological interpretation remains subject to other norms of validity and adequation. It is certainly one of the most questionable aspects of Gadamer's notion of *Darstellung* and, needless to say, of his hermeneutics. I, for one, would never confuse my meaningless "interpretation" of a Beethoven symphony, by listening to it, with what Solti is performing with his orchestra. However, my primary aim here is not to problematize the notion of *Darstellung*, but to single out its different meanings and importance for *Truth and Method*. In this differentiation, a third dimension of *Darstellung* needs to be presented: *Darstellung* as revelation.

Darstellung as Revelation (and Representation)

The third essential element of *Darstellung*, possibly its most essential, lies in the *revelation* it represents. One could speak of its *epiphanic, ontological* or *veritative* dimension. The presentation or *Darstellung* of an artwork is not only the *performance* executed by an artist (1) or an *interpretation* carried out by someone (2), it is also first and foremost the revealing presentation *of* something (or someone). If the presentation for someone though an interpretation, in the second sense we just alluded to, can be called its *downstream* presentation (that is, for its readers and listeners), the presentation *of* something could be called its *upstream* presentation. For Gadamer, the artwork is always the presentation *of* something or some reality. It is never self-confined, it brings us to discover something, indeed the truth of something, and it presents something that is never merely aesthetic. Yet, and most importantly, what the artwork reveals is not something that could be grasped independently from the artwork, argues Gadamer, since it is only through the artwork and its craft that we gain access to it. Gadamer claims that the revelatory presentation of something in an artwork even represents the most real presentation of this thing, indeed its true re-presentation by bestowing upon it something like an increase in Being (a *Seinszuwachs*), and certainly in luminosity. In the presence of a true artwork, one can only sigh, as Gadamer often writes, "indeed, that's the way it is," "*so ist es!*" This is what can overwhelm us when we are reading a novel of Carson McCullers, attending a play of Molière, or contemplating Picasso's *Guernica*. Actually, all artworks would be illustrations of this eye-opening presentation that reveals to us, as if for the first time, the essence of things, the truth that remains, and that the artwork, and it only, truly captured.

One also finds examples of this revelatory dimension in less glamorous artforms such as photography or caricature. While always exaggerating, in what it depicts and what it says, a caricature can reveal the characteristic reality of a person or of a situation, the one that remains. In very much the same way, there are photographs of which it can be said that they grasp the essence of a situation or of a person. One could think here of the well-known photograph of an irreverent Einstein pulling his tongue or of Alfred Eisenstaedt's famous depiction of a Victory-Day kiss in Times Square, which captured the spirit of the liberation brought about by the end the Second World War. By contrast, when one encounters a rather unsuited photograph of someone (or of one's self), one can sigh: "no, that's not you! that's not her." That is quite a declaration indeed! It is obviously a picture of the person in question (at least in the trite nominalistic sense), but somehow it doesn't catch its true essence and presents it in a way that does not do it justice. This is something that strikes us immediately.

Gadamer has no qualms whatsoever to use the much-maligned notion of essence in this context. In his view, the presentation of an artwork always succeeds in revealing the essence of something (or at least some aspect of it) and is only an artwork to this extent. This is what leads Gadamer to endow the artwork with a strong knowledge and truth claim: the artwork enables us to discover, better still, to rediscover a reality that would have remained inaccessible without this epiphanic and ontological revelation (*Darstellung*) accomplished by the work and its overabundance of light, its *Lichtzuwachs* as it were.

Gadamer shows this by focusing on the increase of Being that the "representative" portrait bestows upon a monarch or a person in a position of authority. It serves Gadamer's argument here that the sovereign or public person already exerts a function of representation (here, the translation of *Darstellung* with *representation* is certainly the best): a queen, a king, a president, a bishop represents the authority in a given domain and this is what the artwork—especially the official portrait—has to convey (one can think here, for instance, of the lavish presentation of Cardinal Richelieu by Philippe de Champaigne). The sovereign will be represented with sumptuous clothing, a somewhat haughty yet benevolent stare, and the self-assurance of its standing. By representing the queen, the emperor, or the cardinal, the artwork thus draws on the representative function that is exerted ex officio by that person (or group, or event), but that only the artwork can express, that is, "represent" with all its distinction and brilliance. Official portraits thus *represent* people or events that are meant to be understood as representations and must be shown in this representative function.

It is striking that this is also true of paintings or artworks that represent religious figures or important events of the history of salvation (a crucifixion, a resurrection, etc.). This is also true of Greek gods. We might now see statues or sculptures of them in a museum and judge them on their aesthetic merits. But they used to be put in temples devoted to them where they *represented* the god in question and stood for it. It was thus important to represent the divinity with all its important attributes and glory. Of course, nobody could nor can compare these statues to any "originals," as one can perhaps do with a portrait, since these gods or godly figures (half-gods, heroes, etc.) are only presented or represented through their artistic representations, which are obviously far more than aesthetic. This is also true of the many artworks that present episodes of the history of salvation, which is the case of so much of the history of Western art. Let's take as a very classical example everyone will be familiar with the *Last Judgment* in the Sistine Chapel. Is this the depiction of a true reality? Certainly, there is no original since it represents what will happen at the end of time, when the saved are going to be separated from the damned. Nonetheless, it is an event that can be represented and indeed *calls* for such a representation since it is only by being represented that it unfolds its meaning for the believer. Just as the sovereign needs to be represented, the Last Judgment, the Last Supper, the destruction of Sodom and Gomorrah *need* to be represented, for our salvation. The good artwork is the one that grasps and conveys what needs to be represented. This is how the *Darstellung* comes to be a revelation.

One could perhaps raise here the critical question whether this epiphanic dimension of *Darstellung* holds for all art forms. The question can especially be raised concerning abstract art, which does not appear to represent anything. One could also think of all those works of modern art that explicitly reject the claim that they would represent anything besides themselves. To drive home this point, some artworks are given titles such as "without title," "no title," or "Composition 59" (if they even have titles at all). What or who is then presented or represented? What receives an increase in Being? Gadamer would perhaps respond that these opaque artworks (if one can even speak of works, since some also reject this characterization), by the mere fact that they are exposed and thus presented, call for an interpretative effort on the part of the spectator (the second interpretative dimension of *Darstellung* comes here into play) who will then discover a new reality, uncovered by the artwork itself, which can very well be that of "the absurd opacity of the world." The provocation entailed in a work entitled "without title" also represents a reality in itself!

It would be a decent answer, yet the question remains: is an artwork always the epiphanic and essential (re)presentation of something? The question has to be raised regarding music: what does a musical work actually represent? The question pertains, of course, to what Gadamer would call absolute music (music without a text), since it goes without saying that Haendel's *Messiah* represents something that, for the Christian faith, needs to be presented for our salvation, or that a *Lied* or an opera puts a text or history into music. However, does absolute music always refer to something that would receive an increase in Being through it? It is striking to note in this regard that Gadamer has little to say about music in *Truth and Method* and his work more generally,[8] where the prime examples of artistic truth and knowledge are found in poetry, literature, the figurative arts, and the performing arts that pertain to theater, where something is represented. One might encounter here a limit of his aesthetics and its guiding notion of *Darstellung*, at least of its revelatory meaning since it is obvious for Gadamer that music needs to be performed and played out (*Darstellung* in the first sense of performance).

Darstellung as a Festive Event

A fourth and last element of *Darstellung* needs to be presented. It concerns what one can call the *festive* and participative dimension of artistic *Darstellung*. It has something to do with the three dimensions that were already mentioned, the performance, the interpretation, and the epiphanic revelation of something, but it adds to them the notion that the artwork is never an atemporal artefact closed upon itself in that it implies a particular temporality, a festive nature, and a participation on the part of those who witness it and that likens it to a *happening*, if not a form of ritual. The contemplation of or the participation in an artwork takes us out of our daily routine and ushers us into a new form of time, which resembles that of a celebration, a feast, or a festival (three terms one can use to render Gadamer's notion of *Fest*). One attends a concert or a play with others, as if it were a sacred or ritual event. As eloquent illustrations of this type of *Darstellung* or festive event, one could think of Greek tragedies, which were always played at the time of the Dionysia, the festival in honor of Dionysus, or, in Christian times, of the playing of Bach's Christmas Oratorio (preferably, of course, at Christmas time and in a place of worship) or of a Passion in the Holy Week. All of these are (or were) festive events in their own right—they are of course performed (1), interpreted (2), and are revelations of something (3)—and to take part in them is to participate in something like a festival (4) or celebration with its special temporality. For Gadamer, the presentation of an artwork is always something like an event (*Geschehen*) that goes beyond our limited selves and takes us into its celebration, even when one is only contemplating a picture or musing over a poem that calls for meditation and reflection. The main notions Gadamer develops to describe this experience of filled and transforming time are those of repetition (*Wiederholung*) and contemporaneity, which we cannot study here more closely for reasons of space. Let it suffice to recall that the presentation of artworks often repeats or represents the same works (the same plays, tragedies, symphonies, we also reread poems and novels, revisit pictures, monuments, etc.), much like ritual celebrates the same holy days and festivals, yet every presentation and repetition is unique. It is well-known that Gadamer takes up Kierkegaard's notion of contemporaneity[9] to emphasize the point that we are taken and taken in by the work in the here and now (even if we attend or read a very ancient work), we become part of this presentation and come out transformed by this experience, as we are by the spirit of a celebration or a feast that holds sway over us.

There are thus at least four cardinal dimensions to Gadamer's notion of *Darstellung*, which are woven into one another, but that one can distinguish for the sake of clarity: performative, interpretative, revelatory (and thus representative), and festive. To say that there is no artwork without presentation means that every artwork must be (1) performed (that is, executed and played out by comedians and interpreters), (2) interpreted or read (by spectators), and (3) experienced as a revelation (of the true being or essence of something), and (4) that it unfolds (*sich darstellt*) in the manner of a celebration or a festival that fills us with its atmosphere and aura.[10] Gadamer's contention seems to be that this broad notion of *Darstellung* holds for every artwork.

One can thus ask, in a critical spirit, if Gadamer's thesis holds up. We already alluded to the limit-cases of abstract art and absolute music, which seem to cast doubt over the notion that an artwork is always the revelation of a true reality beyond itself. One can also ask whether all those components of *Darstellung* can hold under the aegis of a single concept. Can one, for instance, see without further ado the same type of presentation in the execution of an artwork by artists, who play and interpret a given artwork, and in the reading of this performance by interpreters? Even if there is interpretation in both, it does not appear to be of the same kind.

What I would now like to point out, in closing and in broad outline, is how Gadamer's loaded notion of *Darstellung* continues to have a paramount importance for his reflections on understanding and language in the second and third parts of *Truth and Method*, where the notion of *Darstellung* appears less in the forefront, by name at least, while remaining essential.

Presentation in the Second Part of *Truth and Method*

The second part of *Truth and Method* is dominated by notions such as prejudice, tradition, application, and *Wirkungsgeschichte* or effective history.

These are all aspects of the interpretative work that, according to Gadamer, the hermeneutics of the nineteenth century wanted to keep in check, in the name of objectivity. For this hermeneutics, the essential task of the interpreter was to re-create the original meaning of the work. This meaning could be distorted unless the interpreter followed a stringent methodology, whose task was precisely to control the sway of prejudices, tradition, possible application to the present, and the lingering effects of a *Wirkungsgeschichte*. If one follows one's prejudices and the possibly distorting influence of tradition, one could miss the original meaning of the work. This is why interpretation would need to be disciplined by a method that keeps in check and, in the best-case scenario, eliminates the prejudices of the interpreter.

Gadamer defends, for his part, an entirely different conception of interpretation (and hermeneutics), one that doesn't insist on the potentially distorting nature of application, but, on the opposite, on its decisive role in the coming about of meaning. Interpretation is not for him the reproduction of a meaning that would exist independently from this interpretation, it is nothing but the bringing out of meaning that is required by the work itself. Here it is the performative dimension that guides Gadamer: just as an artwork needs to be played out (or executed) by an interpreter, the meaning of a text or of a historical event would only come out if it is *dargestellt* or presented by a historian, a philologist, a translator, or an interpreter. For Gadamer, it goes without saying that this presentation of meaning doesn't imply a break with the work of history (*Wirkungsgeschichte*) but stands in its continuity. It is this work of history that has shaped the prejudices, the reception, the types of application, and translation that make it possible for a work to speak to and at a given time and thus to unfold its meaning. It is to be noted here, against the too subjectivist or Nietzschean readings of Gadamer, which are common, that for Gadamer it is always *the meaning of the work itself* that has to be presented, not the prejudices nor the point of view of the interpreter that have to be in the forefront. In this latter case, it remains entirely appropriate to speak of an interpretation that might be distorting, too modernizing, or too dominated by the quirks of the interpreter or the director. What Gadamer wants to highlight is the notion that interpretation—in art as in the humanities—is an essential moment in the concretization and the bringing about of meaning, one that is required by the work itself and in which one should not see a subjective add-on. The notion that art—and more specifically the performing arts—calls for a presentation, in the strong performative and revelatory sense of *Darstellung* we delineated, guides Gadamer's account of the humanities.

To be sure, this conception raises its own issues: is it obvious that an interpretation always has to be seen as an emanation stemming from the work itself? One could think here, in art, of the many modernizing presentations of classical plays and operas whose aim seems to be more to provoke the modern-day spectator than to do justice to the original work. The question also applies to the historical and philological disciplines that for Gadamer make up the bulk of the *Geisteswissenschaften* or the humanities. As we saw, a classical author like Plato has elicited many interpretations, or presentations, that openly contradict one another, say, those of Natorp, Cherniss, Krämer, or Gadamer. Can one say that these are all presentations that are called for by the work of Plato, just as there are many different renditions of Beethoven's Seventh Symphony? This debate is inseparable from the critical reception of Gadamer's work and cannot be adjudicated here. The only point I want to make in the present context is to underline the critical importance of the notion of *Darstellung* for the understanding of interpretation that is put forward in the second part of *Truth and Method*: a work only comes out in its *Darstellung*, in its actual presentation, whereby this does not imply any bad subjectivism since, for Gadamer, it is the work itself that calls for such a presentation for its meaning to come to life.

Presentation in the Final Part of *Truth and Method*

The role played by the notion of presentation is even more subtle in the last part of *Truth and Method* devoted to language. If this role appears at first more discreet, it is no less fundamental and will come out in force, almost with a vengeance, in the final pages of the work when Gadamer will claim, in what can be seen as the conclusion of the work, that "Being is self-presentation, *Selbstdarstellung*, i.e., language."

The entire argument of the last part of *Truth and Method* is directed against an instrumental understanding of language, which sees in it a mere sign of thinking, a sign that would only serve to point out realities that could be thought of independently from the linguistic medium, by thought alone. Gadamer stigmatizes here the nominalism of Western thinking about language ever since Plato.[11] For nominalism, as Gadamer understands it, words are merely names (*nomina*: what's in a name? . . .) or signs created by thinking (or a culture, which amounts to the same thing) to denote realities, which are always individual, material, and given in time and space. More general concepts, the ones that medieval thought called universals, would be nothing but names, abstract names, which would ultimately refer back to these individual realities: thus, the abstract notion of a tree would not exist in itself, it would only unite under the aegis of a common concept all those individual realities in which one could recognize the defining traits of a tree. In this view, language is merely an instrument of thought, a way to designate things that is superadded to the things and even to thinking itself, since thinking could be separated from words. This view thus presupposes an instrumental and even technical relationship between thinking, words, and things.

To this understanding of language as sign and instrument, Gadamer opposes, rather discreetly, another vision of language that follows the lead of his understanding of *Darstellung* in the first part of the work. According to Gadamer, words could be seen not only as signs, but also as images (*Bild*) or copies (*Abbild*), if not icons (from the Greek *eikôn*), of the things themselves. Gadamer forcefully underscores the opposition between the two understandings, while also stating how difficult it is to think through: "A word is not just a sign. In a sense that is hard to grasp, it is also something almost like a copy or image (*Abbild*)" (GW 1, 420; Gadamer 2013, 434). Gadamer views in the nominalist understanding of language "an epoch-making decision about thought concerning language,"[12] which would fail to do justice to its true being. This opposition between sign (*Zeichen*) and image (*Bild*) is thus fundamental, albeit somewhat underdeveloped in the last part of *Truth and Method*. The reason for this is that Gadamer is perhaps more at pains to deconstruct the dominating nominalist understanding of language than to unfold his own conception of language as "image (*Bild*)."

It is here that Gadamer's notion of *Darstellung*, and of course his reflections on the notion of *Bild* in the first part, can help us fill in the silences of the third part. This first part indeed bestowed utmost importance to the "ontological valence (*ontologische Valenz*)" of the notion of image (*Bild*).[13] By ontological valence, Gadamer understands the idea that the image or the picture confers to that which it represents an "increase in being," by making it come out in all its truth.[14] One will recall here the epiphanic or revelatory dimension of *Darstellung*: the image or the picture (*Bild*), does not have less being than what it represents and of which it is a copy (*Abbild*), it has *more*, it *represents* it, Gadamer provocatively argues. It can even be seen, underscores Gadamer by relying on a magnificent Neoplatonic notion, as an "emanation of the original" (GW 1, 145; Gadamer 2013, 141). The true image emanates from the original while also letting it appear in its truth, as if for the first time, since it is the prerogative of the image to capture and present this truth and being. One could say that the pictures and images have "more being" than the things they represent (which would, of course, not be true in the trivial nominalistic understanding of being), since the images are the ones that remain and impose themselves to our attention. Here, the decisive dimension is the revelatory, epiphanic and representative aspect of *Darstellung*.

It is also in this sense that one must understand the being of language for Gadamer (that is, as an emanation of the things and not of autonomous thinking). When we speak with one another—and when we speak, we always speak to one another—we do not use signs that are created by our understanding, we speak directly of the things as they are and manifest themselves in language. One has to understand this "manifestation of things" in the subjective sense of the genitive as a self-manifestation of things: it is the things themselves that come to language. Nonetheless, it is the linguistic element that bestows upon them an increase in being, since it is only by becoming language that these things gain being, reality, and presence: everything that is real for us is a reality that is said or sayable in some language. Gadamer does not insist here on the framing or schematization of reality, which our thinking or brain would accomplish by reading the world in such or such a way—this is an understanding of language as a symbolic form (that is, as a schematization of the mind), which Gadamer recognizes in Cassirer and criticizes. No, the accent lies on the ontological revelation that happens in language, thus on the self-manifestation of things in language.[15]

The strong notion of *Darstellung*, of art as presentation and representation, can thus help us understand the meaning of Gadamer's more famous, albeit not often well understood *dictum* according to which "Being that can be understood is language." This thesis doesn't mean that being is always framed by some language that would make us see it in such or such a way. Gadamer's thesis is less about language than about Being, the first word and indeed the subject of his famous dictum: Being, which can be understood, presents itself in language. It is *thanks* to language that we have access to the Being, but the Being to which we gain access is indeed *Being itself*. Language thus pertains in a way—a mysterious way, perhaps—to Being in the sense that it emanates from it.

Gadamer can thus conclude *Truth and Method* on a strong thesis, which takes up the notion of *Darstellung* unfolded in its first part: "Being is *language, that is self-presentation (Sprache, d. h. Sichdarstellen ist)*" (GW 1, 490; Gadamer 2013, 502). If this can be said with good reason to be the conclusion of *Truth and Method*, which as a whole is a *presentation* of this truth, then *Darstellung* represents its first and final word.

Notes

1. There is one felicitous exception: González Valerio 2006. The notion doesn't appear in Lawn and Keane 2011.
2. See Fruchon's note in his translation of Gadamer 1996, 120–21.
3. "A traves de ellos [los jugadores] el juego simplemente accede a su manifestación" (Gadamer 2003, 145).
4. "Es parte del poceso óntico de la representación, y pertenece esencialmente al juego como tal" (Gadamer 2003, 161). "*Es ist ein Teil des Seinsvorgangs der Darstellung, und gehört dem Spiel als Spiel wesenhaft zu*" (GW 1, 122).
5. "Esso è una parte del processo ontologico della rappresentazione e appartiene essenzialmente al gioco in quanto gioco" (Gadamer 1983, 148).
6. "*Das Spiel kommt durch die Spielenden lediglich zur Darstellung*" is translated by "*è il gioco che si pro-duce attraverso i giocatori*" (Gadamer 1983, 133).
7. On this cardinal notion, see Grondin 2005.
8. Regarding this "ephiphanic" virtue of the artwork, there is another question that can be raised here: why doesn't Gadamer also recognize that this dimension pertains to science itself? Isn't it its primary task to reveal the essence of things and of nature? To what extent, for instance, is an artistic presentation of the moon or of the human body more revelatory and original than a scientific one (which can itself be highly aesthetic)?
9. Kierkegaard thinks mainly of a religious and ethical contemporaneity, which is not only aesthetic. Gadamer radicalizes Kierkegaard by showing that even aesthetic temporality is itself never only aesthetic.
10. The last Gadamer takes up this notion of aura from Walter Benjamin. See, for instance, Gadamer 2007.
11. On this instrumental thinking of language, which for Gadamer amounts to a forgetfulness of language, see Grondin 2022 and 2024.
12. For the important context, see the following observations: "The legitimate question whether the word is nothing but a 'pure sign' or instead something like a 'copy' or an 'image' (*Bild*) [which appears to correspond to Gadamer's understanding] is thoroughly discredited by the *Cratylus*. Since there the argument that the word is a copy is driven ad absurdum, the only alternative seems to be that it is a sign. Although it is not especially emphasized, this consequence results from the negative discussion of the *Cratylus* and is sealed by knowledge being banished to the intelligible sphere. Thus, in all discussion of language ever since, the concept of the image (*eikon*) has been replaced by that of the sign (*semeion* or *semainon*).

This is not just a terminological change; it expresses an epoch-making decision about thought concerning language. That the true being of things is to be investigated 'without names' means that there is no access to truth in the proper being of words as such—even though, of course, no questioning, answering, instructing, and differentiating can take place without the help of language" (GW 1, 418; Gadamer 2013, 431).

13. See the chapter "The Ontological Valence of the Picture" (Gadamer, 2013, 135–44).

14. "Hence presentation (*Darstellung*) remains essentially tied to the original represented in it. But it is more than a copy. That the presentation is a picture—and not the original itself—does not mean anything negative, any mere diminution of being, but rather an autonomous reality. So, the relation of the picture to the original is basically quite different than in the case of a copy. *It is no longer a one-sided relationship.* That the picture has its own reality means the reverse for what is pictured, namely that it comes to presentation (*Darstellung*) in the representation (*Darstellung*)." (I reproduce here the English translation, which does not point out to the reader that it uses, with good reason, two English terms, presentation and representation, to render Gadamer's notion of *Darstellung* in this last segment). "It presents itself there . . . But if it presents itself in this way, this is no longer any incidental event, but belongs to its own being. Every such presentation is an ontological event and corresponds to the ontological dignity of what is represented. By being presented it experiences, as it were, an *increase in being*. The content of the picture itself is ontologically defined as an emanation of the original" (GW 1, 145; Gadamer 2013, 141, slightly modified translation).

15. On this ontological dimension of Gadamer's thinking, which has received many different interpretations, see Grondin 2022 and 2024.

Bibliography

Gadamer, Hans-Georg. "The Artwork in Word and Image." In *The Gadamer Reader: A Bouquet of the Later Writings*. Translated and edited by R. E. Palmer, 192–226. Evanston: Northwestern University Press, 2007.

———. *Truth and Method*. Revised ed. Translated by J. Weinsheimer and D. G. Marshall. New York: Bloomsbury, 2013.

———. *Verdad y método*. Translated by A. Agud Aparicio and R. de Agapito. Salamanca: Ediciones Sígueme, 2003.

———. *Verità e metodo*. Translated and edited by G. Vattimo. Milano: Bompiani, 1983.

———. *Vérité et méthode*. Translated by P. Fruchon, J. Grondin, and G. Merlio. Paris: Seuil, 1996.

———. *Wahrheit und Methode. Gesammelte Werke*. vol. 1 [GW 1]. Tübingen: Mohr Siebeck, 1986.

González, Valerio María Antonia. *El arte develado. Consideraciones estéticas sobre la hermenéutica de Gadamer*. Barcelona: Herder, 2006.

Grondin, Jean. "*La fusion des horizons. La version gadamérienne de l'adaequatio rei et intellectus?*" *Archives de philosophie* 68, no. 3 (2005): 401–18.

———. "The Basic Structure and Argument of *Truth and Method*." In *Gadamer's Truth and Method. A Polyphonic Commentary*. Edited by C. R. Nielsen and G. Lynch, XV–XXXIII. Lanham: Rowman & Littlefield, 2022.

———. "The Universality of Hermeneutics and Rhetoric in the Thought of Gadamer." *Symposium* 8, no. 2 (2004): 325–38.

———. *Metaphysical Hermeneutics*. London: Bloomsbury, 2024.

Lawn, Chris and Niall Keane, eds. *The Gadamer Dictionary*. London–New York: Continuum, 2011.

2

Gadamer's Hermeneutical Aesthetics *as* Practical Philosophy

Stefano Marino

Gadamer's Universal Hermeneutics in *Truth and Method*

The name of Hans-Georg Gadamer has often been associated to *one* philosophical work: *Truth and Method*, his long and complex treatise published in 1960. *Truth and Method* surely represents Gadamer's most systematic philosophical effort and thus definitely deserves to stand out in the entire catalog of his works. However, Gadamer also authored many significant writings, later collected in his *Gesammelte Werke* (GW) in ten volumes (1985 to 1995) and also in other important collections. As I will try to show, paying attention to some developments of his philosophical hermeneutics before and after *Truth and Method* can be important also for an assessment of his hermeneutical aesthetics.

Truth and Method is structured in three parts, respectively corresponding to different fields and steps of development of Gadamer's ambitious universal hermeneutics. In general, Gadamer's fundamental philosophical task is "to seek the experience of truth that transcends the domain of scientific method *wherever* that experience is to be found, and to inquire into its legitimacy" (GW 1, 1; Gadamer 2004, XXI, emphasis added). As he explains, his hermeneutical inquiry is focused on the "modes of experience that lie outside science": "modes of experience in which a truth is communicated that cannot be verified by the methodological means proper to science," "experience[s] of truth" that transcend "the domain of scientific method" (GW 1, 1; Gadamer 2004, XXI). In fact, "the problem of hermeneutics"—which, for Gadamer, is basically the problem of understanding [*Verstehen*]—is "not merely a concern of science," but rather something that "goes beyond the limits of the concept of method as set by modern science" and that "belongs to human experience of the world in general" (GW 1, 1; Gadamer 2004, XX).

The first part of *Truth and Method* constitutes the aesthetic part of Gadamer's book (that is, the part of the book that is specifically focused on certain fundamental problems concerning aesthetics and the philosophy of art)[1] understood in light of the basic hermeneutical phenomenon of understanding. This part of Gadamer's *opus magnum* starts from a historical reconstruction and a philosophical interpretation of the significance of the "humanist tradition" and the "guiding concepts of humanism"; then, it focuses on a penetrating critique of the "subjectivization of aesthetics" in the modern age, with a specific critique of the notions of *Erlebnis* and "aesthetic consciousness [*ästhetisches Bewußtsein*]," as inadequate to fully grasp the breadth of "aesthetic experience [*ästhetische Erfahrung*]"; finally, it arrives to the retrieval of the question of artistic truth and the development of a hermeneutical ontology of the artwork. Should one want to summarize the vast and complex contents and ramifications of the first part of *Truth and Method*, one could probably cite Gadamer's famous statement: "Aesthetics has to be absorbed into hermeneutics [*Die Ästhetik muß in der Hermeneutik aufgehen*]" (GW 1, 170; Gadamer 2004, 157).

In *Truth and Method*, Gadamer famously criticizes the gradual tendency in modern and contemporary culture to devalue and discredit any type of knowledge that does not seem to satisfy the rigorous (and, to some extent, also narrow) conditions of scientific methodology. In fact, Gadamer's fundamental aim is to understand and, so to speak, rescue "the variety of experiences—whether of aesthetic, historical, religious, or political consciousness"—that are irreducible to the procedures of science and technology: namely, experiences "of a unique kind, certainly different from . . . the knowledge of nature" (GW 1, 103–104; Gadamer 2004, 84–85). The aforementioned general tendency in modern and contemporary culture, for Gadamer, has especially conditioned in a negative way the evaluation of art's claim to truth; a key role in this process, according to Gadamer, has been played by Kant's aesthetic thinking and its aftereffects on nineteenth- and twentieth-century philosophical and scientific debates.

The first trace of Gadamer's interest in Kant's aesthetics can probably be traced back to a short essay entitled "On Kant's Foundation of Aesthetics and the Meaning of Art" (1939), in which Gadamer pays a special attention to §16, §17 and §42 of the *Critique of the Power of Judgment*, analyzing some important Kantian themes upon which he would also focus his attention on his later writings. So, in his 1958 essay "On the Problematic Character of Aesthetic Consciousness" Gadamer points out the epoch-making meaning of Kant's third *Critique* (GW 8, 9–17; Gadamer 1982b, 31–40). Then, in his 1960 essay "The Truth of the Work of Art"—first published as introduction to the Reclam edition of Heidegger's famous work "The Origin of the Work of Art" (2002)—Gadamer claims that it is necessary to "gain some insight into the prejudices that are present in the concept of a philosophical aesthetics," or even "to overcome the concept of aesthetics itself," thus turning to the *Critique of the Power of Judgment*, which "established the problem of aesthetics in its systematic significance" (GW 3, 253; Gadamer 1994, 100). But it is especially in the first two chapters of *Truth and Method* that Gadamer harshly questions the Kantian subjectivization of aesthetics, which, for him, essentially (and problematically) provided the conceptual basis for the main developments in the philosophy of art of the last centuries. For Gadamer, Kant's "transcendental justification of aesthetic judgment" implied a limitation of "the idea of taste to an area in which, as special principle of judgment, it could claim independent validity," and this limitation gave birth to an epoch-making and "radical subjectivization" of our experience with art (GW 1, 46–47; Gadamer 2004, 36).

The second part of Gadamer's *opus magnum*, then, is mostly centered on the relation of hermeneutics with the study of history and the "human sciences [*Geisteswissenschaften*]." It starts from a critical analysis of Romantic hermeneutics and its application to the study of history; then, it focuses on the attempt to overcome a narrowly understood epistemological approach through phenomenological research; finally, it arrives to the recovery of what Gadamer calls the fundamental hermeneutical problem and the development of a veritable theory of hermeneutical experience gravitating around the concept of "historically effected consciousness [*wirkungsgeschichtliches Bewußtsein*]."

Apropos of the latter concept, it may appear surprising at first sight that Gadamer's account of hermeneutical experience culminates in the notion of "historically effected consciousness," that is, in a notion that makes explicit use of the term *consciousness*. In fact, as noted by Giovanni

Matteucci (2004, 140), the basic dichotomy "consciousness versus experience" seems to underlie *Truth and Method* on the whole. Not by accident, this was precisely one of the main objections raised by Martin Heidegger, Gadamer's teacher, against his former pupil's philosophy;[2] in fact, when asked in 1965 if he was proud of his former pupil's philosophical hermeneutics, Heidegger reportedly replied: "Perhaps, but do you know his term *wirkungsgeschichtliches Bewußtsein*? . . . It is straight out of Dilthey!" (Palmer 2010, 122–23). Then, in a 1970 Heidelberg seminar organized by Gadamer, Heidegger raised the objection that Gadamer's philosophy, on the whole, failed to avoid a "fall back into consciousness [*Rückfall in das Bewußtsein*]" (Dottori 1996, 201).[3] Richard Palmer (2010, 123) has also recalled that he once "asked Gadamer himself about Heidegger's remark. Gadamer replied that Heidegger had already expressed to him that he did not like the implications of Gadamer's use of the term *Bewußtsein* (consciousness). The term suggested that Gadamer was falling back into thinking about the human subject within a world of objects. Gadamer had apologized to Heidegger and now to me: he did not like the term 'consciousness' either—but 'I could not find a better term!,'" Gadamer explained.

Anyway, apropos of the seemingly small disagreement between Heidegger and Gadamer about the use of the notion of *Bewußtsein*—that, in my view, is actually symptomatic of more essential disagreements and distinctions between them on fundamental doctrines such as the history of metaphysics understood as history of the "forgetfulness of Being [*Seinsvergessenheit*]" (see Marino 2015)—it is noteworthy that Gadamer himself partially recognized the problematic character of using the term *consciousness* to shape the concept of "historically effected consciousness." In fact, in some later discussions on, and clarifications of, his particular use of the term *Bewußtsein* (GW 2, 10–11, 495–96), Gadamer explained that "the effective historical consciousness . . . has more Being than being conscious; that is, more is historically affected and determined than we are conscious of as having been effected and determined" (GW 3, 221; Gadamer 1994, 58). So, in order to prevent a potential misinterpretation of his concept of hermeneutical experience and a reduction of the latter to the sole aspects of historical tradition and textual interpretation, Gadamer explains: "The problem is really universal," and this means that hermeneutical consciousness—that is, "the consciousness that is effected by history"—is something connected

> not only [with] the artistic tradition of a people, or historical tradition, or the principle of modern science in its hermeneutical

preconditions, but rather [with] the whole of our experience [*das Ganze unseres Erfahrungslebens*], [with] our own universal and human experience of life . . . What I am describing is the mode of the whole human experience of the world. I call this experience hermeneutical for the process we are describing is repeated continually throughout our familiar experiences. (GW 2, 226, 228, 230; Gadamer 1976b, 10, 13, 15)[4]

After this digression on *wirkungsgeschichtliches Bewußtsein* (the culminating concept of the second part of *Truth and Method*), let us return now to the general structure of Gadamer's 1960 masterpiece, which also includes a third and final part. The third part of *Truth and Method* starts from the idea of language as the medium of hermeneutical experience; then, it includes a critical examination of the development of the concept of language in the history of Western philosophy (with a special focus on Plato's *Cratylus* and medieval conceptions of language as *Verbum*); finally, it arrives to outline a theory of language as horizon of a hermeneutical ontology and experience of the world, culminating in the ambitious idea of the universal character of hermeneutics precisely due to the universality of language. Should one want to summarize the broad and ramified contents of the third part of *Truth and Method*, one could probably cite Gadamer's famous statement: "Being that can be understood is language [*Sein, das verstanden werden kann, ist Sprache*]" (GW 1, 478; Gadamer 2004, 470).

Aesthetics and Hermeneutics, Being and Language, Facts and Interpretations

In the previous section I have provided a quick sketch of the structure and main contents of *Truth and Method*. What has emerged is that, in Gadamer's view, art, history, humanities, language—and also ethics, law, religion, politics, if one widens the picture on the basis of his later writings that testify "an almost 'political' or cosmopolitan broadening of his hermeneutics" (Grondin 2003, 329)—*all* belong somehow to the "forms of inner self-enlightenment and to the intersubjective representation of human experience" (GW 2, 461; Gadamer 2004, 566). In this respect, what Gadamer builds up is "a philosophical position, a 'universal hermeneutics,' a theory about being and the human condition" (Sokolowski 1997, 224).[5] Apropos of the universal significance that he ambitiously assigns to the project of a philosophical hermeneutics, in the foreword to the second edition of *Truth and Method* (1965) Gadamer writes:

> how is understanding possible? This is a question which precedes any action of understanding on the part of subjectivity, including the methodical activity of the "interpretive sciences" and their norms and rules . . . [U]nderstanding is not just one of the various possible behaviors of the subject but the mode of being of *Dasein* itself. It is in this sense that the term "hermeneutics" has been used here. It denotes the basic being-in-motion of *Dasein* that constitutes its finitude and historicity, and hence embraces the whole of its experience of the world . . . [T]he universality of hermeneutics cannot be arbitrarily restricted or curtailed . . . [W]hat is here affirmed—that the province of hermeneutics is universal and especially that language is the form in which understanding is achieved—embraces "pre-hermeneutic" consciousness as well as all modes of hermeneutic consciousness. (GW 2, 439–41, 444; Gadamer 2004, XXVII–XXVIII, XXIX, XXXI)

Just like the third part of *Truth and Method*—and thus Gadamer's hermeneutical philosophy of language—is somehow summarized by his famous statement "Being that can be understood is language," in a similar way also the first part of *Truth and Method*—and thus Gadamer's hermeneutical philosophy of art—is somehow summarized by his equally famous motto "Aesthetics has to be absorbed into hermeneutics." However, just like the famous statement on being and language has often been interpreted in partially incorrect ways, thus leading to veritable misunderstandings of Gadamer's real philosophical aims, in a similar way also his famous motto on aesthetics and hermeneutics has sometimes been misunderstood, thus disguising (rather than revealing) Gadamer's real philosophical intentions.

Apropos of "Being that can be understood is language," it is a well-known fact that, although relying on different presuppositions and although aiming at different theoretical goals, both Frankfurt critical theorists (like Habermas during the famous "Hermeneutics and Critique of Ideology" dispute of the late 1960s and early 1970s) and so-called new realists have critically interpreted Gadamer's statement as supposedly expressing a sort of "linguistic idealism" (Ferraris 1998, 22, 29, 46). This critical interpretation—that, however, according to other scholars amounts to a veritable misunderstanding[6]—has conditioned in a serious way the "history of effect [*Wirkungsgeschichte*]" of Gadamer's philosophical account of language, up to the point that Gadamer himself sometimes felt the need to clarify that "Being that can be understood is language," for him, "is certainly not a metaphysical assertion," but simply "describes, from the medium of understanding, the unrestricted scope possessed by the hermeneutical standpoint" (GW 8, 7; Gadamer 2007, 130).[7] As Gadamer explains, "language is by nature the language of conversation," and it "has its true being only in dialogue, in *coming to an understanding*" (GW 1, 449–50, 478; Gadamer 2004, 443, 470), so that "we could even say that we are a living dialogue" (Gadamer 2003, 48). In a late important interview with Gadamer on his *Gesammelte Werke* and their *Wirkungsgeschichte*, Grondin observed and asked: "In the third major part of *Truth and Method* . . . being, understanding, and language appear to be completely interwoven with each other. Many have interpreted this as a kind of 'panlinguisticism.' Above all, they are led in this direction by your famous formula, which is indeed the most often-cited quotation from your work, namely: 'Being that can be understood is language.' What do you mean by this formula?" (Gadamer 1997, 285; Gadamer 2007, 416). Gadamer's reply to Grondin is noteworthy:

> Above all it means: being that can be experienced and understood, and it means that Being speaks. Only via language can being be understood. This formula that you cite is certainly a little ambiguous in its meaning, but an important aspect of speculative assertions is that they can come to speech from various sides . . . I have never thought and never ever said that everything is language. Being that can be understood, insofar as it can be understood, is language. This contains a limitation. What cannot be understood can pose an endless task of at least finding a word that comes a little closer to the matter at issue. (Gadamer 1997, 286; Gadamer 2007, 417)

As I said, certain reductive interpretations of the aforementioned motto about aesthetics and hermeneutics that summarizes the first part of *Truth and Method* have also conditioned in a serious way the reception of Gadamer's philosophy of art. For example, the idea that "Aesthetics has to be absorbed into hermeneutics" has been critically interpreted as supposedly expressing a sort of "hermeneutical nihilism," comparable to "the most nihilistic and illogical of all Nietzsche's statements (namely, that according to which there are no facts, but only interpretations)," and basically meaning that, for Gadamer, "artworks have to be merely absorbed into their interpretations," that is, "into their users and their immediate surroundings" (Ferraris 2007, 31, 60n).

In my view, an interpretation of this kind is problematic for various reasons and at various levels. First, it overemphasizes the relevance of a single Nietzschean aphorism—namely, the one that famously reads: "No, facts are precisely what is lacking; all that exists consists of interpretations [*Nein, gerade Thatsachen giebt es nicht, nur Interpretationen*]" (Nietzsche 1974, fr. 7 [60], 323; 1910, §481)—as if it were not possible to also find different (or even opposite) statements in the thought of a fragmentary and anti-systematic philosopher like Nietzsche. As a consequence, *all* Nietzsche's thought sometimes seems to be questionably reduced to just *one* sentence, emphatically defined as the "*Ur*-thesis" of his philosophy and, moreover, of *all* postmodern thinking influenced by Nietzsche (see Ferraris 2012, 5, 11).

Second, it seems to establish an immediate and complete correspondence between Gadamer's and Nietzsche's maxims, thus: (1) comparing in an all too direct way two statements that are *not* exactly focused on the same questions and indeed have different aims, problematically overlapping them (Ferraris 1998, 28); (2) merely equating Gadamer's hermeneutical views on being and language with Gianni Vattimo's development of hermeneutics into "weak thought" as a "philosophy of history" based on the "nihilistic destination of the West" (Ferraris 1998, 22), which is grounded indeed to a large extent on Nietzsche's aforementioned (and surely debatable) view on facts and interpretations (Vattimo 1994, 131). As Donatella Di Cesare (2013, 208) has noted, "[w]hile Vattimo separates hermeneutics from phenomenology, he gives considerable space to Nietzsche's philosophy of interpretation. Accordingly, he conceives of hermeneutics as a 'philosophy of interpretation.' Yet *hermeneutics is not a philosophy of interpretation*," at least not in the sense of the Nietzschean motto on facts versus interpretations,[8] "and [Gadamer's] hermeneutics has never understood itself as such. This is probably the greatest misunderstanding that still burdens the reception of hermeneutics"—and that, as we have just seen, may also arrive to negatively affect the reception of Gadamer's hermeneutical aesthetics.[9]

Third, an interpretation of Gadamer's statement "Aesthetics has to be absorbed into hermeneutics" like the aforementioned one—that abruptly identifies it with Nietzsche's motto "[F]acts are precisely what is lacking; all that exists consists of interpretations"—seems to overestimate the real range of Nietzsche's influence on Gadamer, which is *not* comparable to the influence and the appeal held by Nietzsche on many other twentieth-century philosophers (see Ferraris 2009, 63–145). In fact, Gadamer probably "stands just as far from Nietzsche as he stands close to Plato and Hegel," because he "sees in Nietzsche's hermeneutic radicalism the reverse side of Cartesian metaphysics . . . Measured by the absoluteness of [metaphysical] truth, everything else will appear as mere interpretation and become relativized to a perspective. Here lies the complicity of metaphysics and nihilism, which [Gadamer's] hermeneutics *cannot accept*" (Di Cesare 2013, 208, emphasis added).

Gadamer's peculiar unconcern to Nietzsche plays a relevant role for the purpose of a proper and adequate understanding of his philosophical hermeneutics (see GW 4, 448–49; Gadamer 1998b, 124; Gadamer 2002b, 27; Gadamer 2006, 73). It is surely remarkable that Gadamer sometimes distanced himself in a quite explicit way from Nietzsche's radicalism. For example, Gadamer observes that "we all run the risk of a terrible intellectual *hubris* if we equate Nietzsche's anticipations . . . with life as it is actually lived with its own forms of solidarity," also adding that here, "in fact, [his] divergence from Heidegger is fundamental" (Gadamer 1983b, 264). In this context, it is also noteworthy that Gadamer distanced himself from the so-called hermeneutics of suspicion, which has been strongly influenced by Nietzsche and has played an important role in twentieth-century philosophy. So, in his essay "The Conflict of Interpretations," Gadamer explains that "it was mainly Nietzsche that brought about [a] new style of interpretation," namely one that aims at "unmasking *pretended* meaning and signification" (Gadamer 1982a, 299). However, Gadamer critically asks: "how can we hope to reconcile this radicalism of interpretation as unmasking" with the kind of hermeneutics precisely presented in *Truth and Method*, that is, "with an attitude of participation in a cultural heritage which forms and transforms itself in a process of mediation?" (Gadamer 1982a, 301). "In posing this question," Gadamer explains, "we are confronted by the two extremes," represented, on the one hand, by "interpretation in the Nietzschean sense," whereas, on the other hand, "there is the experience of life in communicative processes, the actual working out of daily life, where communication . . . structures the whole of social reality and encompasses the cultural features of this reality" (Gadamer 1982a, 303).[10]

Hermeneutics as Practical Philosophy before and after *Truth and Method*

In the previous section I have tried to briefly explain why, in my view, certain interpretations of Gadamer's hermeneutical aesthetics (and also of his hermeneutical philosophy of language) are problematic and questionable, also hinting at the fact that certain misunderstandings have conditioned in a negative way the reception of Gadamer's philosophy. On this basis, in this section and the next one I will try to provide a slightly different interpretation, basically suggesting to seriously take into consideration Gadamer's idea of hermeneutics *as* practical philosophy—an idea that was mostly implicit before *Truth and Method* and in Gadamer's 1960 *opus magnum*, but was presented in a clear and explicit way in his writings of the 1970s and 1980s. In fact, if aesthetics has to be absorbed into hermeneutics, and if hermeneutics has to be understood on the basis of the model of practical philosophy, this implies that, for Gadamer, the true role, value, and significance of aesthetic experience derives from its fundamental connection with the universal and all-encompassing human dimension of practice [*praxis*]. An observation by Günter Figal is remarkable in this context, as Figal notes that, in Gadamer's philosophy, "hermeneutical consciousness is to be demonstrated as a variation of practical knowledge," so that "philosophical hermeneutics is consequently able to be understood . . . as 'practical philosophy' "; accordingly, hermeneutical experience, "even if it encompasses 'aesthetic' phenomena, is conceived [by Gadamer] on the model of practical philosophy" (Figal 2010, 23).

At this point, it is important to grasp the exact meaning of the notions of "practical philosophy [*praktische Philosophie*]" and "practical knowledge [*praktisches Wissen*]" in the context of Gadamer's thinking. As I said at the beginning of my essay, although Gadamer authored many writings before and after publishing *Truth and Method* in 1960, nevertheless *Truth and Method* stands out in the entire catalog of his works because of its length, complexity, and systematicity. However, this does *not* mean that every aspect of Gadamer's philosophical hermeneutics can be found in the three parts of *Truth and Method*[1]—just like, for example, not all the dimensions of Heidegger's ontology can be found only in *Being and Time*, not all the details of Adorno's dialectics can be found only in *Negative Dialectics*, and so on. So, although the most important features and aspects of Gadamer's aesthetics are surely available in the various chapters, sections, and subsections that form the first part of *Truth and Method*, this must *not* lead to overlooking the relevance of his subsequent writings on aesthetics and poetics, collected in the eighth and ninth volumes of his *Gesammelte Werke*.

Some aspects of Gadamer's hermeneutical conception of *praxis* are already present in *Truth and Method*. However, it is especially in some of his later writings (sometimes connected in a fascinating way to some of his early works) that Gadamer fully explicates the breadth, depth, and significance of his interest in the concept of praxis for a reconsideration and rehabilitation of hermeneutics *as* practical philosophy. The question concerning practical knowledge represents one of the leading questions of Gadamer's entire path of thinking. This question is already at the core of some of his first publications, as testified by his important essay from 1930 precisely entitled "*Praktisches Wissen*" (GW 5, 230–48). Thirty years later, the same question plays a fundamental role in the influential section of *Truth and Method* on the hermeneutical relevance of Aristotle's ethics, in which Gadamer deals with "the problem of *application*, which is to be found in all understanding," that is, the problem of "applying something universal to a particular situation" (GW 1, 312, 317; Gadamer 2004, 306, 310). But the question concerning the breadth, value, and significance of *praktisches Wissen* acquires the status of *the* veritable key question of Gadamer's philosophy in the 1970s and 1980s, when Gadamer makes fully explicit what he had left partially implicit in his previous works, thus revealing the nature of his philosophical hermeneutics *as* practical philosophy. Finally, at the end of the 1990s, this question leads Gadamer to publish his own translation of the sixth book of Aristotle's *Nicomachean Ethics* (Gadamer 1998c), a text that he had first studied in Freiburg under Heidegger's guidance in the early 1920s. Not by chance, various scholars of hermeneutics have identified the Aristotelian question of practical knowledge as the "original conception" of Gadamer's philosophy (Chang 1994, 95–104) and have defined Gadamer's "interpretation of Heidegger's interpretation of Aristotle" as *the* "key for the comprehension of his own hermeneutic theory" (Stolzenberg 2005, 135).[12]

In his theory of *Verstehen*—which, as we will see, is also closely related to his concept of *Erfahrung*—Gadamer often makes reference to Aristotle's conception of the fundamental dimensions of human life (*theoria, praxis, poiesis*) and their corresponding virtues (*episteme, phronesis, techne*). For example, when Gadamer claims that *Verstehen* and *Erfahrung* stand "in an ineluctable opposition . . . to the kind of instruction that follows from general *theoretical* or *technical* knowledge" (GW 1, 361; Gadamer 2004, 350, emphasis added), he apparently relies on a concept of understanding and experience as *practical* knowledge. Apropos of this, Jean Grondin (2002,

36–41) has importantly distinguished in Gadamer's philosophy three slightly different notions of understanding: *Verstehen* "as intellectual grasp" (which, however, plays a minor role in *Truth and Method*), "as agreement," and finally, most noticeably and most meaningfully, "as practical know-how"; according to Grondin, Gadamer mostly uses "a 'practical' notion of understanding to shake up the epistemological notion that prevailed in the tradition of Dilthey and the methodology of the human sciences," and "[a] very important source for this Gadamerian notion of practical or applicative understanding" is precisely "Aristotle's notion of practical understanding [*phronesis*]."

Now, the interpretation of the question concerning practical knowledge that I would like to suggest here argues that Gadamer's conception of *praktisches Wissen*—as the basis for his subsequent definition of philosophical hermeneutics *as* practical philosophy—can be understood in two slightly different ways, corresponding to two levels or dimensions of his conception of *praktische Philosophie*. On the one hand, *praxis* and *phronesis* are strictly and exclusively related to ethics and politics, that is, with what Aristotle's practical philosophy properly consists of. This is especially clear in Gadamer's writings specifically dedicated to the interpretation of Aristotle's texts, often establishing a comparison also with Plato's works (with extraordinary philological skills, thanks to Gadamer's studies with the great philologist Paul Friedländer). On the other hand, in some of his essays more generally dedicated to the conception of hermeneutics *as* practical philosophy—and, in that context, to the question of practical reason [*praktische Vernunft*]—Gadamer seems to adopt the concept of *praxis* in a wider sense, that is, using it as a notion that is suitable to indicate an all-encompassing dimension of human existence, of which ethics and politics strictly understood are only a part.[13]

As we have seen in the second section of the present contribution, the great ambition of Gadamer's "universal hermeneutics" is that of unifying a variety of experiences by understanding them as different modes of the basic hermeneutical phenomenon of *Verstehen* that "pervades *all* human relations to the world" (GW 1, 1; Gadamer 2004, XX, emphasis added). James Risser has rightly observed that "the issue of a philosophical hermeneutics," for Gadamer, "is to identify at a fundamental level the operation that unites . . . the experiences of philosophy, art, and history as experiences of truth that extend beyond methodological considerations . . . as experiences of understanding" (Risser (2010, 6) and, more precisely, of *practical* understanding. In fact, Gadamer's *entire* philosophical project is the project of a hermeneutics that "embraces *the whole* of the human *life-world* as its *practical understanding* of itself in *all* of its dimensions" (Bruns 2004, 44, emphasis added). In his seminal essay "Hermeneutics as Practical Philosophy" Gadamer offers some elucidations on this point, explaining that

> practice formulates . . . the mode of behavior of that which is living in the broadest sense. Practice, as the character of being alive, stands between activity and situatedness. As such it is not confined to human beings, who alone are active on the basis of free choice [*prohairesis*]. Practice means instead the actuation of life [*energeia*] of anything alive, to which corresponds a life, a way of life, a life that is led in a certain way [*bios*]. Animals too have *praxis* and *bios*, which means a way of life . . . The way of life of human beings is not so fixed by nature as is that of other living beings. This is expressed by the concept of *prohairesis*, which . . . means "preference" and "prior choice" [and] which can be predicated only of human beings. (Gadamer 1976a, 81; 1983c, 90–91)

From the point of view of this broader and more comprehensive meaning of *praxis*, the latter represents for Gadamer "*the* all-inclusive, distinctive characteristic of the human being" (GW 7, 226; Gadamer 1986a, 175, emphasis added). It is precisely in such a broader sense of *praxis*—and, correspondingly, of practical knowledge and practical reason—that this concept is sometimes understood by Gadamer as synonymous of hermeneutical experience, which, in turn, in Gadamer's universal hermeneutics does *not* coincide only with the experience of the interpretation of texts, but rather refers to "the way experience in the *life-world* is lived" (Gadamer 1993, 31; Gadamer 2001, 52). This leads in the direction of a complex hermeneutical "phenomenology of the mediation of sense" and "phenomenology of culture" (Figal 2001, 103–104) that aims to account for different forms of unmethodical and non-scientific experience (including our experience with the various arts) by including them in the universal dimension of understanding *as* practical knowledge and experience (GW 2, 327). For example, in the afterword to the third edition of *Truth and Method* (1972) Gadamer writes:

> practice [*praxis*] represents an independent contribution to knowledge . . . Relying on the tradition of practical knowledge helps guard us against the technological self-understanding of the modern concept of science . . . I can appeal to the fact that the *fore-knowledge* [or] *prescientific knowledge* . . . stemming from

the way *language* orients us in the world . . . comes into play *wherever the experience of life is assimilated*, linguistic tradition is understood, and social life goes on. Such fore-knowledge is certainly no higher court where science is tried; it is itself exposed to every critical objection that science raises, but it is and remains the vehicle of *all understanding* . . . Philosophy . . . does pertain to *the whole of our experience of life and our world*, but like no other science—rather like *our very experience, articulated in language, of life and the world* . . . [O]ne cannot ignore such "knowledge," *in whatever form it expresses itself*: in religious or proverbial wisdom, in works of art or philosophical thought. (GW 2, 455, 459, 461; Gadamer 2004, 560–61, 564–66, emphasis added)

Hermeneutical Aesthetics and the Anthropological Basis of Our Experience of Art

After having inquired, in the last two sections, into the general structure of Gadamer's hermeneutics (on the basis of the three parts of *Truth and Method*) and his conception of hermeneutics *as* practical philosophy that powerfully emerges in the 1970s, let us return now to the questions addressed in the first section of the present contribution and, particularly, to the famous statement "Aesthetics has to be absorbed into hermeneutics." As we have seen, in the first part of *Truth and Method* Gadamer develops a critique of "the approach of modern philosophy of consciousness," an approach that, for him, "fails to thematize the broader constitutive conditions of aesthetic experience" (Hance 1997, 134) and, consequently, fails to do justice to the vastness and richness of aesthetic experience.

The central role played by the concept of *Erfahrung* in Gadamer's philosophy, in general, has already emerged in the final paragraphs of the previous section. In fact, in order to do justice to the vastness and richness of our unmethodical *Verstehen*—which, although "not concerned primarily with amassing verified knowledge, such as would satisfy the methodological idea of science," is nevertheless also "concerned with knowledge and truth"—it is necessary "to take the concept of experience more broadly" (GW 1, 1, 103; Gadamer 2004, XX, 84) than modern culture has done, due to the powerful influence of science and technology. For Gadamer, in other words, it is necessary to understand experience *not* just as the relation of "an object that stands over against a subject for itself" (GW 1, 108; Gadamer 2004, 103), as the basic epistemological framework of modern science invites us to do. In fact, *Verstehen* and *Erfahrung* are characterized by the fact that "a 'subject' does not stand over against an 'object' or a world of objects," but rather "something *plays* back and forth between the human being and that which he or she encounters in the world" (Gadamer 1993, 26–27; Gadamer 2001, 49, emphasis added).

A section of *Truth and Method* is specifically focused on the concept of experience and the essence of hermeneutical experience. It is indeed a decisive section, emphatically defined by Gadamer himself as a section that "takes on a systematic and key position" in his investigation and represents "the centerpiece of the whole book" (Gadamer 1993, 32; Gadamer 2001, 53). The starting point of Gadamer's inquiry into the notion of experience is the observation that, quite paradoxically, "the concept of experience," notwithstanding its wide diffusion and its everyday use, is "one of the most obscure we have" (GW 1, 352; Gadamer 2004, 341). This situation, according to Gadamer, basically derives from the fact that the concept of experience "plays an important role in the natural sciences," and, accordingly, since the seventeenth century "has been subjected to an epistemological schematization that . . . truncates its original meaning" (GW 1, 352; Gadamer 2004, 341). From this point of view, "the main deficiency in theory of experience hitherto," for Gadamer, "is that it is entirely oriented toward science" (GW 1, 352; Gadamer 2004, 341). Sometimes Gadamer expresses this idea by saying that, in the modern age, the concept of *experience* has been wrongly reduced to the idea of *experiment* in natural science. As Gadamer explains, the concept of experience is

> the least well known concept in philosophy as a whole, and this is because the so-called sciences of *experience* took the *experiment* as their starting-point and made it a paradigm for experience. These *sciences* only grant space to an experience if they can obtain from it methodically guaranteed answers to questions. But *on the whole, our life is not like this*. Our lives are *not* lived according to scientifically guaranteed programs and secure from crises; rather, *we have to undergo our experiences ourselves*. (Gadamer 1993, 32; Gadamer 2001, 53, emphasis added)[14]

As we have seen in the first section of the present contribution, modern aesthetic thinking, for Gadamer, has been characterized on the whole by a problematic process of subjectification: that is, by a general tendency to reduce the (intersubjective, indeed communitarian) richness and complexity of aesthetic experience to the mere (subjective) capacity of a supposedly pure aesthetic consciousness. For Gadamer, as I said, a central role in this process was played by Kant's aesthetics, inasmuch as Kant,

> in the subjective universality of the aesthetic judgment of taste, discovered the powerful and legitimate claim to independence that the aesthetic judgment can make over against the claims of the understanding and morality . . . What sets the beautiful apart . . . manifests itself in a subjective factor: the intensification of the *Lebensgefühl* [life feeling] through the harmonious correspondence of imagination and understanding . . . We must acknowledge that this justification of the autonomy of art was a great achievement in the age of the Enlightenment . . . Basing aesthetics on the subjectivity of the mind's powers was, however, the beginning of a dangerous process of subjectification. (GW 3, 253–54; Gadamer 1994, 100–101)

Among the various implications and consequences of the advent of a subjectivistic and anti-experiential (or, so to speak, not adequately experiential) approach to the aesthetic dimension, Gadamer emphasizes the gradual confinement of art in the realm of the imaginary, the unreal, the mere appearance, that is, "fiction" (GW 1, 90; Gadamer 2004, 73). On the one hand, the modern process of legitimization and autonomization of the aesthetic dimension surely had some positive effects, leading to "the creation of specific 'sites' for art" that are often "carefully separated from the rest of civic reality, which is dominated by the hard realities of science and economics"; on the other hand, however, the same process had also negative consequences, leading to conceive of art "as appearance *sui generis*," as "an autonomous world of production and creation," and gradually cutting it off "from the rest of reality" (Grondin 2003, 36–37). So, the aforementioned "specific 'sites' for art"—such as "the 'universal library' . . . the museum, the theater, the concert hall," and so on—have assumed the form of spaces in which "the 'aesthetic differentiation' performed by aesthetic consciousness also creates an external existence for itself" (GW 1, 92–93; Gadamer 2004, 75–76). Namely, spaces in which "the work loses its place and the world to which it belongs":

aesthetic differentiation is an abstraction that selects only on basis of aesthetic quality as such. It is performed in the self-consciousness of "aesthetic experiences" . . . By disregarding everything in which a work is rooted (its original context of life, and the religious or secular function that gave it significance), it becomes visible as the "pure work of art." In performing this abstraction, aesthetic consciousness . . . differentiates what is aesthetically intended from everything that is outside the aesthetic sphere. It abstracts from all the conditions of a work's accessibility. Thus it is a specifically aesthetic kind of differentiation. It distinguishes the aesthetic quality of a work from all the elements of content that induce us to take up a moral or religious stance towards it. (GW 1, 91, 93; Gadamer 2004, 74, 76)

Shifting his attention from the theoretical questions concerning the conceptual foundations of modern aesthetics to the practical implications of this discourse concerning the artists' experiences and activities, in the first part of *Truth and Method* Gadamer emphasizes some difficult situations often experienced by artists in the modern age. In fact, beside the undeniably positive aspect of the achievement of unprecedented levels of creative freedom (especially in the age of twentieth-century avant-garde art), Gadamer also recalls some negative aspects concerning the artists' loss of their place in the world. According to Gadamer, "the complete independence of his [or her] creativity" has gradually made the artist become "an outsider" or "a bohemian," turning him/her into "an ambiguous figure" who must unceasingly struggle to create "new symbols or a new myth that will . . . create a community"; however, "the particularity of such communities," for Gadamer, "merely testifies to the disintegration that is taking place" (GW 1, 93–94; Gadamer 2004, 76). So, in the end, the modern artist

> does not live within a community, but creates for himself a community as is appropriate to his pluralistic situation. Openly admitted competition combined with the claim that his own particular form of creative expression and his own particular artistic message is the only true one, necessarily gives rise to heightened expectations. This is in fact the messianic consciousness of the [contemporary] artist, who feels himself to be a "new savior" (Immermann) with a claim on mankind. He proclaims a new

message of reconciliation and as a social outsider pays the price for this claim, since with all his artistry he is only an artist for the sake of art. (GW 8, 98; Gadamer 1986b, 7)[15]

As I said, in *Truth and Method* Gadamer still had *not* thematized in an explicit way the idea of hermeneutics *as* practical philosophy (in the broad meaning of the notion of *praktisch* that has been previously explained). Nevertheless, it is not impossible to understand in light of that idea his aforementioned critical observations on the artwork's loss of its place in the world caused by the negative impact of the abstraction processes of "aesthetic differentiation [*ästhetische Unterscheidung*]." Anyway, it is in particular Gadamer's long and complex essay "The Relevance of the Beautiful"—not by accident, coeval to his "turn" to practical philosophy as *the* model for philosophical hermeneutics in the early 1970s—that probably offers the most explicit and stimulating insights in this direction (GW 8, 94–142; Gadamer 1986b, 3–53).

In "The Relevance of the Beautiful," Gadamer articulates a hermeneutical reflection on art and aesthetic experience that gravitates around three key concepts: play, symbol, festival [*Spiel, Symbol, Fest*]. Remarkably, Gadamer lets emerge here the promising and rich anthropological background of his hermeneutical aesthetics, explicitly speaking of the need to inquire into "the anthropological foundation upon which the phenomenon of art rests" and the "profound anthropological dimension" of aesthetic experience (GW 8, 96, 136; Gadamer 1986b, 5, 47). For the limited purposes of the present contribution, what matters is especially the connection established by Gadamer between regaining "the anthropological basis of our experience of art" and recovering the fundamental importance of "the genuine experience of community" in order to truly understand "the proper function of art" in the whole of human life (GW 8, 113, 140–41; Gadamer 1986b, 22, 50–51). In fact, it is only through the recognition of its essential embeddedness in the dense, lifeworldly, communal, and communicative context of human practices that the experience of art can be properly understood in all its meaningfulness. With regard to this, it is not hard to see that certain practical and also performative aspects that characterize Gadamer's ideas about art and aesthetic experience also allow to establish fruitful comparisons between his hermeneutical aesthetics and, for example, John Dewey's pragmatist aesthetics, based on the idea of art *as* experience (on this topic, see Romagnoli 2022).

Coherently with the interpretation of Gadamer's hermeneutical aesthetics that I have tried to advance in the present essay, it is especially the connection between the notions of community, communication, and festival—understood as important to grasp "the nature of aesthetic experience" (GW 8, 112; Gadamer 1986b, 21)—that emerges as one of the most powerful and distinctive features of "The Relevance of the Beautiful." So, Gadamer observes that artworks were once "encountered within a religious or secular context as an adornment of the life-world," without being "divorced from [their] context of life" or being appreciated in a detached and disenchanted way as "simply 'art' " (GW 8, 110; Gadamer 1986b, 19). For Gadamer, "art occupied a legitimate place in the world," and hence was able "to effect an integration between community . . . on the one hand, and the self-understanding of the creative artist on the other," whereas "this self-evident integration . . . no longer exists" (GW 8, 97–98; Gadamer 1986b, 6). However, if we aim to overcome the narrowness of a conception of art that tends to abruptly differentiate it and isolate it from the broader context of actual life experience, for Gadamer we have to rediscover "the idea of universal communication" that is inherent to art and the "experience of community" that plays such a decisive role to form "the real nature of art" (GW, 103, 131; Gadamer 1986b, 12, 40).

As I said, in "The Relevance of the Beautiful" it is especially the concept of festival that Gadamer strategically uses to emphasize these aspects of his hermeneutical view of art and aesthetic experience. Apropos of this, Gadamer eventually offers some examples that include "the great works of Greek tragedy," "Attic drama [that] united its audience," "[t]he great Western polyphonic tradition that derives from Gregorian church music . . . and the Passion music of J. S. Bach," and, quite surprisingly (and displaying a notable open-mindedness), also contemporary popular music, that is, "the records of modern songs so popular with the young people of today" that equally have the "capacity to establish communication" and create a "genuine experience of community" (GW 8, 140–41; Gadamer 1986b, 50–51).

In conclusion, what emerges from Gadamer's critique of "aesthetic consciousness" is the need to recover a wider and more comprehensive concept of "aesthetic experience," one that is capable, among other things, to overcome the modern tendency to separate the artwork from the *practical* and *lifeworldly* context that it belongs to and that actually provides the artwork with its full meaningfulness and significance for human life. If aesthetics, for Gadamer, has to be absorbed into hermeneutics, it is surely *not* to nihilistically dissolve the artwork into an uncontrolled and unbalanced flow of subjective interpretations, but rather to reintegrate it into a robust set of shared practices and experiences, in order to strengthen our self-understanding and especially our mutual understanding with each other.

Notes

1. Aesthetics is basically understood by Gadamer as a philosophy of art, rather than as a philosophy of perception, on the basis of its etymological derivation from the Greek term *aisthesis*. A noteworthy exception, from this point of view, is represented by Gadamer's essay "Man and His Hand in Modern Civilization," in which he deals with the question concerning the crisis of aesthetic experience today, but *not* intending *aesthetic* experience as *artistic* experience (as Gadamer usually does), but rather understanding the latter as *sensory, perceptual* experience. For example, Gadamer explains here that the "omnipotent bureaucracy and stagnating progress in technology and civilization" have determined "a loss in cultivated senses," so that today we must reinstate a "genuine equilibrium between our sensuous and moral powers," in order to attempt "to humanize our lives in our state, society, and administration" (Gadamer 1983a, 145, 147–48; Gadamer 1998a, 119, 121). As Gadamer writes: "The senses have a certain intelligence . . . Cultured senses: that ultimately means developing the human capacity for choice and judgment . . . Little has fundamentally changed since Schiller hoped aesthetic education would give us a way of progressing toward freedom from the soulless mechanism of the state apparatus" (Gadamer 1983a, 144–45, 148; 1998a, 118–19, 121).

2. Another famous and relevant objection raised by Heidegger against Gadamer's philosophy is that of secretly aiming to "absorb" everything in hermeneutics, thus remaining "trapped" in a traditionally dialectical—and hence, for Heidegger, metaphysical—framework. In fact, in a letter to Otto Pöggeler dated January 11, 1962, Heidegger comments on *Truth and Method*: "It is indeed curious [*merkwürdig*] to see how Gadamer takes up the metaphysics of Being [*Seinsmetaphysik*] at the end of his book without further examination and understands language as a transcendental determination of Being" (I borrow this information from Grondin 2010, 200, 201n).

3. In this context, it is also worth mentioning Gadamer's letter to Heidegger dated June 28, 1957, in which he optimistically stated that he reckoned to conclude his *opus* in a few weeks, but then added that Heidegger would have probably considered it as an insufficiently radical philosophical effort (Gadamer 2002a, 26–27). Anyway, although Heidegger sometimes distanced himself from Gadamer's thinking, it must be also emphasized that, when asked about his most gifted student, he recommended precisely Gadamer (see Heidegger's letter to Stadelmann dated September

1, 1945, in Heidegger 2000, 395). Moreover, Heidegger explicitly recognized that Gadamer had given excellent interpretations of his own thought, for instance with regard to the philosophy of art (see Heidegger's letter to Gadamer dated September 3, 1960; in Heidegger 2005–2006, 37).

4. "The theme [of] the humanities . . . dominated in *Truth and Method*," especially in its second part; although "the development toward a *philosophical* hermeneutics, which leaves the 'bounded' problem of the humanities behind it," was already present in *Truth and Method*, it is apparent that Gadamer still presented his project in 1960 "as one of a 'hermeneutics of the humanities'" (Grondin 1995, 31–32, 37). This was probably misleading for some readers of *Truth and Method*, who could not immediately recognize the universal ambition of Gadamer's philosophical hermeneutics. Also, Gadamer later observed: "I used to think from the perspective of the *Geisteswissenschaften* as the central problem, more so than I do now . . . Now, when I lecture on hermeneutics, I can raise this entire debate to a more adequate level . . . Insofar as hermeneutics is more than a theory of the human sciences, it also has the human situation in the world in its entirety in view" (Gadamer 1992, 150, 152).

5. The universal character of Gadamer's hermeneutics must *not* be confused with a claim for absoluteness, which would contradict his constant emphasis on the inescapable "*finitude of our . . . experience*" (GW 1, 461; Gadamer 2004, 453). In fact, the hermeneutical claim for universality (GW 2, 219–31; Gadamer 1976b, 3–17) does *not* coincide "with totality": as Gadamer noted, "[t]his does not concern an encyclopedic collection of all that is knowable. That would only lead one back to the metaphysical concept of reason and so to the doctrine of the *intellectus infinitus*" (GW 8, 401; Gadamer 2000b, 152).

6. Quite interestingly, for example, Brice R. Wachterhauser (1994; 2002) has interpreted vice versa Gadamer's hermeneutical account of knowledge and language (again, summarized by the motto "Being that can be understood is language") as clearly expressing a form of epistemological and ontological realism.

7. "When I wrote the sentence, 'Being that can be understood is language,'" Gadamer explains, "what was implied by this was that what is can never be completely understood. This is implied insofar as everything that goes under the name of language always goes beyond whatever achieves the status of a proposition. That which is to be understood is that which comes into language, but of course it is always that which is taken as something, taken as something true [*wahr-genommen*]. This is the hermeneutical dimension—a dimension in which Being 'shows itself'" (GW 2, 334; Gadamer 2007, 162).

8. Of course, this must *not* lead us to overlook and understate the role played by notions such as *Auslegung* and *Interpretation* in Gadamer's hermeneutics, which, as such, are surely important both in *Truth and Method* and in many other writings. Rather, the point is to emphasize: (1) the primacy of understanding [*Verstehen*], as the fundamental hermeneutical dimension, over interpretation; and

(2) the difference between Gadamer's idea of interpretation (mostly influenced by Dilthey and other hermeneutical thinkers) and Nietzsche's.

9. *Weak Thought* (in Italian: *Il pensiero debole*) is the title of a collection of essays edited by Gianni Vattimo and Pier Aldo Rovatti in 1983; however, the expression has been frequently used to indicate, in general, the whole development of Vattimo's nihilistic hermeneutics. Di Cesare's clarifications are surely of great relevance, most of all with regard to the Italian reception of Gadamer's thinking that has been surely influenced by the "mediation" of Vattimo (who, by the way, is also the Italian translator of *Truth and Method*). In fact, Di Cesare's detailed remarks allow us to clearly notice some relevant differences between Gadamer's hermeneutics and Vattimo's "weak thought"—which, among other things, is based on a veritable apology of nihilism, viewed as today's "only possibility of freedom" (Vattimo 1991, 29)—also in order to appreciate the autonomy and originality of Vattimo's own philosophy. Apropos of Vattimo's relation to Gadamer, see his autobiographical reflections (Vattimo 2010, 28–29, 103, 108–10).

10. According to Gadamer, "going behind, unmasking . . . is something besides communication," and "the preeminent model" must always remain the model of "the *dialogue*," which we must assume as "the basis of our social life" and understand as "sharing in a social act . . . In this sense," Gadamer observes, "the critique of ideologies, psychoanalysis, and every radical form of critique" directly or indirectly inspired by Nietzsche "needs to be reintegrated into [the] basic process of social life" (Gadamer 1982a, 303–304). On the same topic, see also Gadamer's essay "The Hermeneutics of Suspicion," where Gadamer differentiates "hermeneutics in the classic sense of interpreting the meaning of texts" from the "radical critique of and suspicion against understanding and interpreting," and then explains that "[t]his radical suspicion" and the "effort to unmask the pretentions hidden behind so-called objectivity" were "inaugurated by Nietzsche" (Gadamer 1984, 54, 58).

11. According to Richard J. Bernstein, the "practical-moral orientation" represents "the approach that pervades so much of Gadamer's thinking and helps to give it unified perspective," *but* "in *Truth and Method*, Gadamer's primary concern is with the understanding and interpretation of works of art, texts, and traditions . . . Ethics and politics are not in the foreground of his investigations . . . But it is also clear that if we pay close attention to Gadamer's writings before and after the publication of *Truth and Method*, we will see that from his very earliest to his most recent writings he has consistently shown a concern with ethics and politics, [returning] again and again to the dialectical interplay of hermeneutics and *praxis*" (Bernstein 1983, 150–51, 166).

12. On many occasions, Gadamer has emphasized the relevance of Heidegger's early hermeneutics of facticity for the development of his own philosophical project. In his introduction to Heidegger's so-called *Natorp-Bericht* (a text from the early 1920s but first published only in 1989, after Heidegger's text had been considered lost for decades), Gadamer has indicated his first encounter with Heidegger's

phenomenological interpretations of Aristotle as the original source of his *whole* philosophy (Gadamer 1989, 229). Sometimes Gadamer arrived to compare his reading of Heidegger's *Natorp-Bericht* in 1922 to "being hit by a charge of electricity" (GW 3, 263; Gadamer 1994, 113), also emphasizing the decisive importance of his attendance to Heidegger's 1923 lecture course *Ontologie (Hermeneutik der Faktizität)* and seminars on Aristotle's ethics (see GW 2, 485; GW 10, 4–5, 21, 32, 61, 66). As emphatically noted by Günter Figal, "[w]hoever wants to understand Gadamer's conception of philosophical hermeneutics must go back to the year 1923. In the summer semester of this year in Freiburg, the later author of *Wahrheit und Methode* attends Heidegger's lecture course on 'Ontology,' which comprises, at its core, the development of a philosophically understood hermeneutics" (Figal 2010, 8).

13. See GW 2, 301–18; Gadamer 1983c, 113–38. GW 4, 175–188; Gadamer 1999, 18–36; GW 4, 216–28; Gadamer 1983c, 69–87; GW 10, 238–46, 259–66; Gadamer 1983a, 67–76; Gadamer 1998a, 50–61; Gadamer 1976a, 78–109; Gadamer 1983c, 88–112.

14. As Gadamer explains: "In the sciences, of course, we are fully aware of the superiority of carrying out logically secured demonstration. But we also know about . . . many important human experiences other than those in science . . . One must grant to all of these their right to be. One simply cannot make everything into an object of knowledge" (GW 10, 172; Gadamer 2007, 404).

15. On this basis, in some of his aesthetic writings Gadamer pessimistically defines our culture as "a withering aesthetic culture" that is typical of "the industrial age that we live in" (GW 3, 330; Gadamer 1994, 192). This seems to be one of the symptoms of the critical condition of our civilization today, as Gadamer also observes in a late essay from the mid-1990s, "The Concept of Art in Transition" (Gadamer 2000a, 152–53).

Bibliography

Bernstein, Richard J. *Beyond Objectivism and Relativism: Science, Hermeneutics and Praxis*. Philadelphia: University of Pennsylvania Press, 1983.
Bruns, Gerald L. "On the Coherence of Hermeneutics and Ethics: An Essay on Gadamer and Levinas." In *Gadamer's Repercussions*. Edited by B. Krajewski, 30–54. Berkeley–Los Angeles–London: University of California Press, 2004.
Chang, Ting-Kuo. *Geschichte, Verstehen und Praxis. Eine Untersuchung zur philosophischen Hermeneutik Hans-Georg Gadamers unter besonderer Berücksichtigung ihrer Annäherung an die Tradition der praktischen Philosophie*. Marburg: Tectum, 1994.
Di Cesare, Donatella. 2013. *Gadamer: A Philosophical Portrait*. Trans. N. Keane. Bloomington–Indianapolis: Indiana University Press.

Dottori, Riccardo. "La questione della dialettica in Hegel, Heidegger, Gadamer." Appendix to Hans-Georg Gadamer. In *La dialettica di Hegel*. Translated and edited by R. Dottori, 189–214. Genova: Marietti, 1996.

Ferraris, Maurizio. *La fidanzata automatica*. Milano: Bompiani, 2007.

———. *L'ermeneutica*. Roma–Bari: Laterza, 1998.

———. *Manifesto del nuovo realismo*. Roma–Bari: Laterza, 2012.

———. *Nietzsche e la filosofia del Novecento*. Milano: Bompiani, 2009.

Figal, Günter. *Objectivity: The Hermeneutical and Philosophy*. Trans. T. George. Albany: State University of New York Press, 2010.

———. "Phänomenologie der Kultur. *Wahrheit und Methode* nach vierzig Jahren." *Sein, das verstanden werden kann, ist Sprache. Hommage an Hans-Georg Gadamer*, 100–106. Frankfurt a.M.: Suhrkamp, 2001.

Gadamer, Hans-Georg. *A Century of Philosophy: Hans-Georg Gadamer in Conversation with Riccardo Dottori*. Translated by R. Coltman and S. Koepke. London–New York: Continuum, 2003.

———. "A Letter by Professor Hans-Georg Gadamer." Appendix to Richard J. Bernstein. *Beyond Objectivism and Relativism: Science, Hermeneutics and Praxis*, 261–65. Philadelphia: University of Pennsylvania Press, 1983b.

———. *Aristoteles. Nikomachische Ethik VI*. Translated and edited by H.-G. Gadamer. Frankfurt a.M.: Klostermann, 1998c.

———. "Ausgewählte Briefe an Martin Heidegger." *Jahresgabe der Martin–Heidegger–Gesellschaft* 17 (2002a): 1–62.

———. *Gadamer in Conversation: Reflections and Commentary*. Translated and edited by R. E. Palmer. New Haven–London: Yale University Press, 2001.

———. *Gesammelte Werke* [GW]. 10 vols. Tübingen: Mohr Siebeck, 1985–1995.

———. "Heideggers 'theologische' Jugendschrift." *Dilthey–Jahrbuch* 6 (1989): 228–34.

———. *Heidegger's Ways*. Translated by J. W. Stanley. Albany: State University of New York Press, 1994.

———. *Hermeneutics, Religion, and Ethics*. Translated by J. Weinsheimer. New Haven–London: Yale University Press, 1999.

———. *Hermeneutik, Ästhetik, Praktische Philosophie. Hans-Georg Gadamer im Gespräch*. Edited by C. Dutt. Heidelberg: Winter, 1993.

———. *Hermeneutische Entwürfe*. Tübingen: Mohr Siebeck, 2000a.

———. *Im Gespräch: Hans-Georg Gadamer und Silvio Vietta*. München: Fink, 2002b.

———. "Interview: The 1920s, the 1930s, and the Present: National Socialism, German History, and German Culture." In *Hans-Georg Gadamer on Education, Poetry, and History: Applied Hermeneutics*. Translated by L. Schmidt and M. Reuss. Edited by D. Misgeld and G. Nicholson, 135–53. Albany: State University of New York Press, 1992.

———. "I tormenti di un maestro. Intervista a Hans-Georg Gadamer." In *L'ultimo sciamano. Conversazioni su Heidegger*. Edited by A. Gnoli and F. Volpi, 61–93. Milano: Bompiani, 2006.

———. *Lob der Theorie. Reden und Aufsätze*. Frankfurt a.M.: Suhrkamp, 1983a.

———. "On the Problematic Character of Aesthetic Consciousness." *Graduate Faculty Philosophy Journal* 9 (1982b): 31–40.

———. *Philosophical Hermeneutics*. Translated and edited by D. E. Linge. Berkeley–Los Angeles–London: University of California Press, 1976b.

———. *Praise of Theory: Speeches and Essays*. Translated by C. Dawson. New Haven–London: Yale University Press, 1998a.

———. *Reason in the Age of Science*. Translated by F. G. Lawrence. Cambridge, MA–London: The MIT Press, 1983c.

———. "The Conflict of Interpretations." In *Phenomenology: Dialogues and Bridges*. Edited by R. Bruzina and B. Wilshire, 299–304. Albany: State University of New York Press, 1982a.

———. "The Drama of Zarathustra." In *Nietzsche: Critical Assessments*. Vol. 1. Edited by D. W. Conway and P. S. Groff, 124–37. London–New York: Routledge, 1998b.

———. *The Gadamer Reader: A Bouquet of the Later Writings*. Translated and edited by R. E. Palmer. Evanston: Northwestern University Press, 2007.

———. "The Hermeneutics of Suspicion." In *Hermeneutics: Questions and Prospects*. Edited by G. Shapiro and A. Sica, 54–65. Amherst: University of Massachusetts Press, 1984.

———. *The Idea of the Good in Platonic–Aristotelian Philosophy*. Translated by P. C. Smith. New Haven–London: Yale University Press, 1986a.

———. *The Relevance of the Beautiful and Other Essays*. Translated by N. Walker. Edited by R. Bernasconi. Cambridge: Cambridge University Press, 1986b.

———. "Towards a Phenomenology of Ritual and Language." In *Language and Linguisticality in Gadamer's Hermeneutics*. Edited by L. K. Schmidt, 19–50. Lanham–Oxford: Lexington Books, 2000b.

———. *Truth and Method*. Revised ed. Translated by J. Weinsheimer and D. G. Marshall. London–New York: Continuum, 2004.

———. *Vernunft im Zeitalter der Wissenschaft*. Aufsätze. Frankfurt a.M.: Suhrkamp, 1976a.

———. "Zu Kants Begründung der Ästhetik und dem Sinn der Kunst." *Festschrift Richard Hamann zum sechzigen Geburtstage am 29. Mai 1939*, 31–39. Burg bei Magdeburg: Hopfer, 1939.

Grondin, Jean. "Gadamer's Basic Understanding of Understanding." In *The Cambridge Companion to Gadamer*. Edited by R. J. Dostal, 36–51. Cambridge: Cambridge University Press, 2002.

———. "Nihilistic or Metaphysical Consequences of Hermeneutics?" In *Consequences of Hermeneutics: Fifty Years after Gadamer's* Truth and Method. Edited by J. Malpas and S. Zabala, 190–201. Evanston: Northwestern University Press, 2010.

———. "On the Composition of *Truth and Method*." In *The Specter of Relativism: Truth, Dialogue, and Phronesis in Philosophical Hermeneutics*. Edited by L. K. Schmidt, 23–38. Evanston: Northwestern University Press, 1995.

———. *The Philosophy of Gadamer*. Chesham: Acumen, 2003.

Hance, Allen. "The Hermeneutic Significance of the *Sensus Communis*." *International Philosophical Quarterly* 37, 2, 146 (1997): 133–48.

Heidegger, Martin. "Ausgewählte Briefe Martin Heideggers an Hans-Georg Gadamer." *Jahresgabe der Martin-Heidegger Gesellschaft* 20 (2005–2006): 1–41.

———. "Empfehlungen für Gadamer, Krüger und Löwith (1945)." *Gesamtausgabe*. Vol. 16, 395–97. Frankfurt a.M.: Klostermann, 2000.

———. "The Origin of the Work of Art." In *Off the Beaten Track*. Translated and edited by J. Young and K. Haynes, 1–56. Cambridge: Cambridge University Press, 2002.

Marino, Stefano. "Gadamer on Heidegger: The History of Being as Philosophy of History." In *Aesthetics, Metaphysics, Language: Essays on Heidegger and Gadamer*, 49–68. Newcastle: Cambridge Scholars Publishing, 2015.

Matteucci, Giovanni. "Processi formativi e ontologia dell'arte." In *Gadamer: bilanci e prospettive*. Edited by M. Gardini and G. Matteucci, 133–56. Macerata: Quodlibet, 2004.

Nietzsche, Friedrich. "Nachgelassene Fragmente. Herbst 1885 bis Herbst 1887." In *Kritische Gesamtausgabe Werke*. Vol. VIII, 1. Edited by G. Colli and M. Montinari. Berlin–New York: De Gruyter, 1974.

———. *The Will to Power*. Translated by A. M. Ludovici. London: Oscar Levy, 1910.

Palmer, Richard E. "Two Contrasting Heideggerian Elements in Gadamer's Philosophical Hermeneutics." In *Consequences of Hermeneutics: Fifty Years after Gadamer's* Truth and Method. Edited by J. Malpas and S. Zabala, 121–31. Evanston: Northwestern University Press, 2010.

Risser, James. "Gadamer's Hidden Doctrine: The Simplicity and Humility of Philosophy." In *Consequences of Hermeneutics: Fifty Years after Gadamer's* Truth and Method. Edited by J. Malpas and S. Zabala, 5–24. Evanston: Northwestern University Press, 2010.

Romagnoli, Elena. "From a Remote Pedestal to Everyday Life. The Social Role of Art in Gadamer and Dewey." *European Journal of Pragmatism and American Philosophy* XIV, 1 (2022): 1–16.

Sokolowski, Robert. "Gadamer's Theory of Hermeneutics." In *The Philosophy of Hans-Georg Gadamer*. Edited by L. E. Hahn, 223–34. Chicago–LaSalle: Open Court, 1997.

Stolzenberg, Jürgen. "Hermeneutik der praktischen Vernunft. Hans-Georg Gadamer interpretiert Martin Heideggers Aristoteles–Interpretation." *"Dimensionen des Hermeneutischen." Heidegger und Gadamer*. Edited by G. Figal and H.-H. Gander, 133–52. Frankfurt a.M.: Klostermann, 2005.

Vattimo, Gianni. *Not Being God: A Collaborative Autobiography (with Piergiorgio Paterlini)*. Translated by W. McCuaig. New York: Columbia University Press, 2010.

———. *Oltre l'interpretazione. Il significato dell'ermeneutica per la filosofia*. Roma–Bari: Laterza, 1994.

———. *The End of Modernity: Nihilism and Hermeneutics in Postmodern Culture*. Translated by J. R. Snyder. Baltimore: Johns Hopkins University Press, 1991.

Vattimo, Gianni, and Rovatti, Pier Aldo, eds. *Il pensiero debole*. Milano: Feltrinelli, 1983.

Wachterhauser, Brice R. "Gadamer's Realism: The 'Belonginess' of Word and Reality." In *Hermeneutics and Truth*. Edited by B. R. Wachterhauser, 148–71. Evanston: Northwestern University Press, 1994.

———. "Getting It Right: Relativism, Realism and Truth." In *The Cambridge Companion to Gadamer*. Edited by R. J. Dostal, 52–78. Cambridge: Cambridge University Press, 2002.

3

The Aesthetics of the Invisible in Hans-Georg Gadamer

Mariannina Failla

Darstellung

In this essay I intend to explore a highly interesting aesthetic perspective of Gadamerian philosophy: the human being's relationship with Beauty and the latter's capacity to bring us into contact with the infinite, with the Good. Therefore, we must examine to what degree self-displaying, aesthetically exhibiting the supersensible, aids a consideration of the peculiar position adopted by Hans-Georg Gadamer toward metaphysics.[1] Besides, Gadamer himself claimed that the most suitable theoretical arena for reflecting on metaphysics is precisely the relationship between the Good and the Beautiful. His pregnant philosophical interest, present since his earliest doctoral studies, turned to the problem of the Good, the Good for a concrete and finite human being, and thus to the question of the relationship between Good and pleasure, Good and wisdom, to the comprehension of *phronesis*, not only the Aristotelian concept of ethical virtue, but also the same Platonic dialectic, in itself considered a virtue and thus the unavoidable source of the Aristotelian conception of the Good. Shining through these words there is already a sense of Gadamer's ethical interest: considering the Good as something that appears in the sensible, is embodied in the finite, and thus thinking of it in relation to the Good, in other words aesthetically.

All the same, in exposing the cardinal points of the relationship between Good and Beautiful the intention is not to touch on the theme of the political horizon of art, as it emerges from the reflections on "Plato and the Poets." This is because the true interest here lies in reflecting on the theoretical structure of the relationship between Being–Good–Beauty in order understand the eventual redeeming potential with regard to the nihilism Gadamer skillfully retraced in ideas that run from Nietzsche to Weber, on the one hand, and the mystical drifts of the poetic thinking of Heidegger, on the other. The reformulation of the concept of Being, capable of escaping nihilist or mystical siren song, is generated in Gadamer thanks to a sensitivity toward Renaissance humanism, according to which the finiteness of the human being, his/her caducity, is also the site of his/her fullness. This is a highly delicate question, which often divides critics. On the one hand, the strong call of humanism to the relationship in the circularity between the human being and the divine appears to have left its traces in Gadamerian reflections. In affirming this, I refer to Gadamer's relationship with a humanist philosopher who drew his constant interest: Nicholas of Cusa. I will return to his philosophy in the development of my argumentations as it constitutes a precious source of inspiration precisely to Gadamer's reflection on the concept of Being and the relationship between Good and Beauty.[2] On the other hand, in reflecting on the relationship between infinite and finite, Gadamer seeks an authentic autonomy from any religious appurtenance (see Grondin 1999). Evidence of this twofold necessity is offered by his interpretation of Rilkean poetry.[3] "The poetry of Rilke"—Gadamer claims in his 1993 essay "Reiner Maria Rilke after Fifty Years"—"is a 'warning' to recognize the distance from God and to place ourselves rightly in that distance" (GW 9, 313, my translation). This distance from God "corresponds . . . with the celebration of 'what is here' and 'being here'" (GW 9, 314, my translation); it corresponds with the acceptance of pain and death, the assumption of the idea of having to resist and support finiteness without any religious consolation (GW 9, 314). The refusal of religious consolation betrays the refusal of religious ideologies and confessional appartenances, though it does not wish to negate the relationship with the divine and with the infinite.

First, the awareness of the distance from God, intoned by Rilke, still presupposes the divine as the "infinite in the spirit" and not as God revealed; second, it belongs to the notion of "being here" assuming for oneself the law of one's heart, the heart to which the angels speak. They are not only beings beyond the human, who constantly overcome it, but also its testimonial; human beings, in fact, do not limit themselves to the despairing acceptance of death; their role is to depict and to revive in the visible all that has become invisible. We are the bees of the invisible, Rilke states. And this is precisely the direction of Gadamer's questioning of the relationship between finite and infinite, and the relation between Good and Beautiful. If we ask: "How are we to think of the supersensible *eidos* of Good? How do make intelligible beings enter into the relationship with humans, also in the sensible, historical, and finite world? How to be bees of the invisible?"[4], then the answer rings out: thanks to the Beautiful. It is from the Beautiful that we can borrow the possilbity of the Good to root itself in the concrete, to participate in the sensible, as we read in the young Gadamerian interpretation of the *Philebus*. The Good, in fact, acquires the possibility to be imagined as the supersensible manifest in the sensible, in the concrete, in the particular, thus as an idealism that is investigable and identifiable in the rooted finiteness of humanity, thanks precisely to the exhibitive capacity of the Beautiful. In *Truth and Method*, Gadamer affirms, in fact, how the example of the Beautiful serves to clarify the *parousia* of *eidos* "and to provide an evident notion of it that contrasts with the logical difficulties of participation in the 'unfolding' of 'being'" (GW 1, 485; Gadamer 2004, 476). The Beautiful, its idea, would thus have the function of resolving the opposition of Being and becoming and find a point of contact, a suture [*geschlossen*] between the sensible and the supersensible.

Beyond the romantic-idealist echo of these themes (see Schelling 1962 and 1977), it is Gadamer himself who indicates the path for intending the relationship between Good and Beautiful: he sets out from Plato to flow into the Christian interpretation of the metaphysics of light, identifying later in Renaissance humanism and in particular in the theological speculation of Nicholas of Cusa an important philosophical spark for a new reflection on the relationship between the human and the divine that sets the backdrop to the theme of the Beautiful as the suture between visible and invisible.

Anagogic

First, Gadamer ties the Beautiful to *eu zen*, to that good life connected with education [*paideia*], and pulls away from the sphere of the useful. "Beautiful things are those whose value shines on its own." (GW 1, 482; Gadamer 2004, 472–73).[5] The use of the verb *shine* already contains signs of the relationship between Beauty and light. All the same, before searching for a tie with the metaphysics of light, Gadamer wishes to underline the ethical value of being remarkable.

"The concept of the beautiful thus assumes a very close relationship with the good" (GW 1, 482; Gadamer 2004, 472–73); being inherently remarkable, the Beautiful, like the Good, subordinates anything else to itself. In the comment on Plato's *Philebus*, also presented in *Truth and Method*, Gadamer takes a step further and affirms that the Beautiful has a certain *Vorzüglichkeit*, that is, a preferability with respect to the Good, because it is more susceptible to being understood, while the Good remains inherently out of our grasp. "It is part of the very essence of the beautiful to be something that appears [*Erscheinendes zu sein*]" (GW 1, 482; Gadamer 2004, 472–73). In the search for the Good what appears is not the unspeakable, the elusive, what is beyond Being, but the Beautiful, that is, that supersensible that, however, by its very nature, is manifest in the sensible. The Good finds an anagogic correspondence in the Beautiful, Gadamer claims. The term *anagogic* must not be ignored; without a doubt it relates to induction and in this sense may recall the Socratic *dialectic*. As Aristotle acutely noted (*Metaphysics*, 1078 b27) in seeking to clarify what is [*ti esti*] goodness, friendship, courage, etc., Socrates always set out from single examples, to arrive at the definition of courage, friendship, etc. He did this through inductive argumentation, based on the verb *epagoghein*, which can have both a passive and active use. The passive form appears in the *Posterior Analytics*, in particular in lines 71 a8 and 81 b2; in this context *epagoghein* always implies someone or something that is brought, led, and in the case of Socrates it would be the interlocutor who is brought toward a diverse awareness of himself. In the *Topics*, in which Aristotle dedicates himself to rhetorical argumentations, *epagoghein* is, however, also given an active use (108 b10), and in the same line in the *Topics* 108 b10 it appears twice, once to state that (1) single examples are "brought" for the purpose of (2) "bringing out," rendering universal notions clear. This would exemplify the two meanings of the verb *epagoghein*, which can be found in argumentative, persuasive, inductive strategy, attributable to Socrates. In bringing single examples, the other is led (passive form) to the awareness of the partiality of personal vision and in adducing single examples we "also bring them out" (active form of the verb *epagoghein*), make them clear, explicate the universals, the essences that permit the definitions of what we are searching for. In the passive form, the verb signifies precisely "leading out from." This is what Socrates does: he leads the interlocutor out of his own contradictions. In the active form, *epagoghein* signifies bringing single examples with the purpose of "bringing out or making clear" the universals (Aristotelian *Topics*). This is the other moment of Socratic dialectics: arriving *with awareness at the universal definition of anything.*

The term *anagogic* has, nonetheless, had its own resonance precisely within that Neoplatonic metaphysics of light that Gadamer indulges in in the final part of *Truth and Method*. It has a theological reference in this anagogic tradition and concerns the allegorical symbolic capacity to represent the divine. In fact, the term *anagogic* is used in *De Sole* by Marsilio Ficino to indicate the theological pregnancy of allegory with respect to the discursive definitions of God. Like many concepts from early humanism, it is a synthesis of diverse philosophical motivations and traditions. The reference to light as a symbol is declaredly linked to *De Mysteriis* by Iamblichus, to the confrontation with the negative theology of Pseudo-Dionysius the Areopagite and the Augustinian interpretation of the *Genesis*, as well as the Aristotelian *De Anima*.[6]

The *De Sole*, nonetheless, begins with the philosophical value of silence that, in the end, is also the point of arrival of the mysticism of the One. The exercise in silence signifies not only that we must not takes risks with the divine beyond that limit which light itself makes visible to inspired minds, but the exercise in silence also appears to warn us not to capture and express the concealed divine light with reasonings, but with entirely sensible and empirical similitudes, inspired by the Muses, and thus aesthetic. This introduces the idea that Beauty has capacities to reveal Being and not merely reproductive ones.

In Gadamer, the anagogic function of the Beautiful with respect to the Good, the visible with respect to the invisible, while underlining the value of the symbolic as the revealer of Being, thus despite undertaking parallel avenues to those of Ficinian humanism, is not realized in the medium of silence, that is, it forcefully avoids the mystic backdrop of the Renaissance return to Plato. The Beautiful expresses its anagogic strength toward Being, toward the Good through the medium of *logos* and language. In other words: stating that the Beautiful has an anagogic function with respect to the Good signifies attributing the symbol, the allegorical, not the role of a copy of Being, but as the authentic place of the sensible *sayability* of Being. And it is precisely from this perspective that he penetrates into the heart of the work of Cusa to capture the comprehensive value of the concept of the symbol.

Emblematic, in fact, is the reference by Nicholas of Cusa to the value of the symbol as mathematical language that approximates the understanding of the divine, without ever achieving it. If we could access the divine only through symbols (Heymericus de Campo, *Tractatus de sigillo aeterniattis I*, Cod. Cus. 106, f. 77r), then the most convenient are mathematical signs precisely for their indubitable certainty. Cusa thus places us in the role of mathematics and the symbolic value of its signs, and in so doing, introduces us into the human being's learned ignorance of God (see De Cusa 1959, 24).

The first thing that must be noted is that Cusa conceives of the cognitive process as a comparative proportion capable of approximating the uncertain to the certain; when he speaks of knowledge he does not use the word *unknown*, but, precisely, the couple certainty-uncertainty, letting it be understood that there exists an infinitesimal graduality to certainty. It is the reflection on God, a necessary and highest being, that drives Cusa to move from the couple certain-uncertain to the couple known-unknown. The finite is the realm of the certain and the uncertain. The infinite is completely outside of it, as Aristotle had already stated in *De Coelo* and in *Physics*. Proportion expresses union and separation, Cusa claims, convenience and alterity, unity, and multiplicity. It cannot be intended without the number, and for this belongs to the finite. God, however, is not a number. He has nothing to do with numeric relations. If the number is a relation of convenience and alterity, of identity and diversity, of measure and proportion, etc., it becomes the origin not only of relations among scales, but also the origin of all things—as Pythagoras claimed, according to Aristotle's testimonial in *Metaphysics I* (5, 985 b26 ff). The number, however, is not the origin of the divine. If God were an origin–number of things, he would thus somehow be fully knowable through mathematical categories, including those of incommensurability and the infinite. God is, instead, the unknown origin that escapes proportion and the number. It can be said that the category of Euclidean origin of incommensurability is utilized by Cusa to know God as unknowable. While knowledge is certain of finite things, mathematics does not help us to positively know the infinite as such. If this is the state of things, where does our desire for knowledge find its peace? Peace, that is, the full satisfaction of the virtue of all knowledge, is ignorance. Only by knowing that we do not know do we reach the fulness, the *arete*, of our capacity for judgment. Through the awareness of our ignorance, a gifted awareness—expressed with the maximum knowledge of the intellect, like mathematics—we manage to calm the desire for knowledge. The doctrine of mathematics makes us night birds hungry for light: knowing we are nocturnal in the search for light is the maximum perfection of human judgment.

Mathematics does not only fulfil the negative role of being the learned ignorance of the infinite. It also plays a positive role precisely with respect to the possibility to grasp and see God. In the *Possest* (1460)—only slightly successive to *De Docta Ignorantia* and a cardinal text for Gadamerian interpretation—Cusa considers mathematics both negatively, as the human ignorance of all things divine, and positively, as the *image* and *reflection* of God's knowledge of things. Mathematics is that symbolic language that is also a mirror, an enigmatic reflection of the precise knowledge of all things created; it is the admirable art of God in creating the world. Thus, the participation [*methexis, participatio*] of the finite in the infinite, of the sensible in the supersensible is the idea that Gadamer holds firm when considering Cusa's works and their applicability (see Gadamer 1987b, 303). Gadamer's theoretical attention is, therefore, clearly turned toward Cusa's theological theories. This is precisely because in returning to a thematic of Augustine's, he shifts the problem from the unity and complication of God to the Verb, to *logos*, to language. Both Ficino and Cusa are in the end exegetes of Plotinus, and they connect themselves with the mystical currents of Neoplatonic theology, what is more supporting the infinite simplicity of God and negating the comparison between God and the number. However Cusa—Gadamer affirms—demonstrates a satisfying solution to the problem of the multiple in God himself, that in Ficino, I continue, above all in his commentary on *Parmenides*, remains under the aegis of the Plotinian One. In this commentary, Ficino distinguishes between One and Being, One and entity, faithfully reproducing the spirit of Plotinus's *Ennead V*. This distinction would find modifications and variations not only in Cusa's idea of the unitrinity and the relationship between One and entity, but also and perhaps more decisively in the *De Ente et Uno* by Pico della Mirandola.

To follow the Gadamerian suggestion, that is, to see in Cusa, rather than in other humanists, the capacity to contrast medieval resistance and place Beauty, the harmonic proportion of the many, the plural, in God, in the One, that is, to see in Cusa the humanist attempt par excellence for an ontological foundation of the Beautiful, it is also significant to investigate Cusa's use of speculative geometry. According to it, the same knowledge of God is based on proportion and measure, inherent concepts of Beauty. The reference to speculative geometry represents above all the search for that *pars construens* of theology, capable of giving a positive meaning to our inevitable ignorance of God. Speaking of speculative geometry, Cusa inserts the notion of measure within the heart of the simplicity of God: maximum simplicity is the reason for everything; and reason is measure.

Certainly, the concept of measure takes us back to the Beautiful and its intimate relationship with the Good, that probably ended up guiding

Gadamer in his exegesis of the complication of the divine One. Cusa stated: to conceive of the One in its three and one complication, we can think of the One as the unity and coincidence of its contradictory nature. In the divine we must embrace the contradictory with a simple concept that is anterior to it; for example, distinction and indistinction are not to be intended as contradictory, but as antecedents to contradiction itself at their very simple origin that is the One, in which distinction is no different from indistinction and where even minimum and maximum coincide. Thus, if we comprehend the coincidence between contraries, we can also comprehend in the clearest manner how trinity and unity are one and the same reality. In fact, where distinction is indistinction, trinity is unity. Some efficacious means for intending the divine *complicatio*, its unitrinity, are indicated in *Apologia Doctae Ignorantia Discepoli ad Discepulum*; this text speaks of infinite simplicity and the singularity of God appealing to contradictions that present God as singular non-singular, finite infinite, end without end, indistinct distinction. This makes it possible to state: if Beauty is measure, proportion, harmony, implies a multiple, "only the Cusanian doctrine of the *complicatio* of the multiple in God" would provide us—Gadamer claims—with the means for placing Beauty in Being, or in the Being of all beings, in God. Gadamer appears sensible to the opening laid out by Cusa: the possibility to find a notion of the One that inherently admits the presence of the plural without determining it as alterity.

The central idea, not only of the *Sermon on Beauty*, but also of the *De Docta Ignorantia*, is that the infinite wisdom of God is the simplicity that complicates all forms and that is the proper measure of all things.

Verb

In the final pages of *Truth and Method*, Gadamer makes an admission and states: though the Greek philosophy of *logos* only partially reveals the base of hermeneutics, that is of language, the authentically hermeneutic sense of *logos* emerges from the Platonic theories of Beauty. They, continues Gadamer, constitute a subterranean current capable of crossing medieval teachings and emerging thanks precisely to Neoplatonic mysticism; a mysticism to which Gadamer assigns the doctrines of Nicholas of Cusa, underlining his ties with the school of Chartres. Neoplatonism, as a vehicle for the authentic meaning of the Platonic theory of Beauty, for Gadamer had the capacity to elaborate the conceptual vocabulary required by the idea of the finiteness of human existence (see GW 1, 490; Gadamer 2004, 480–81).

This vocabulary sought in Cusa's analysis of the One-Trinity an essential point of reference also for the Gadamerian reflection on language. The idea of the divine complication in the simplicity of God relies on the idea of God as able-to-be, already constructed at the beginning of *De Docta Ignorantia* relative to the concept of God as maximum-minimum. Foreign to this idea are the reflections of Boethius and Augustine on the trinity, sedimented in the argumentations of Thierry of Chartres on individual substance, to which Cusa alludes in the portion of *De Docta Ignorantia* dedicated to the problem of the three in one unity of God. This leads us, according to the free interpretation of Gadamer, to the centrality of the word and listening to the *Verbum*. Fulness, abundance—affirms Cusa—suit the one. Unity, intended in a particular manner, that is as entity, as action, as the form of being, actual existence, coincides with the maximum. Thus, we can say: unity coincides with the maximum as the actual existence of all possible forms, it is, therefore, freed of any determination, that is, of any reference and contraction, and so nothing opposes it.

If unity is the actual form of all of its possible forms, free from any determination, then it is the being non contracted and not determined of all possibilities. For this reason, it precedes any relation and, therefore, any opposition. Freed of any opposition, the maximum is the absolute being of all things and is comparable to the necessary entity. If the one is free of any opposition, the minimum is not opposed to the maximum, but coincides with it. The maximum is the one absolute that is everything, in which all things are, that is, the absolute maximum is the entity of all things. The minimum is in all things. Because the minimum is absolute, it is also the action of all *things possible*. It contracts nothing from anything, all things derive from it. It is important to note that in what has just been stated, the adjective *possible*, linked by Cusa to the notion of power, appears in the description of the minimum, or better yet, in the absoluteness of the minimum, and the term entity, linked to the notion of action, of the actual form of being, appears in the desorption of the maximum as an absolute.

The coincidence between entity and possibility so clearly declared in *De Docta Ignorantia*, in my opinion introduces, even if *in nuce*, the successive theory of God as *Posse est*, that is, as *able-to-be*, where action and divine power coincide. First, Cusa takes from *Posse est*, the idea, already present in the concept of Maximum, according to which God is free of any opposition. Things that appear to be opposites are, in Him, identical; in Him negation is not opposed to affirmation. In the *able-to-be* there is neither distinction, nor separation. The very simplest meaning of the composed name *possest* is "power is, that power can be." And because what is is in action, the able-to-be is the same as the able-to-be in action. God is absolute power in action. God is maximum-minimum. Able-to-be is a name—Cusa affirms—sufficiently appropriate according to the human conception we can have of God. *Possest* is a name that embraces all and each of the names, and together none of them. When God wishes to speak of himself he says, "I am God almighty," "I am who I am," "I am he who is." In Greek we find the writing "I am the entity." God is in fact the form of being, that is, the form of any formable form. Entity as pure actuality.

From this theory Gadamer does not accept the vision of God as a necessary, and thus formal, actual entity. Instead, he underlines the unavoidable unity of the necessary entity and the possible, infinite power. From the assertion according to which the maximum entity is the actual form of its infinite possibilities, Gadamer derives the idea of God as infinite virtuality, infinite possibility, which is immediately compared to language, or better yet, to its ontological nature. If, on the one hand, the conception of God—as possibility and infinite virtuality—initiates a complex debate on the role of matter and void in God himself, on the other hand it connects—according to Gadamer—the notion of the possible, of power, with that of the word. Cusa belongs to theology of the work, Gadamer claims. He adopted a position with respect to a central question, widely debated among the Platonists and Aristotelians: the problem the way of being of the universals. Cusa would claim—Gadamer tells us—that the ancient philosophers would not have understood the work of the *Verbum*, of the word and thus also that of the creation.

> The *Verbum* in fact is *Verbum creans*; it is not a simple and mere being together of all forms of being and all possibilities. The *Verbum* is a word that creates from will. The ancients would have managed to think of the birth of the world in a definitive manner only as the development of a necessity, this is the limit they are unable to overcome, even if from Anaxagoras onward they focus on the spirituality of the foundation of the world. (Gadamer 1987b, 303–304, my translation)

Cusa, instead, would interpret Platonic and Neoplatonic tradition in an original manner, separating himself from the Plotinian theory of emanation. According to Cusa, the ontological structure of creating is different: "creation can be represented as the essence of the word." Enchantment, "the prodigy of the word," is in fact "that of producing new forms, transforming them, nothing less, make them present, call them into being [*ins Sein ruft*] without there being something existing" (Gadamer 1987b, 304, my translation). Behind the idea of creation lies the necessity to compare Being, the divine Being, thus the first Being, to power, to creative power and this latter to language, to the word. Cusa "dared to propose the more acute (but also more sober) linguistic formulation of *possest*, that is, the total unity and compenetration of power and being and, at the apex of the reflection, it appears to him that power itself (the *posse ipsum*) is the unlimited and infinite condition of all being. Becoming aware, interiorising this condition in all being is the grand possibility of the human spirit" (Gadamer 1987b, 305, my translation). Gadamer is highly sensible to the idea of Being as infinite virtuality. He saw in language, in the relationship between the *Verbum* and sensible, finite *verba*, a more fitting image for this ontological conception and for the consequent relationship between finite and infinite. Turning to what he refers to as the "theology of the word"—continued by Cusa—Gadamer is in reality interested in the destruction-re petition [*Destruk tion-Wie der holung*] of the Augustinian exegesis of the *Verbo*. "Repeating" Augustine means considering the *Verbum*, the *Idea giovannea*, as that Being manifest only in the spoken word and thus continually manifest and continually transcending its own manifestations. Augustine serves to establish a relationship between the mystery of the Trinity and language, and Thomas serves to analyze this relationship from the point of view of its human finiteness. In Gadamer, the relationship between Being and language becomes a return to the inherent possibilities of the tradition that travels from Augustine into Cusanian philosophy. The spoken word is the mirror of the interior immaterial word. It is the reflected image, the *speculum*, to be intended as its exhibition [*Darstellung*] or better yet as sensible, temporal self-presentation, of Being itself. In natural historical languages, it is not Christ but the Being that becomes flesh, connecting with humans through comprehension. In the sensible word it is the Being that is self-represented, manifest, and who can and must be comprehended. But how is the relationship of the mirroring of Being in the word configured? Why is the word a mirror of Being? Gadamer accounts for the speculative character of the word by channeling the interpretation that moved from Augustine to Cusa in the Hegelian reflection on predication and in *Truth and Method* employs the relationship between subject and predicate as it was conceived by Hegel in the treatment of the *philosophischen Satzes*. The speculative character of language begins with predication, with the subject and the predicate, with substance and its determination, inverting functions, position, and significance, without ever truly breaking free of the metaphysical horizon of the relationship between Being and its manifestations. In the philosophy of Hegel, Gadamer tells us, the relationship subject-predicate is overturned: substance is no longer the subject that through predication is subjected to determinations from a plurality of points of view; substance becomes the predicate itself, determination, in which the truth of the subject *zur Darstellung kommt*.

Asserting "God is one" does not signify that being one is an *Eigenschaft* of God, but that Being, the essence of God is "being a unity," one is a speculative predicate of God, that is, it is that determination in which God expresses his Being and not one among his diverse qualities. It is interesting that Gadamer later underlines Hegel's recourse to rhythm to account for the self-dissolution of the predicative form and its passage to speculative assertion. The form of assertion self-dissolves because speculative assertion does not predicate something of something, but represents [*zur Darstellung bringt*] the unity of the concept, and leads, case by case, toward the expression of its truth. Rhythm becomes a metaphor of the unity/truth of the concept as the harmony that results from the continuous alternation of metric and accent (see GW 1, 470–71; Gadamer 2004, 462–63).

By listening to the interior *Verbum*, to the theology of the word, we have arrived at the pregnant theme of the philosophy of Gadamer, identified at the outset: the temporal manifestation of Being in language, of the infinite in the finite. A theme this German philosopher wished to explore by seeking, in the relationship between Good and Beautiful and in the philosophy of Nicholas of Cusa, a vocabulary suited to the needs of the present and by making the word *Verbum* an infinite power, a fundamental point of reference for the lexicon of our modern era.

Notes

1. On the debate on Gadamer's relationship with metaphysics, see the essays by Günter Figal, Jean Grondin, and Claudio Tuozzolo included in the volume "Il cammino filosofico di H.-G. Gadamer," special issue of the journal *Paradigmi* (Figal 2008; Grondin 2008; Tuozzolo 2008).

2. In this regard I would like to recall the fundamental steps of the idea of the circularity between human and God, so important to all of humanism and to Cusa himself. In the *Corpus Hermeticum* the words of Poimandres describe the relationship between human and God, placing it within God himself, his mirroring, loving, and recognition. The Nous, as we find written in the *Corpus*, generated a

human similar to him and with whom he fell in love as with a son. It was beautiful because he had the image of the Father. God fell in love in reality with his own form and he gave him all of his work. Human form, a mirror of the divine, is the *medium* of God's love for himself and of the donation of forms to all creation. The role of the created and of the creatures as a *medium* of pleasure and divine calm is also present in Meister Eckart. In his *Expositio on Genesis* there is however a shift in meaning in the reflection of God in all creatures and the created, recounted by Poimandres. On the seventh day God returned to himself in a reflected movement, pleased with himself for all that he had created and seeking to rest in this pleasure. Turning to what he had created, to the dual, to day and night, to the multiple, God sought rest shared with pleasure for himself, that is the pleasure of his very Being, with a fundamental ontological pleasure. In this moment—following Eckhart—God became a physician, or better yet a surgeon, and could not avoid this. How, in fact, could he be pleased with himself, rest in his being, if what he had created, which is duality, evil, not exist? God must, therefore, depend on the capacity to amputate, targeting the perfection of everything. Both the *Corpus* by the Pseudo-Hermit and Eckart, as well as the mysticism of Dionysius, are important sources for Cusa's reflection on the relationship human-God, as it is outlined in a work essential to the Gadamerian interpretation of Cusa's humanist message, that is in *The Vision of God*. Drawing inspiration from a painting by Roger van der Weyden—in which the gaze of the image looks toward any angle from which it is observed—Cusa illustrates how the infinite unity of the Divine offers itself "one" and "the same" in the infinite multiplicity of everything that refers to it. Gadamer commented on this idea as follows: "The peculiar essence of any vision, of any image is the self-encounter of the spirit." In this encounter of gazes between human and the divine, human is creative "*vis*" who "is elevated above the passing and the relative," he moves beyond it. "This elevation does not make him God, but leads him to comprehend beginning with the embodiment of God in Christ" (Gadamer 1987b, 302–303).

    3. For the religious interpretation of Rilke, highly criticized by both Heidegger and Gadamer, see Guardini 1953.

    4. In his letter to Witold Hulewicz dated 13 November 1925 Rilke states: "When one makes the mistake of holding up to the *Elegies* or *Sonnets Catholic* conceptions of death, of the beyond and of eternity, one is getting entirely away from their point of departure and preparing for oneself a more and more basic misunderstanding. The 'angel' of the *Elegies* has nothing to do with the angel of the Christian heaven (rather with the angel figures of Islam) . . . The angel of the *Elegies* is that creature in whom the transformation of the visible into the invisible, which we are accomplishing . . . The angel of the Elegies is that being who vouches for the recognition in the invisible of a higher order of reality" (Rilke 1950, 898–99 ff).

    5. "In all these usages the word is in the same antithesis as is the Greek *kalon* to the idea of *chresimon*. Everything that is not part of the necessities of life

but is concerned with the 'how,' the *eu zen*—i.e., everything that the Greeks reckon part of paideia—is called *kalon*. Beautiful things are those whose value is of itself evident. You cannot ask what purpose they serve. They are desirable for their own sake [*di hauto haireton*] and not, like the useful for the sake of something else. Thus even linguistic usage shows the special status accorded to what is called *kalon*. But even the ordinary antithesis that determines the idea of the beautiful, the antithesis to the ugly [*aischron*], points in the same direction. The *aischron* is what cannot be looked at. The beautiful is what can be looked at, what is good-looking in the widest sense of the word. In German *ansehnlich* [good-looking] is also used to express magnitude (see 'fair-sized'). And in fact the use of the word *schön*—both in Greek and in German—always implies a certain majestic size. Because the element of the *ansehnlich* points to the whole sphere of the *decorus*, the moral, its meaning comes close to being defined by its antithesis to the useful [*chresimon*]. Hence the idea of the beautiful closely approximates that of the good [*agathon*], insofar as it is something to be chosen for its own sake, as an end that subordinates everything else to it as a means. For what is beautiful is not regarded as a means to something" (GW 1, 482; Gadamer 2004, 472–73).

6. On the importance of the symbol to Neoplatonic tradition Gadamer reflects also in the essay "Hegel und die Heidelberger Romantik," included in GW 7, 395–405.

Bibliography

De Cusa, Nicolai. "Apologia Doctae Ignorantiae." In *Opera Omnia. Vol. 2*. Edited by Raymond Klibansky. Leipzig: Felix Meiner, 1932.

———. "De Docta Ignorantia." In *Opera Omnia. Vol. 1*. Edited by Paul Wilpert. Hamburg: Felix Meiner, 1959.

———. *Opera Omnia. Vol. 19. Sermones IV*. Hamburg: Felix Meiner, 2002.

Figal, Günter. "Gadamer fenomenologo." *Paradigmi* 3 (2008): 81–95.

Gadamer, Hans-Georg. *Ästhetik und Poetik II: Hermeneutik im Vollzug. Gesammelte Werke. Vol. 9* [GW 9]. Tübingen: Mohr Siebeck, 1993.

———. "Hegel und die antike Dialektik." In *Gesammelte Werke. Vol. 3*, 3–28. Tübingen: Mohr Siebeck, 1987a.

———. *Metafisica e filosofia pratica in Aristotele*. Milano: Guerini e Associati, 2000.

———. "Nicolaus Cusanus und die Gegenwart." In *Gesammelte Werke. Vol. 4*, 297–305.Tübingen: Mohr Siebeck, 1987b.

———. *Schmerz. Einschätzungen aus medizinischen, philosophi scher und therapeutischer Sicht*. Heidelberg: Winter, 2003.

———. *Truth and Method*. Revised ed. Translated by. J. Weinsheimer and D. G. Marshall. London-New York: Continuum, 2004.

———. *Wahrheit und Methode. Gesammelte Werke. Vol. 1* [GW 1]. Tübingen: Mohr Siebeck, 1990.
Grondin, Jean. *Hans-Georg Gadamer. Eine Biographie.* Tübingen: Mohr Siebeck, 1999.
———. "Hans-Georg Gadamer e la metafisica." *Paradigmi* 3 (2008): 97–108.
Guardini, Romano. *Rainer Maria Rilkes Deutung des Daseins. Eine Interpretation der Duineser Elegien.* München: Kösel, 1953.
Rilke, Rainer Maria. *Briefe.* Edited by Rilke-Archiv in Weimar. Wiesbaden: Insel-Verlag, 1950.
Schelling, Friedrich Wilhelm J. *Briefe und Dokumente. Vol. 1. 1775–1809.* Bonn: Bouvier, 1962.
———. *Bruno. Werke. Vol. 3* (nach der Originalausgabe in neuerer Anordnung). Edited by Manfred Schröter. München: Beck, 1977.
Tuozzolo, Claudio. "Hans-Georg Gadamer, Emilio Betti e il futuro dell'ermeneutica filosofica." *Paradigmi* 3 (2008): 109–27.

4

The "Unshapely Form" of the Work of Art
Parsing the Structure of an Irresolvable Paradox

JOHN ARTHOS

The paradox of my title lies in Heidegger's and Gadamer's accounts of the work of art as something at the same time both fixed and moving.[1] On the one hand, "'to set' means here: to bring to a stand [*'Setzen' sagt hier: zum Stehen bringen*]" (Heidegger 1977, 21; Heidegger 1971, 36). Heidegger asserts that this "standing-there, this taking and maintaining a stand that stands erected high in itself, is what the Greeks understood as Being" (Heidegger 2000, 62–63). On the other hand, "truth is set to work in such a work [*Und doch ist in solchem Werk . . . die Wahrheit ins Werk gesetzt*]" (Heidegger 1977, 22; Heidegger 1971, 37). Now, this movement is not a movement spinning in place—for truth "unfolds itself in an inexhaustible variety" (Heidegger 1971, 47). But how does this increase happen if the work, as Heidegger and Gadamer never tire of telling us, brings matters to a stand? Heidegger himself states this problem as a paradox: "For art is both the setting to work of the truth, and the composed shelter of the work as it comes to stand in the work in itself for itself [*Weil Kunst z. B. ist das* Ins-Werk-setzen *der Wahrheit und im Werk die Bergung in sich selbst zu sich selbst zu stehen kommt*]" (Heidegger in Inwood 1999, 18; Heidegger 2003, 69).

In the 1930s Heidegger seized on the structure of the work as a locus for exploring the riddle of being-in-the-world itself, that is, the riddle of our incongruous *Anwesend*, our temporal *Unheimlichkeit*. As Gadamer would later explain it, the "standing-in-itself of the work betokens at the same time the standing-in-itself of beings in general" (Gadamer 1994, 108). So if we unpack the paradox of art we are peering into the structure of the ontological difference itself.[2] As we see Heidegger and Gadamer working out the character of the paradox of the work as a passageway between Being and beings, I think we are actually seeing the hermeneutic alternative to dualism and monism, something Gadamer will call in 1992 "a third type of being" (Gadamer 2007, 209). To defend this claim, I will show how the two sides of the polarity of coming to a stand and setting to work are defined, how they constitute a middle, and what this middle is.

Coming to a Stand

To see art as a way to capture our fleeting lives in a timeless medium is a conventional *topos*. As finite creatures we want to find ways to arrest the transient flux of temporal being. Sebastian Flyte in *Brideshead* says, "I should like to bury something precious in every place where I've been happy and then when I was old and ugly and miserable, I could come back and dig it up and remember" (Waugh 1973, 24–25). A contemporary version of this fixing role is Alexis Nowicki's justification for writing an autobiographical account of a relationship: "I felt so scared of losing the memories I had, since I was suddenly the only person who had them. I was so scared of forgetting them, and also of remembering instead what [someone else had written about them,] so I just felt urgently that I needed to make a record of everything that happened" (Nowicki 2021, §59). We have a philosophical account of this Romantic urge to preserve a memory in a text in Friedrich Schleiermacher's tribute to the poetry of Novalis: "The greater your emotion, the more you are absorbed in it, the more your whole nature is concerned to retain for the memory an imperishable trace of what is necessarily fleeting, to carry over to what you may engage in, its colour and impress, and so unite two moments into a duration" (Schleiermacher 1958, 42). In league with this Romantic inclination but now moving in a phenomenological direction, Heidegger asserts that Being is "the proper self-collected perdurance of the constant [*die eigene in sich gesammelte Gediegenheit des Ständigen*]" (Heidegger 2000, 102; Heidegger 1998, 74). A work "holds its ground," it "brings to a stand," it sets up a world "and keeps it abidingly in force," it sets up a work "to establish it in its structure" (Heidegger 2000, 42,

36, 44). Now, Heidegger renders this impulse problematic, and he quotes Novalis to do so: "Should the highest principle contain the highest paradox in the task? Being a principle that allows absolutely no peace, that always attracts and repels, that always anew would become unintelligible as soon as one had understood it? That ceaselessly stirs up our activity—without ever exhausting it, without ever becoming familiar?" (Novalis in Heidegger 1991, 13). Between these two opposite assertions we are indeed in the vicinity of paradox. The self-subsistence of the work as artifact is imported into hermeneutics as something very much like a foreign body, against which hermeneutics would reflexively rebel—a stand-alone object. Yet here is Heidegger on coming to a stand in "The Principle of Reason": "Cognition is a kind of representational thinking [*Vorstellen*]. In this presentation [*Stellen*] something we encounter comes to stand [*Stehen*], to a standstill [*Stand*]. What is encountered and brought to a standstill in representational thinking is the object [*Gegenstand*]" (Heidegger 1991, 23). For hermeneutics, normally it is representational thinking that reifies thought. Coming to a stand in this context is a form of death. "We murder to dissect" (Wordsworth 1986). But thinking in a positive light about a paradoxical in-between of hermeneutic identity, Heidegger connects the constancy of a work to the exchange between beings and being, and to the appearance of being itself: "Some particular entity, a pair of peasant shoes, comes in the work to stand in the light of its being. The being of the being comes into the steadiness of its shining" (Heidegger 1971, 36).

Gadamer would both affirm the privilege of this feature in the work of art and connect it to its broader ontological relevance: "The standing-in-itself of the work betokens at the same time the standing-in-itself of beings in general" (Gadamer 1994, 108). But most helpfully, he confirms that what is enduring about a work *is* its structure. He connects this structural attribute to Aristotle's definition of beauty—nothing can be added and nothing can be taken away: "Nevertheless, this is only possible on the basis of *a central structure which must be left intact* if we are not to destroy the living unity of the work" (Gadamer 1986, 43, emphasis added).

So, the first axiom in the hermeneutics of the work of art is that there is a central durable structure, which does not change. Gadamer offers a memorable description of this achievement of structure: "One may define the text as a series of signs that fixates the unified sense of something . . . The plaiting of oscillating threads of sound and semantic reference on which the sense of speech is built up is cinched, so to speak, in such fixation" (Gadamer 1982, 339).

Setting to Work

However, it is also axiomatic for hermeneutics that a work can have no essential fixed meaning, because it is always partly constituted by its contexts of reception. To understand is to understand differently. Thus, for Heidegger the work of art is a task that remains unfinished: "[A]rt is truth setting itself to work" (Heidegger 1971, 36). Heidegger reads this processivity in the Aristotelian ontology of *energeia*, but this reading is obviously encouraged by Heidegger's debt to Hegel's attack on fixed essences. Thus "truth setting itself to work" is a way to reject correspondence theories of language [*adaequatio intellectus ad rem*] and representationalist theories of art, "the reproduction of the thing's general essence," by turning to a processive and performative ontology of becoming (Heidegger 1971, 37). It is in this sense that the work-being of the work is "a happening and in no sense a repose" (Heidegger 1971, 48). For Gadamer too, the work of art is "something emerging," something that "oscillates between actuality, reality and activity," that "point[s] to the side of the action in the process of being carried out and not to the 'ergon'—the completed action" (Gadamer 2007, 200, 210).

But how does art express these two opposite modalities? It is a problem with which hermeneutics confronts us. How is the work something permanently fixed yet always in process? If the beauty or power of the form must be of such a quality that it lasts, are we not surreptitiously smuggling in a constant value, something that we judge to be of lasting worth and meaning?

We can read "The Origin of the Work of Art" as a response to this question. Heidegger starts with the premise that the work is not primarily the outcome of an artist's creative genius, that it indeed has its *own* autonomous agency (see, for example, Heidegger 1971, 21). Just as the world worlds, the work works. Heidegger doesn't say this precisely, but something close, *das Sich-ins-Werk-Setzen*, the setting to work of the work itself. The idiom activates the verbal force implicit in the nominal form. But it does something more: *Das Sich-ins-Werk-Setzen* puts in tension the Aristotelian metaphysical principles of rest and motion. And then Heidegger makes clear that this is the level he is working on. Art is a privileged crossing point between Being and beings, which he elaborates as "*das Sich-ins-Werk-Setzen der Wahrheit des Seienden*" (Heidegger 1977, 21).

Heidegger approaches the "curious tangle [*merkwürdige Verstrickung*]" of process and product within the Aristotelian physics of rest and motion, which, in a temporal universe, can, in certain instances, become each other: "Where rest includes motion, there can exist a repose which is an inner concentration of motion, hence a highest state of agitation, assuming that the mode of motion requires such a rest [*Wenn Ruhe die Bewegung einschließt, so kann es eine Ruhe geben, die eine innige Sammlung der Bewegung, also höchste Bewegtheit ist, daß die Art der Bewegung eine solche Ruhe fordert*]" (Heidegger 1977, 34–35; Heidegger 1971, 48). From this premise, Heidegger will come to the categorical conclusion that "[*o*]*nly* what is in motion can rest" (Heidegger 1971, 48, emphasis added). The phenomenon of inner concentration is found eminently in the created work [*das Schaffen*]. Heidegger defines this creation as "*das Hervorgehenlassen in ein Hervorgebrachtes*," which is given in the English translation as follows: "To create is to cause something to emerge as a thing that has been brought forth" (Heidegger 1977, 48; Heidegger 1971, 60). Both substantive forms are processive, but from different temporal perspectives—in the act of emergence, and as finally achieved.

Unshapely Form

Françoise Dastur wondered out loud why the concept of *work* is so central to the original Freiburg version of the lecture. He concluded that Heidegger saw art as a chiasm of beings and Being, connecting the solid, odorous, reliable earth under his feet (potatoes in the cellar), and the phantasmic, evanescent, unreliable ideals of human imagination. In other words, the work of art "does not connect matter and spirit as separated domains, but . . . opens up the free play into which human existence becomes possible" (Dastur 1999, 138). The work doesn't give us this access as a kind of pass-through or portal to a transcendent realm of Being; rather, it creates the conditions for Being's upsurge amidst beings. "[T]o be a work means to set up a world" (Heidegger 1971, 45). This setting up or upsetting of a world is the institution of a conflict structure, what Heidegger calls a "rift-design," a stage on which Being wins an appearance from among beings through a struggle that we are allowed to participate in (Heidegger 1971, 63, 70): "In setting up a world and setting forth the earth, the work is an instigating of this striving" (Heidegger 1971, 50). In the medium of art, this struggle is between an "unshapely form" and its perfect "interfusion" (Heidegger 1971, 28).

Heidegger's phrase *unshapely form* is an intentional oxymoron—a hermeneutic rejection of the dualism of matter and form. What hermeneutics proposes in its place—and here is how Heidegger moves beyond the dialectic of stasis and motion—is the push of an incipiently formed matter toward its fulfillment—the work of the work. Heidegger elaborates this end run around dualism as the relation of work and world—*work* in the double sense of *ins-Werk-Setzen*, and the *Insichstehen des Werkes*, and *world* in the double sense of an incipient intimation of a place of repose, and its ongoing realization (Heidegger 1977, 25). These two kinds of virtuality (incipient and fulfilled) correspond to the different ratios of form and content; work is form- or eidos-heavy, world is content- or meaning-heavy.

We can crudely summarize this work-world relation in Heideggerian terms as follows. The work of the artist, the thing that stands or lasts, is the formal indication, the *formale Anzeige*. The work of the audience, the world that is built from that work-plan, is the *Vollzug*, the fulfilled realization. Of course, for finite humans there is no such thing as a perfect *Vollzug* in our lives; it is always only ever on the way. Both Heidegger and Gadamer admit that there are local or partial fulfillments, but the ideal world that we construct out of our imagination is an ever approaching-receding possibility. Our lives are caught between the two.

In summary, art puts two defining elements in incongruous relation: the fixed text defies our subjective impermanence, but our subjective assimilation of this structure is an unfinalizable process. These countertendencies are the engine of Being's appearance amidst and with beings. Act and thing, process and product, "the particular nature of the mode of being that is common to them" (Gadamer 1993a, 261).

As I turn from Heidegger to Gadamer I want to mark the significance of their respective theories of art for a general hermeneutics as fully in concert. Heidegger's wordplay with *work* and Gadamer's with *play* can be viewed as a passkey to a hermeneutic perspective. We are fortunate in English that the words *work* and *play* are both noun and verb—easily the most efficient linguistic means to express predicative transitivity—process and product in one word. Lacking such a simple device, Heidegger elaborated a rich set of idiomatic expressions: [*das Werkhafte des Werkes; im Werk am Werk; das Sich-ins-Werk-Setzen; das Werksein des Werkes; das Insichstehen des Werkes*], several of which have cognate forms beyond art (e.g., *Die Welt weltet*). The fact that we as temporal beings are allowed, condemned to travel back and forth between process and product is, I would suggest, the nub of hermeneutic logic: the immediacy of the process and the durability of the product compensate for the ephemerality of the process and the exanimacy of the product. Ricoeur would establish a similar dialectic (or chiasm) between person and institution. Gadamer summarizes this all nicely when he refers to "the particular nature of the mode of being that is common to them" (Gadamer 1993a, 261).

Indeed, Otto Pöggeler complained that "The Origin of the Work of Art" did not provide a theory of art at all, and Heidegger agreed. It "deliberately yet tacitly moves on the path of the question of the nature of Being" (Heidegger 1971, 86).[3]

Gadamer's Elaborations of the Paradox

Gadamer adopts Heidegger's conception of the work as a hermeneutic exemplar of the ontological difference, draws out its characteristic entailments, and pinpoints the inherited paradoxical trait of each. I see five of these interrelated traits developed in Gadamer's account of the work (or play) of art from across the writings.

(1) *Incitement to Play*. The animating tension of Gadamer's hermeneutic theory of art, one that thinks with greater specificity about reception, is the difference between the *given* structure of a work (that which stands, that which perdures down through time), and the metamorphosis of the work in the collaborative fusion of artist, art, and audience in history. On the one hand, the exquisite combination of form and content that we recognize in a great work has "a unique, enduring existence" (Gadamer 1982, 339). Gadamer is fond of quoting Aristotle's criterion for the beauty that nothing can be added or taken away from it. When a work achieves this perfection, it endures, it stands: its threads of sound and sense are "cinched" in a fixation that can no longer be undone. On the other hand, in a seeming contradiction, Gadamer warns us that "the poetic structure is formed by us in the act of reading" (Gadamer 1982, 342). The fixed text is only ever partial, "a phase in the execution of the communicative event" (Gadamer 1989, 35). Its "written formulation must take into account the interpretive free space that arises for the 'reader' of the text who has to employ this space" (Gadamer 1989, 35). The inscribed work "is not to be viewed as an end product," but is rather "a mere intermediate product [*Zwischenprodukt*], a phase in the event of understanding" (Gadamer 1989, 31).

Gadamer splits the 'work' of art between (a) the work of art (the object) and (b) the work of the audience (which he rechristens as *play* in order to underline its degrees-of-freedom from the fixed elements of the work) (Gadamer 1993a, 43). A *Gebilde* is a "field of play" for the imagination. In this phrase "field of play" we must read the genitive as more partitive than possessive; structure "field" and structuration "play" are not fully segregated, are porous to each other (Gadamer 1993a, 46). Antigone and Creon represent legitimately conflicting imperatives for audiences; different audiences will read the play differently, and so read their lives differently. The distribution, collaboration, and diffusion of work between field and play gets at the paradox of *Verwandlung ins Gebilde*, which I can summarize this way: a work of art comes together, gains purchase, and endures by "cinching" a certain nagging issue in just the right way, posing an enduring question that we have to answer for.[4] Then it will grab us, arrest us in our tracks, and call us to account. The fixed nature of the work is the perfection of its question, and the malleable, transforming structure of the work is the play of our answers. The work's disruption of our everyday complacency "overwhelms" us, rendering us "defenseless," and sets us "a task for consciousness" (Gadamer 1986, 34, 37; Gadamer 1993a, 127). We too are both frozen in place and set into motion. "Incitement to play [*die Anregung ihres Spieles*]" is the paradoxical structure of "the absolute moment" of the work's work (GW 1, 52; Gadamer 1993a, 128). The work as a fixed text that endures provides the spur, the occasion, the opportunity to become otherwise.[5] The work's fixed identity and its transformation in us are co-determinants.

(2) *Ontological Confusion*. If you look closely at the phrase *Verwandlung ins Gebilde*, you'll see that it is effectively backwards. We are not surprised to learn that someone is transformed by an encounter with a great work; we hear this story all the time. But with *Verwandlung ins Gebilde*, the transformation seems to happen transitively in the work itself, in its very being: "[S]omething is suddenly and as a whole something else" (Gadamer 1993a, 111). The work that Heidegger and Gadamer have told us repeatedly comes to a stand, crystallizes in a unique union of form and matter that wins a lasting place in a culture, is somehow itself altered as it encounters audiences. How do we explain *that*?

The only way to get the transformation going back in the other direction is to undo our hardwired sense of the ontological boundaries of audience and work. We would need a clearer sense of how the physical-material immutability of the Mona Lisa in the Louvre must be blended, merged, fused, intermixed with the fickle waves of cultural interpretation and practical application, with the culture and cultural history, and that mixture, in this strange way of thinking, is the *Gebilde*, the "additional something by virtue of which art clearly becomes what it is for the first time" (Gadamer 1993a, 20).

Some help for this revision work, I think, lies in the metaphor of the fourth wall that Gadamer introduces in the section immediately prior to the *Verwandlung* section. The substitution is quite odd. A wall is a fixed structure, an audience is anything but—the audience comes and goes, brings its various appetites, dispositions, experiences, sensibilities, and is reshaped in the event by the encounter. Even more, an audience that has been changed by the encounter takes that change into the world and changes the world in which that play will be performed.

On the other hand, an audience really is a fourth wall in the sense that it acts as a sounding board [*Resonanzboden*], a test of plausibility, fidelity, and relevance to its own life. Even though an audience, a fourth wall, is malleable, permeable, dissolvable, even though it actuates, extends, translates, applies, still it has a certain material substantiality. It offers resistance. It laughs or fails to laugh. It provides the tests of coherence and probability that determine which works last. It is what Gadamer calls a court of last resort.

So now we have a genuine reciprocity between both sides of the fixed and changeable work, a doubling of this exchange. The script, screenplay, libretto, score, and text all have various built-in types of leeway for the discretion and invention of interpretation but provide fixed material ingredients that prove to last. The audience is a kind of living potentiator that takes this nourishing experience and remakes the world as a result of the engagement, but is also a frequenter, a habitué, a patron of the arts; it comes, it pays its ticket, it gives itself over, it acts happily as the fourth wall. The second aspect of the *Verwandlung ins Gebilde* is a breakdown in the ontological boundaries between work and a work.

(3) *Performative Fusion*. Gadamer throws us a bit of a curve ball by adding a confounding claim about the paradox of the work: "In [the audience] the game is raised, as it were, to its ideality" (Gadamer 1993a, 109). Here the equilibrium we thought we had secured in the dialectic of field and play, mutation and form, seems to be thrown overboard. How does the *mixture* of the fixed and always changing produce an ideal? How are we not now trading in a Platonic dualism?

An almost invisible clue to this riddle is contained in Gadamer's assertion that "the irreplaceable uniqueness of sound and sense can simultaneously hint at an indeterminate polyphony of meaning" (Gadamer 1985, 254). There is a crucial difference between sound and sense. In a lyric poem, sense is tied irrevocably to sound, but sound is in the voice, not on the page. Even when we read silently, our inner ear hears the rhythm of the words. The meaning can only be understood in what Gadamer calls, using a processive form, "sound-structuring [*Klangstrukturierung*]," which means that the sense lies in the performance, *only* in the performance, and in *each* performance (Gadamer 1993b, 250). "It achieves its full being only each time it is played" (Gadamer 1993a, 117). He reminds us that "[a]ll written texts lack modulation, gesture, intonation," so that each "becomes eloquent again in its full sense when a person reads it" in the "living speech-event" (Gadamer 1993b, 246). The actor speaks the part, the pianist plays the piece, the singer sings the song. "[O]nly now is it really there" (Gadamer 1993b, 254).

This "only" is a terrible, incisive, defining burden of *Dasein*, a principle of dependency that underlies the entire hermeneutic project. It is what Heidegger called *weltbezogen*, the fundamental dependency of an object, any object, to its world (Gadamer 1985, 86). The animating question of hermeneutic ontology is how an understanding that is embedded in its context intimates a way to break free; free enough to peer around the corner of its being-in-the-world.

Gadamer's "only" connects this radical dependency and intimation of freedom to the fusion of sound and sense. A text "is not only open to interpretation but in need of it" (Gadamer 1985, 249). The truth and meaning of its words "depend upon and demand being read" (Gadamer 1985, 247). We do not have the full meaning of a poem outside of the performance (in a paraphrase for instance), so we are captive, reader and writer both, to the present of the performance. Literary works, and poems especially, "depend upon and demand being read the right way" (Gadamer 1985, 247). The whole point of the textual revolution is that writing is for reading. The work "emerges in a direct way from our temporality," because it is tied irrevocably to its performance, and it is tied to this temporality. To be sure, a great work "enjoys greater reality than any of its potential realizations can ever claim for itself," but its dependence on performance means that it will be perpetually shuttling back and forth between the two (Gadamer 1986, 109).

(4) *Ideality in the Moment*. Yet performative dependence takes us to another level of the paradox of structure, one at which Gadamer's claim of ideality reaches its paradoxical zenith. On the one hand, Gadamer says that we read out loud because understanding a text is "precisely a matter of bringing it to fulfillment," and "it will only be a complete whole in being read aloud" (Gadamer 1985, 248–49). Yet fulfillment, he tells us explicitly, is a fool's errand. The eminent work, Gadamer says, "demands

something unattainable from the human voice" (Gadamer 1985, 248). No single performance will ever realize it completely. "[W]e never fully grasp the meaning of what is said" (Gadamer 1985, 251). The ideality of the work, therefore, is "inaccessibly ahead [*unerreichbar voraus*]" (Gadamer 1985, 248; Gadamer 1993b, 247).

Because Gadamer says that the work of art gives us both—a complete whole and an impossible ideal—we are driven to the conclusion—and Heidegger has already signaled this solution—that the ideality of the poem has the structure of the *Augenblick*. Indeed, Gadamer finally says this himself. The "magical unity of thought and event" is an "emergence of words" that "can simultaneously hint at an indeterminate polyphony of meaning" (Gadamer 1985, 254). He unites the two imperatives in a single formulation—"a unique value permanence ever emerging into its own presence" (Gadamer 1985, 253). Both permanent and emerging. The whole is, therefore, in the intimation, the formal indication. The final explanation of the *Gebilde* leads us to an inevitable conclusion. The *Gebilde*, the work of art, is paradigmatic of the Lutheran-Kierkegaardian *Augenblick*. Indeed, instead of analogizing the work of art to the structure of the Word (in the Lutheran sense), we ought to look to the hermeneutic relation of work and world to understand this teaching better.

(5) *Gleichzeitigkeit*. It is from this perspective of the *Augenblick* as a glimpse of the *Vollzug* that is inaccessibly ahead that I believe we must read Gadamer's major late essay "The Artwork in Word and Image" (1992). This essay is an extended explication of his notion of *Gleichzeitigkeit*, which is defined explicitly as a paradox, that is, "by an immediate presentness in time and at the same time by a rising above time" (Gadamer 1992, 2). Against Hegel's idealistic "constant, full presence to itself," the experience of the work is lodged restlessly in two mismatched places; "the present here and now," and a space where "the future is in play" (Gadamer 1992, 4–5). The passage between the particular moment, which is "its own life-space," and the intimation of fulfillment is what he calls a third type of being (Gadamer 1991, 18): "The word for present, '*Gegenwart*' [*warten* = waiting], already points to the fact that in it the future is in play. The future, as what is coming, is the present that 'waits' for us, and that we await" (Gadamer 1991, 5). In this "favorable moment" we see something "completely unnamable" that nevertheless "teaches us to see better" (Gadamer 1991, 14, 2, 8). "The Artwork in Word and Image" overflows with ontological insights that far exceed this one clarification, but the climactic arrival at the denomination

a third type of being gives a habitation and a name to the structural puzzle of the hermeneutic work.

Conclusion: The Inaccessibly Ahead

Heidegger and Gadamer both are happy to announce and affirm the lasting purchase of a work as an abiding fixed construction (a work of art is in the first instance a construction that has won that durability), but also that a work (its structure in the second sense) is always being transformed, and it does so because the audience is part of that structure. The paradoxical twist to this second sense of work-structure is that, as the audience is being transformed (in its ongoing relationship to the work, a relationship that must be understood as ontologically indissociable), it is also transforming the work that stands. The only way to understand this double operation (the reciprocity of coming-to-a-stand and setting-to-work, and of structural transformation on both ends) is to reconceive the conventional metaphysical categories under the pressure of their ontological subversion.

The *Gebilde*, Gadamer says in an enigmatic formulation, "enjoys greater reality than any of its potential realizations can ever claim for itself" (Gadamer 1986, 109). Here it would seem that hermeneutic historicity wants to have it both ways, since it is not, as the idealists and historicists would have it, a growing sum, but the ontological difference itself. The strangeness of the hermeneutic structure is that there is transformation all round. We have to conceive of transformation by placing art in the path of the being whose being is an issue for itself. *That* being is not the subject; that being is the encounter of work and audience. The riddle of the fixed and moving work is the riddle of a third type of being, neither dualism nor monism. We cannot put our finger on this place in the middle, because there is no such place, no "third term." We sense it only in the moment.

To explain why an artwork works by "setting-itself-to-work" is to explain the fundamental hermeneutic structure of the human condition. We humans are creatures of imagination and desire because of the improvised tools we have evolved to respond to our locus of being both in a particular time and place that feels to us irreplaceably real and present, and in knowing that that particularity sits between two other kinds of particularity, one that is irrevocable and irrecoverable (although interpretable), and one that is indeterminable (if influenceable). The partial agencies we hold in each of those three particularities—appreciative of irreplaceable value (the present), capable of interpretation (the past), susceptible of influence (the future)—are all interrelated. Because we deeply value the evanescent and precious reality of the immediate present, we tirelessly manipulate what little hold we have over the past and the future to maximize our hold on that presentness:

> Whenever we have to hold something, it is because it is transient and threatens to escape our grasp. In fact, our fundamental experience as beings subject to time is that all things escape us, that all the events of our lives fade more and more, so that at best they glow with an almost unreal shimmer in the most distant recollection. But the poem does not fade, for the poetic word brings the transience of time to a standstill . . . As we know from our own experience of life, the basic task facing us is "to make ourselves at home" in the flood of impressions. (Gadamer 1986, 114)

The work of art, the toil of reason, the observance of ritual, are chief among our patchwork attempts to fabricate some bulwark against the inescapable tide of loss that is our condition. The peculiar structural feature of the hermeneutic work is that it rests in protective repose and yet also restlessly transforms itself. Determined to avoid the dualism of form and content—the aesthetic version of epistemic dualism—hermeneutics refashions the form-content relation as the irresolvable struggle between formal incipience and ideal form.

Notes

1. The Latin *stasis* or *status* captures this paradoxical identity in a word, since status has the root sense of both rest (something is static) and movement (static electricity).

2. Joan Stambaugh glosses this contradiction in the opposition between *Entrückung* and *Berückung* in the *Beiträge*: "The first term expresses movement and corresponds to time; the second involves a kind of stasis and corresponds to space" (Stambaugh 1992, 118). The "essential complexity" of this oxymoron is nothing less than *Da-sein* itself (Stambaugh 1992, 118).

3. See a discussion of this interchange between Pöggeler and Heidegger in Kockelmans 1986, 81.

4. Another word Gadamer uses for this is *invitation*. Great works are "invitations for further meditation" (Gadamer 1985, 250).

5. Gadamer gives us something close to this formula in "The Artwork in Word and Language." A work of architecture "gives one something to think about." When we are struck by a painting we are "drawn into its full reality and into the thought it generates" (Gadamer 2007, 221).

Bibliography

Dastur, Françoise. "Heidegger's Freiburg Version of the Origin of the Work of Art." In *Heidegger toward the Turn: Essays on the Work of the 1930s*. Edited by J. Risser, 119–42. Albany: State University of New York Press, 1999.

Gadamer, Hans-Georg. *Heidegger's Ways*. Translated by J. W. Stanley. Albany: State University of New York Press, 1994.

———. "Philosophie und Literatur." In *Gesammelte Werke. Vol. 8*, 240–57. Tübingen: Mohr Siebeck, 1993b.

———. "Philosophy and Literature." Translated by A. J. Steinbock. *Man and World* 18 (1985): 241–59.

———. "Text and Interpretation." In *Dialogue and Deconstruction: The Gadamer-Derrida Encounter*. Edited by D.P. Michelfelder and R.E. Palmer, 21–51. Albany: State University of New York Press, 1989.

———. "The Artwork in Word and Image—'So True, So Full of Being!'" In *The Gadamer Reader: A Bouquet of the Later Writings*. Translated and edited by R. E. Palmer, 195–224. Evanston: Northwestern University Press, 2007.

———. "The Eminent Text and Its Truth." In *The Horizon of Literature*. Edited by P. Hernadi, 337–47. Lincoln: University of Nebraska Press, 1982.

———. *The Relevance of the Beautiful and Other Essays*. Translated by N. Walker. Edited by R. Bernasconi. Cambridge: Cambridge University Press, 1986.

———. *Truth and Method*. Revised ed. Translated by J. Weinsheimer and D. G. Marshall. New York: Continuum, 1993a.

———. "Wahrheit und Methode." *Gesammelte Werke. Vol. 1* [GW 1]. Tübingen: Mohr Siebeck, 1990.

Heidegger Martin. *Beiträge zur Philosophie (vom Ereignis)*. *Gesamtausgabe* 65. Frankfurt a.M.: Klostermann, 2003.

———. *Contributions to Philosophy (From Enowning)*. Translated by P. Emad and K. Maly. Bloomington: Indiana University Press, 1999.

———. "Der Ursprung des Kunstwerkes." In *Gesamtausgabe. Vol. 5*. Frankfurt a.M.: Vittorio Klostermann, 1977.

———. *Einführung in die Metaphysik*. Tübingen: Max Niemeyer, 1998.

———. *Introduction to Metaphysics*. Translated by G. Fried and R. Polt. New Haven: Yale University Press, 2000.

———. *Phänomenologische Interpretationen zu Aristoteles: Einführung in die Phänomenologische Forschung*. Frankfurt a. M.: Klostermann, 1985.

———. "The Origin of the Work of Art." In *Poetry, Language, Thought*. Translated by A. Hofstadter, 15–88. New York: Harper & Row, 1971.

———. *The Principle of Reason*. Translated by R. Lilly. Bloomington: Indiana University Press, 1991.

Inwood, Michael. *A Heidegger Dictionary*. Oxford: Blackwell, 1999.

Kockelmans, Joseph J. *Heidegger on Art and Art Works*. Dordrecht: Martinus Nijhoff, 1986.

Nowicki, Alexis. "The Patriarchy Can F Itself episode." *Culture Gabfest*. July 2021. [online] https://podcasts.apple.com/us/podcast/culture-gabfest-the-patriarchy-can-f-itself/id279188498?i=1000528837186.

Schleiermacher, Friedrich. *On Religion: Speeches to Its Cultured Despisers*. Translated by J. Oman. New York: Harper & Row, 1958.

Stambaugh, Joan. *The Finitude of Being*. Albany: State University of New York Press, 1992.

Waugh, Evelyn. *Brideshead Revisited*. New York: Little Brown, 1973.

Wordsworth, William. "The Tables Turned." In *Poetical Works. Vol. 1*. Edited by W. Knight. London: Macmillan & Co., 1986 [online] https://www.gutenberg.org/cache/epub/10219/pg10219-images.html#section23.

5

Critiquing Gadamer's Aesthetics
Hermeneutics and the Specificity of the Aesthetic[1]

GEORG W. BERTRAM

Hans-Georg Gadamer developed his hermeneutics out of his engagement with art. He begins his seminal work *Truth and Method* with a critique of Romantic aesthetics and only later turns towards general questions of hermeneutics proper. The book concludes with a broader treatment of the "Ontological Shift of Hermeneutics Guided by Language." Gadamer's approach opens questions about the relation between his hermeneutics as a fundamental ontology of beings who understand and the aesthetics that kicks off his inquiry. Does the aesthetics that Gadamer develops on the basis of his hermeneutics hold water? As John McDowell and others have shown, it is possible to work with Gadamer's hermeneutics without delving into issues of aesthetics (see McDowell 1994, 115–19). Is this a symptom of the absorption of aesthetics into general hermeneutics?[2]

In the run of critiquing the Romantics' subject-centered conception of aesthetic experience, Gadamer fundamentally criticizes the concept of aesthetic difference. Countering notions that aesthetic objects and aesthetic consciousness are unique,[3] Gadamer focuses on the everydayness of the aesthetic. One might say that, for Gadamer, every act of understanding has an aesthetic dimension that lies in its transformative character. Accordingly, he grasps understanding as a process that is in constant flux. This sensibility is poignantly captured in Gadamer's assertion that it is "enough to say that we understand in *a different* way, *if we understand at all*" (Gadamer 2004, 296, emphasis in original).

Gadamer's emphasis on the understanding's mutability is grounded in the insight that every instance of understanding involves an interaction between objects of understanding and understanding subjects. His first argument is that understanding does not begin with the subject approaching an object. Rather, it originates in objects that trigger changes in the subject and in subjects whose varying perspectives open space for objects to appear in innumerable different ways. One concept that Gadamer employed to capture this process is that of question and answer (see Gadamer 2004, 362–71). The object places the subject in question and impels change in the subject, while at the same time, the subject poses its own questions to the object. Conceived in this fashion, understanding always signifies an occurrence in which an object has a singular resonance for a subject. And this is, for Gadamer, the core of the aesthetic. Its truth resounds in an object challenging a subject and evoking a response.

The problem with Gadamer's position, however, lies in its implication that every act of understanding has an aesthetic structure.[4] It does not allow for a distinction between objects that pose a specifically aesthetic challenge and those that only challenge the contents of the subject's understanding. Accordingly, he grasps every challenge posed by an object as an aesthetic challenge in the sense that it occasions transformations of everyday practices. In setting up his concept of understanding this way, Gadamer fails to account for the specificity of aesthetic challenges. At the end of the day, his hermeneutics necessitates reconstructing all aesthetic challenges as challenges to the understanding. But this is erroneous. Aesthetic challenges have a specificity that escapes Gadamer's account.

Moreover, Gadamer's hermeneutics fails to sufficiently explore the constitution and preconditions of the subject. His critique of aesthetic difference dethrones the subject. But in doing so, it obscures the significance of the subject in processes of understanding, because, first, subjects can forge their own perspectives on objects by grappling with, drawing from, and subtracting from the perspectives of others, and, second, engagement with specifically aesthetic challenges is crucial for the development of one's own perspectives. Thus, critiquing Gadamer demands not only an explication of the specificity of the aesthetic beyond aesthetic difference, but also an account of the constitution of subjects and the aesthetic contribution to it.

In the following, I seek to show what it might look like to put together a hermeneutic aesthetics unburdened by the problems of Gadamer's position. What does hermeneutic thought need in order to gain an adequate conception of the specificity of aesthetic challenges? And what perspectives on the aesthetic does hermeneutics offer us? The critique of Gadamer's aesthetics should make it possible to sketch a hermeneutic aesthetics that also has affinities with Hegel's position.[5] The paper concludes by conceiving of the aesthetic as a specific mode of cultural practices by means of which understanding beings call themselves into question. Aesthetic objects and events are produced in order to give impulses to the structures that shape subjects' relations to the world and to others. They thus inform and influence negotiations over the structures of understanding itself without, however, sacrificing their distinctiveness to the general transformative character of understanding. In this sense, the present critique further sharpens the contribution of hermeneutics to debates on aesthetics.

I will flesh out these ideas by first reconstructing Gadamer's critique of aesthetic consciousness. I focus on whether the conclusions that Gadamer draws from his critique are plausible. My negative response to this question leads me to work out some alternative conclusions that might be deduced from Gadamer's critique. This paves the way for an account of what Gadamer's position leaves wanting: namely, an illumination of the specific character of the challenges posed by aesthetic objects. With that in hand, the fourth section of the paper explains how a hermeneutic aesthetics that fills this gap might adopt aspects of Gadamer's hermeneutics. I aim to demonstrate that hermeneutics can conceive of the aesthetic—including aesthetic difference—as practical and everyday. Finally, the paper concludes with an alternative perspective on the hermeneutic critique of Romantic aesthetics.

Gadamer's Critique of Romantic Aesthetics

Gadamer criticizes two foundational concepts of a position that he attributes to Romantic aesthetics. The first is that of aesthetic consciousness. It signifies the notion that subjects receive—in the sense of an experience—the aesthetic aspects of objects as such in consciousness. The second details how subjects receive aesthetic objects. It asserts that aesthetic experiences involve a (structural) reassurance of the subject.

Gadamer's critique is primarily concerned with the second notion. Crucial for him is grappling with the transformative potential of aesthetic objects. He claims that the Romantic position's fatal error is its—implicit or explicit—definition of the aesthetic as something that reassures.[6] Accordingly, he accuses Kant and the Romantics of overlooking the potential of aesthetic objects to set in motion changes in the world outside of aesthetics. Their oversight is, for him, a consequence of the notion that subjects relate to aesthetic objects via consciousness. Because the subject receives aesthetic objects, it has to be attuned to them. For this reason, it is incapable of being changed by the objects; instead, its already existing conceptions are confirmed by them. In this context, Gadamer speaks compellingly of the "unlimited sovereignty" of aesthetic consciousness (Gadamer 2004, 77).

One might counter Gadamer's criticism by recalling that Romantic aesthetics always also insisted that aesthetic experiences transcend the subject. In that line of reasoning, the subject would not be reassured, but sublated. Even though this is undoubtedly the correct interpretation of Romantic aesthetics, Gadamer also rightly discerns a moment of reassurance in the subject's sublation. His point is that, from the perspective of Romantic aesthetics, the subject as such is reassured by aesthetic experiences because it does not, as such, encounter any impulses in them. In other words, aesthetic experiences leave the subject unchanged. Gadamer counters this argument by reinterpreting consciousness as "historically effected consciousness"—a consciousness that undergoes incessant transformation (Gadamer 2004, 335–82).

Gadamer articulates his notion of the transformative potential of aesthetic experiences by drawing on Hegel's concept of experience.[7] He approvingly cites Hegel as recognizing a fundamentally negative aspect of experience in which the experience always alters its subject (see Gadamer 2004, 347–48). Consequently, whoever confronts an object without being changed by it has not, by this definition, had an experience. This, Gadamer states, is precisely the basic structure of encounters with aesthetic objects. Thus, Gadamer writes that "the work of art has its true being in the fact that it becomes an experience that changes the person who experiences it" (Gadamer 2004, 103). In line with his critique of Romantic aesthetics, he says that "our concern is to view the experience of art in such a way that it is understood as experience [in general]" (Gadamer 2004, 85).[8] In short, he seeks to expand the concept of aesthetic experience as a transformative experience.

However, in making the negativity of experience central to his concept of aesthetics, Gadamer, for all that, does not want to lay the foundations for a concept of aesthetic difference.[9] Rather, he wants to gain from his critique of Romantic aesthetics an insight into the constitution of human understanding more generally. He grasps Romantic aesthetics as an expression of a false conception of understanding, which he thinks determined

Romantic hermeneutics and historicism. Gadamer accuses this false notion of being bound to the idea that subjects have to enable objects to appear in their singularity.[10] Subjects gain understanding by becoming a neutral surface for objects. Gadamer calls this an "epistemological problem" that must be overcome (Gadamer 2004, 235).

Gadamer thinks doing so is possible by abandoning both the affirmative concept of aesthetic experience as well as the concept of the subject as a neutral entity. Accomplishing these two maneuvers necessitates leaving behind the notion that object and subject are self-enclosed figures that stand opposite one another in a relation of indifference. In turn, this leads Gadamer to grasp the subject's act of relating to an object as a transformative practice—independent of whether the subject engages with the object with intentionality (like in some acts of understanding) or whether the object is directed at engaging the subject (like in aesthetic experience). On the whole, Gadamer's hermeneutics asks us to grasp every subject-object relation as one in which objects transform subjects. This fundamental position eliminates the possibility of meaningfully distinguishing between a more specific aesthetic engagement with objects and general instances of understanding.

Gadamer's critique of the reassurance hypothesis thus has a problematic outcome: it fails to do justice to the specificity of the aesthetic. His hermeneutics categorizes all understanding—both of the everyday and the exceptional varieties—as transformative. Since he categorizes all transformation in understanding as aesthetic, this leads him to conceive of all understanding as aesthetic. Gadamer arrives at this point by claiming that understanding is always bound up with an act of questioning, which gives it an aesthetic dimension. The strength of this position is its acknowledgment of the everydayness of the aesthetic. However, in doing so, it loses the capacity to say anything about the specific contribution of the aesthetic to human practices. This problematic conclusion poses the question as to whether the critique of Romantic aesthetics can take another path that does not lead to the absorption of the aesthetic into everyday practices. How can one preserve the specificity of the aesthetic while at the same time rejecting the Romantic—in the broadest sense—position on aesthetics?

An Alternative Reading of the Critique of Romantic Aesthetics

In short, Gadamer's critique of Romantic aesthetics targets the notion that aesthetic experiences reassure the subject (in its consciousness-structure).

Against the Romantics, Gadamer counters that, like objects of understanding, aesthetic objects always pose a challenge to the subject. But this simply recapitulates the other key feature of the Romantic position—namely, that aesthetic objects are directed at a subject that chooses to engage with them. Even though Gadamer does not have a robust concept of the subject, the notion that understanding begins with challenges posed by objects or other subjects remains problematic. In Gadamer's account, the genesis of challenges presupposes that object and subject stand over against one another, which for its part presupposes that subjects have a constitutive disposition to be challenged. Even though Gadamer seeks to overcome the confines of epistemology, he holds fast to the notion that subjects are constituted through the challenges that objects confront them with.

At first glance, it seems trivial to say that objects (including artistic ones) stand opposite to subjects. Calling something an object seems to presuppose its difference from a subject. Thus, it seems reasonable to ask what is wrong with the Romantic focus on the object that Gadamer partially shares. But the entire constellation rests on an assumption that needs to be unveiled and overcome. Positing that subjective (pre)conceptions are challenged by objects makes it impossible to draw the important distinction between objects that are constitutive for subjects and objects that pose challenges for constituted subjects, broadly understood.

Gadamer criticizes the Romantics for their exaggerated valorization of subjectivity and—relatedly—of aesthetic consciousness, but he does not criticize the uniform one-sided concept of challenge bound up with the Romantic account of aesthetic experience. Asserting that every instance of understanding is transformative because it is rooted in the confrontation with a challenge is ultimately just a continuation of the Romantic position. But it is precisely at this juncture that the Romantic position needs to be left behind.

Doing so requires dismantling the isolated status of the subject in Romantic thought. The Romantic perspective is one-sided because it abstracts from dynamics that are constitutive of the subject.[11] Contrary to the message of Romantic aesthetics, the aesthetic should be conceived as just one aspect of these dynamics, which come into being because subjects always stand among many other subjects and themselves are only constituted through interactions with others. These interactions involve practices through which fundamental orientations of all understanding (which we might conceive of as self-understandings) are reflexively determined, critiqued, and changed.[12] The aesthetic belongs among these practices of social interaction—a point that the Romantic position fails to capture.[13]

The Romantic perspective is untenable because it defines the aesthetic on the basis of a subject that is presumed to precede it. Instead, the aesthetic should be conceived of as a moment in the constitution of the subject. Presupposing a subject and then building a concept of the aesthetic upon it thus fails to do justice to the aesthetic. Developing an adequate grasp of the relevance of the aesthetic necessitates a more dynamic conception of subjectivity that acknowledges its formation through social structures and practices.

One might retort that Gadamer, too, does not begin his account of the aesthetic with the presumption of an already constituted subject. Indeed, for him, the concept of the subject does not really play a central role at all. Supporting this are Gadamer's claim that "our understanding . . . is not an act of subjectivity" (Gadamer 2004, 293) and his criticism of the "focus of subjectivity" as a "distorting mirror" (Gadamer 2004, 278). But this changes nothing about the fact that the object-subject dynamic guides Gadamer's explication of the aesthetic and understanding. Evidence of this is his definition of understanding as having a question-and-answer structure and his concept of the history of effect. But this account of the dynamic constitution of subjectivity through practices—among them aesthetic practices—is itself truncated because it fails to consider how subjectivity is formed and the role of self-critique therein.

I think it is helpful to take a different perspective on the critique of Romantic aesthetics outlined here. Romantic aesthetics begins with the assumption that engagement with aesthetic objects is a special type of experience for a subject. The experience is distinct because it opens up established relations to the world and pulls the subject away from habituated practices. The dynamic realized in aesthetic experiences can involve de-subjectification, fracturing the relations that define the subject's habituated relationship to itself and the world (see Menke 2013, 61–66).

Even if this Romantic—or Romantic-adjacent—interpretation of aesthetic experience discerns something transformative in the aesthetic, it remains caught in the notion that the transformation in question emanates from the subject. In contrast, Gadamer asserts that subjects of understanding undergo constant transformation. His position suggests that we have to decide between two options: either transformations are bound up with a transcendence of subjective forms, or they entail changes that the subject experiences through external impulses. But this binary choice is incomplete, because it fails to consider the possibility that subjects can, on their own accord, occasion transformations and thus constitute themselves through these acts. I call this self-critique, or, more precisely, I use the concept of self-critical impulses to describe impulses through which a subject effectuates transformations in itself. The aesthetic should be conceived of in terms of self-critical impulses. It is not sufficient to juxtapose Romantic aesthetics with the radical plasticity of the subject. The point is not to align the subject with forms that are constantly being altered via objects' impulses. Rather, the subject must be grasped as standing in constant (critical) relation to the fundamental forms of understanding that are constitutive of itself.

This rereading of the consequences of the critique of Romantic aesthetics is significant because it illuminates both a problem of understanding as well as a problem of aesthetic practice. If one assumes that subjects always stand in some kind of constitutive relation to forms, then it seems clear that they can become fixed in these forms, thus hindering their own capacity to change. In other words, subjects can relate to themselves such that their forms of understanding ossify. This has specific consequences for contents of understanding. The self-critical impulses that subjects initiate can also end up reifying these contents. The plasticity and mobility of subjects are not, as Gadamer tells us, necessarily enduring. They must be constantly enacted and practiced to be retained. This is the task that subjects face.

Returning to the transformative impulses occasioned by aesthetic objects, this means that they do not necessarily trigger change. Aesthetic formations can be brought forth and received in such a way that they lead to an ossification of contents of understanding, forms, and practices. They can also reinforce subjects' rigidity. These points further limit the claims of Romantic aesthetics by underscoring that the aesthetic does not guarantee the liberation of subjects from themselves and from the subordinating forms of social structures. Rather, the aesthetic has the potential to generate moments of, to paraphrase Kant, "self-imposed immaturity."

Thus, a self-consistent critique of Romantic aesthetics cannot limit itself to championing the transformative character of aesthetic objects. Instead, it needs to demonstrate how the transformative impulses bound up with them can sometimes hinder change. It should not be taken for granted that aesthetic practices lead to change. However, this does not require a return to the position that aesthetic objects reassure the subject in its knowledge and prejudgments. Rather, the point to be made is that the subject can question itself through aesthetic practices and, in doing so, might also bolster its own resistance to change. Articulating the meaning of this claim, though, first necessitates a look at the specificity of the challenges posed by aesthetic objects.

The Specificity of Aesthetic Challenges

In light of this revised critique of Romantic aesthetics, one should reflect on how to distinguish between the transformative character of all understanding and the transformative character of encounters with aesthetic objects. Continued relevance is held here by the critique of approaches that can be read as Romantic in the broadest sense, which often support the position that aesthetic understanding is wholly separate from everyday understanding (see Sonderegger 2000, 270–76). Taken to its conclusion, one can say that the routines of understanding that guide us and bind us in everyday life are called into question by aesthetic experiences.

However, the notion that aesthetic understanding is fundamentally distinct from all other understanding runs into two problems. First, it makes it seem as if, in aesthetic experiences, we exit everyday life entirely and, in the best-case scenario, thus contribute to a revision of everyday norms. But this renders incomprehensible the place of aesthetic practices in everyday life. The next step is to conclude that aesthetic practices—in the broadest sense—that belong to everyday life should simply be excluded from the realm of the aesthetic altogether. Adorno's concept of the "culture industry" is a paramount example of this (see Horkheimer and Adorno 2002, 107–15). Whether explicitly or implicitly, it situates use-oriented forms of art (including all types of popular literature that rely on everyday language) outside the realm of art. Second, the insistence on the uniqueness of the aesthetic often carries the implication that in aesthetic experiences, understanding simply does not function. The reasoning goes that because forms of understanding belong to the everyday and because the everyday is suspended by art, art is not an object of understanding. In Adorno's pithy formulation, "the communication of artworks . . . occurs through noncommunication" (Adorno 2002, 5). But this fails to do justice to many types of art. After all, watching a play, following thematic developments in a poem, and analyzing iconography in paintings all involve moments of understanding.

Avoiding this exclusion of understanding from art demands defining the specificity of the aesthetic on the basis of something else besides a break with everyday forms of understanding. The reflections in the preceding section offer some clues to developing a more stable concept. Engagement with aesthetic objects should not be conceived of as a mode of understanding or as a break with forms of understanding, but as a mode of self-critique directed towards forms and structures of understanding. In our engagement with aesthetic objects, we reflect on and then revise forms and structures of understanding. I call the forms and structures in question "orientations of human practices."

The challenges posed by aesthetic objects are, from this perspective, posed to foundational orientations of human practices.[14] Aesthetic practices enable humans to grapple with *how* they understand. They open up inquiries into the intersubjective relations that condition all understanding, into core concepts like reality, truth, and contradiction, and into other structures that hold significance for understanding others and the world. In short, the challenges posed by aesthetic objects concern the concepts, preconceptions, and practices that guide our understanding.

Two notions are decisive for this approach to the specificity of the aesthetic. First, the aesthetic and the challenges posed by it are directed at foundational orientations; thus, their transformative impulses do not concern contents of understanding. It is precisely this point that Gadamer's aesthetics fails to sufficiently capture. In no unclear terms, Gadamer says that "*all . . . understanding is ultimately self-understanding*" (Gadamer 2004, 251, emphasis in original). But this is incorrect. Although all understanding is indeed related to self-understandings, it is not identical with them. Not every act of understanding addresses and critically challenges self-understandings as such. However, this statement does hold for aesthetic practices.

Second, Gadamer is right to say that all critical reflection on self-understandings—conceived of as foundational orientations—is directly related to contents of understanding. The thematization of self-understandings is not some kind of rarified discourse but is bound up with everyday acts of understanding. One might turn Gadamer's claim on its head and assert: all self-understanding is an act of understanding. All engagement with orientations that determine the subject's relations to others and the world involves direct contact with others, with the world, and with the contents of understanding that are thereby gained and constantly revised. In this respect, self-understandings are challenged by engagement with the world and, in turn, they themselves can challenge contents of understanding.

For example, consider the connection between music and affect. Music is an artistic praxis that thematizes affects as foundational orientations in our relations to others and to the world.[15] It challenges how we experience affects and thus helps restructure them in new ways. In this accomplishment, music does not simply stand by itself; rather, it stands in direct relation to the affective lives of those who engage with music, whether as listeners or as practitioners. On the one hand, the novel articulation of affect evoked by music can alter the affective lives of recipients and players. On the other, affective life has the potential to change how we hear music and how it thematizes affects.

The specificity of aesthetic challenges thus lies in how they address foundational orientations, elements of human practices and humans' relations to the world. Objectness plays a central role in their realization. In the arts, objects generate impulses that occasion engagement with foundational orientations. Performative arts, too, have an object dimension inherent in the structures they produce, which their recipients engage with (see Bertram 2019, 126–45). Artistic objects do not prescribe how orientations should look. Rather, they confront subjects with structures that pose challenges to orientations. The impulses generated by the arts are, one might add, always associated with indeterminacy. As Adorno regularly reminds us, they "stand under the prohibition on graven images" (Adorno 2002, 104). They do not propose on their own accord particular revisions of orientations; rather, they open space for such revisions through their impulses. The impulses generated by aesthetic objects place orientations in question and thus call forth an indeterminacy that enables subjects to critique and determine anew foundational orientations of human practices.

Refining Hermeneutic Aesthetics

What might a hermeneutic position that does justice to the preceding arguments look like? To what extent can Gadamer's hermeneutics be adjusted such that it accounts for the specificity of aesthetic challenges? Decisive for a revision of hermeneutic thought in aesthetics is to cease conceiving of human cultures' practices of understanding as entirely aesthetic. This will avoid the problem of absorbing aesthetic understanding into more general structures of understanding.

As discussed above, the notion that understanding is a transformative act is central to Gadamer's hermeneutics. This concept should be retained. However, it should be interpreted such that aesthetic transformations and general transformations in understanding do not become indistinguishable. Refining Gadamer's approach necessitates differentiating between changes that the subject effects on its own, on the one hand, and, on the other, changes that constantly shift the subject's relation to others and to the world. Still, this differentiation should not wholly dispose of the constitutive connection between both types of change.

I've already sketched what this undertaking might involve in the previous two sections. I'd thus like to dedicate some time to another perspective. Hermeneutic philosophies put forward a foundational intertwining of subject and object, mind and world. In this respect, Gadamer travels on a path blazed by Martin Heidegger,[16] though he places stronger emphasis on the dynamic that follows out of the interweaving of subject and object. Hegel's philosophy can help explain why. Hegel, too, reads the interrelation of subject and object—in good hermeneutic fashion—as an all-encompassing dynamic. However, he underscores that this presupposes an immanent relation between subject and object, and, thus, that it requires the rejection of the notion that changes are impelled by external factors. For this reason, Hegel asserts that the dynamic is driven by "self-movement" (Hegel 1977, 28).

In line with Gadamer's critique of Hegel's concept of absolute spirit (see Gadamer 2004, 349–50), one might reject the notion of self-movement as a relic of idealism. Does this not imply that the subject unfurls, out of itself, the dynamic of the relation between subject and object? This suspicion, though, falls short of Hegel's thought. If self-movement comes into being through the relation between subject and object, it cannot emanate in isolation from one side or the other. Thus, it is incorrect to say that Hegel prioritizes the subject. Similarly, it is also wrong to say that the dynamic of self-movement is rooted in the primacy of the object (in the sense of a given).

Hegel, then, confronts us with the question of how to grasp a dynamic that at once proceeds from both subject and object. An initial negative remark might help remove the potential for confusion: the dynamic is set in motion neither by impulses of the object nor by the initiative of the subject. Rather, it is propelled by actions of the subject that address and pose challenges to objective impulses. Only through the interaction of impulses from both sides does self-movement begin. This explication, though, remains quite formal.

Considering art might help concretize it. Through artworks and artistic performances, humans produce objects that generate impulses. Let's return to the example of music. Humans make music in order to develop their affective lives. Music thematizes affective states and, in doing so, opens these affective states to new encounters with the world. Only through interactions with aspects of the world that trigger certain affects can musical impulses achieve their transformative potential. The challenges posed by artistic music do not themselves initiate movement in the subject's relation to the world. Rather, they presuppose a world in which affects have significance. Impulses generated by music thus proceed both from subject and object at the same time. They enable objects to change subjects' affective reactions, without the objects simply causing these changes. They are, at the same time, initiated by the subject themselves through the musical exploration of affects.

The conclusion for art as a whole is that engagement with art gives impulses to subjects to renegotiate their relations to others and to the world. Questioning orientations thus does not mean that subjects simply determine for themselves what the replacement is going to be. Rather, the impulses of art open subjects to others and to the world. The self-movement initiated by art thus makes impulses from subjects and objects interact with one another, which in turn releases impulses from both sides. Ultimately, self-movement follows from an interaction between subject and object. Art thus reveals itself to be, briefly put, a practice of the subject calling itself into question.[17] This self-questioning is brought about by objects that unsettle the subject's orientations and thus contribute to their revision.

The ability of objects to offer resistance without simply causing changes themselves is decisive for Hegel's concept of self-movement. So long as objects only cause changes from the outside, there is no self-movement. And the same holds when a subject moves itself and thereby initiates movement that is indistinguishable from stasis. Key to the development of spirit in Hegel's philosophy is that it relates to nature as its other. In less abstract terms, this means that the orientations that guide subjects are regularly reconceived as orientations that have validity and application in the outside world. Art contributes to reconceptions in precisely this sense. It paves the way for orientations to be put in question, opening them to the world in such a way that they can be revised. As the discussion of music illustrates, engagement with the challenges posed by art concerns not only concepts that are foundational for the subject's relation to the world, but also affective, physical, and imaginative orientations of human practices.

The revision of Gadamer's hermeneutic approach to aesthetics and understanding detailed here revolves around the key distinction between processes of understanding and processes of negotiating and altering the orientations foundational for every act of understanding. A hermeneutics that accounts for the specificity of aesthetic challenges thus reformulates the hermeneutic circle as a "circle of circles," in Hegel's words (see Hegel 2010, 43, §15). Understanding is not just constituted by the application of preformed concepts to a new situation. Rather, constitutive for understanding are also the challenges that call into question the orientations that guide a subject's understanding. Revisions of accepted contents of understanding do not simply set forth foundational orientations of understanding unquestioned. Rather, they involve repeatedly subjecting these orientations to changes that stem from impulses that are both produced and sought out. Thus, the circle in which contents of understanding are changed is embedded in a circle in which the orientations that guide understanding are always confronted with new impulses.

Nelson Goodman articulated a concept that is helpful for conceptualizing the interaction of both circles. Writing on the relation between inductive and deductive aspects of logic, he introduced a concept that has since been called "reflective equilibrium" (Goodman 1983, 62–66). The concept refers to the process of weighing simple logical judgments against formalizations and generalizations in logic. In his analysis, neither generalizations nor simple judgments have the final word. Rather, the task is to discern where alterations need to be made in the tension between them. From the perspective of the reconfigured hermeneutics laid out here, this sort of reflective equilibrium plays a part in all processes of understanding. Understanding does not just occur through constant change. Rather, it arises out of the tension between revisions to contents of understanding and critical questioning of the orientations that guide these changes.

The Critique of Romantic Aesthetics Revisited

In *The Sickness unto Death*, Kierkegaard criticizes the Romantic position as one of aestheticism, though his reasoning differs from Gadamer's. Kierkegaard speaks of the Romantic extremes of "despair at not willing to be oneself" and "despair of willing despairingly to be oneself" (Kierkegaard 2013, 330, 359). In stark terms, one might say that Gadamer's hermeneutics never departs from these two extremes. His reconstruction of understanding as a process of constant change can be read as an attempt to avoid considering processes of self-formation. From the perspective of Kierkegaard's critique, Gadamer remains, in a sense, stuck in the Romantic framework. One path to escaping it might be taking hermeneutic thought to the point where it departs from Romantic assumptions.

According to Kierkegaard, doing so requires abandoning the alternative between subject-capture and subject-abandonment. Kierkegaard's solution is for the subject to give itself over to other powers in order to be itself. For him, the recourse to other powers has an essentially religious dimension (see Kierkegaard 2013, 378–84). But his thinking can be reinterpreted to signify an openness towards the subject's other in a Hegelian sense. The act of calling oneself into question that arises out of engagement with the challenges posed by art brings the subject into a position in which it is itself precisely in being challenged by an other.

In his analysis of processes of understanding, Gadamer emphasizes that the "in-between" is its "true locus" (see Gadamer 2004, 295). His theory of the "fusing of horizons" captures this notion in cogent language (see Gadamer 2004, 306). However, as elucidated here, focusing on the "in-between" fails to bring the specificity of aesthetic challenges to light. This article has sought to make the reason clear: The "in-between" does not tell us how the subject challenges its own orientations in order to return to itself in its being-challenged. Accounting for the retention of self through the act of self-questioning involved in all understanding requires *not* situating understanding in an "in-between," but rather grasping it as a product of the tension between subject and object. By remaining itself in questioning itself, the subject at once opens itself to the object and critically subordinates its orientations to the impulses of the object. For non-Romantic hermeneutics, it is this tension that brings forth understanding.

This line of reasoning gives the aesthetic its own place within hermeneutic theory. It neither absorbs the aesthetic into general processes of understanding, nor does it fall into reflection on the abyssal foundation of humans' relation to the world à la Heidegger (see Heidegger 2002, 14–16, 23–24). Grasped in its specificity, the aesthetic constitutes an important dimension of the ongoing renegotiation of humans' relations to others and to the world. This is the fruit of the critique of Gadamer's aesthetics. Conceptualizing aesthetic challenges as impulses for transformation prohibits viewing them as mere moments of a more general transformative process. Rather, they need to be conceived of as parts of critical reflection on the foundational orientations that guide humans in all acts of understanding.[18]

Notes

1. Translated from German by Adam Bresnahan.

2. Gadamer seems to himself point in the direction of such absorption. He writes: "Aesthetics has to be absorbed into hermeneutics" (Gadamer 2004, 157).

3. Here and in the following, the concept of aesthetic objects includes aesthetic events such as performance.

4. Kristin Gjesdal speaks in this context of an "aestheticizing model of understanding" (Gjesdal 2009, 3).

5. For a reading of Hegel's aesthetics as a contribution to what a hermeneutic aesthetics might look like see Bertram 2020, 196–211.

6. Reassurance means, in a sense, that the subject undergoing an aesthetic experience remains present to itself. For a critique of Gadamer on this point see Gjesdal 2005, 293–310.

7. On Hegel's conception of experience, see the remarkable passage in the introduction to the *Phenomenology of Spirit* (Hegel 1977, 55–57).

8. Nicholas Davey calls this thought the "re-orientation of aesthetics" (Davey 2013, 42–64).

9. This is underscored when compared to an anti-hermeneutic position like Christoph Menke's, for whom aesthetic negativity is identical with aesthetic difference (see Menke 1998).

10. Schleiermacher's position is an especially illustrative example of Romantic hermeneutics (see Schleiermacher 1977, 175–214).

11. On these dynamics see Bertram 2013, 197–213.

12. On the significance of self-understandings see Bertram 2018, 389–410.

13. For a compelling treatment of art's contribution to self-understanding see Feige 2012.

14. This thought is supported by Hegel's philosophy. Hegel views art as a practice of self-thematization and thus as a practice of absolute, self-moving spirit (see Pinkard 1994, 221–68).

15. On musical expressivity's relation to affect, see Zwinggi 2016. The notion that music articulates affects is treated in detail in Bertram 2015, 231–51.

16. On the foundational connection of spirit and world in Heidegger's *Being and Time*, see Haugeland 2013, 17–39.

17. Self-questioning can also be understood as a principle of improvisation (see Bertram 2024 [forthcoming], IV. 2.4).

18. I am thankful to Adam Bresnahan for his careful translation of the text and for providing important comments for improving it.

Bibliography

Adorno, Theodor W. *Aesthetic Theory*. Translated by R. Hullot-Kentor. New York: Continuum, 2002.

Bertram, Georg W. "Absoluter Geist als sich vollbringender Skeptizismus." In *Objektiver und absoluter Geist nach Hegel*. Edited by T. Oehl and A. Kok, 389–410. Leiden–Boston: Brill, 2018.

———. *Art as Human Practice: An Aesthetics*. Translated by N. Ross. London: Bloomsbury, 2019.

———. "Die Einheit des Selbst nach Heidegger." *Deutsche Zeitschrift für Philosophie* 61, 2 (2013): 197–213.

———. *Die Freiheit des Verstehens. Hermeneutik und kritische Theorie*. Berlin: Suhrkamp, 2024.

———. "Rethinking Hegel's Modern Conception of Art." In *Hegel's Political Aesthetics: Art in Modern Society*. Edited by Stefan Bird-Pollan and Vladimir Marchenkov, 196–211. London: Bloomsbury, 2020.

———. "Was heißt es, Musik als eigenständige Artikulationsform des Denkens zu begreifen? Ein musikphilosophischer Versuch im Anschluss an Heidegger." *Allgemeine Zeitschrift für Philosophie* (2015): 231–51.

Davey, Nicholas. "Gadamer's Re-Orientation of Aesthetics." In *Unfinished Worlds: Hermeneutics, Aesthetics and Gadamer*, 42–64. Edinburgh: Edinburgh University Press, 2013.

Feige, Daniel Martin. *Kunst als Selbstverständigung*. Paderborn: Mentis, 2012.

Gadamer, Hans-Georg. *Truth and Method*. Revised ed. Translated by J. Weinsheimer and D. G. Marshall. New York: Continuum, 2004.

Gjesdal, Kristin. "Against the Myth of Aesthetic Presence: A Defence of Gadamer's Critique of Aesthetic Consciousness." *Journal of the British Society for Phenomenology* 36, no. 3 (2005): 293–310.

———. *Gadamer and the Legacy of German Idealism*. Cambridge: Cambridge University Press, 2009.

Goodman, Nelson. *Fact, Fiction, and Forecast*. Cambridge, MA: Harvard University Press, 1983.

Haugeland, John. "*Dasein's* Disclosedness." In *Dasein Disclosed: John Haugeland's Heidegger*. Edited by J. Rouse, 17–39. Cambridge, MA: Harvard University Press, 2013.

Hegel, Georg Wilhelm Friedrich. *Encyclopedia of the Philosophical Sciences in Basic Outline, Part I: Science of Logic*. Translated and edited by K. Brinkmann and D. O. Dahlstrom. Cambridge: Cambridge University Press, 2010.

———. *Phenomenology of Spirit*. Translated by A. V. Miller. Oxford: Oxford University Press, 1977.

Heidegger, Martin. "The Origin of the Work of Art." In *Off the Beaten Track*. Translated and edited by J. Young and K. Haynes, 1–56. Cambridge: Cambridge University Press, 2002.

Horkheimer, Max, and Theodor W. Adorno. "The Culture Industry: Enlightenment as Mass Deception." In *Dialectic of Enlightenment: Philosophical Fragments*. Translated by E. Jephcott, 94–136. Stanford: Stanford University Press, 2002.

Kierkegaard, Søren. "The Sickness unto Death." In *Fear and Trembling and the Sickness unto Death*. Translated by W. Lowrie, 235–468. Princeton: Princeton University Press, 2013.

McDowell, John. *Mind and World*. Cambridge, MA: Harvard University Press, 1994.

Menke, Christoph. *Force: A Fundamental Concept of Aesthetic Anthropology*. Translated by G. Jackson. New York: Fordham University Press, 2013.

———. *The Sovereignty of Art: Aesthetic Negativity in Adorno and Derrida*. Translated by N. Solomon. Cambridge, MA: The MIT Press, 1998.

Pinkard, Terry. *Hegel's Phenomenology: The Sociality of Reason.* Cambridge: Cambridge University Press, 1994.

Schleiermacher, Friedrich. "On the Concept of Hermeneutics, with Reference to F.A. Wolf's Instructions and Ast's Textbook." In *Hermeneutics: The Handwritten Manuscripts.* Translated by J. Duke and J. Forstman. Edited by H. Kimmerle, 175–214. Missoula: Scholars Press, 1977.

Sonderegger, Ruth. *Für eine Ästhetik des Spiels. Hermeneutik, Dekonstruktion und der Eigensinn der Kunst.* Frankfurt a. M.: Suhrkamp, 2000.

Zwinggi, Stefan. *Musik als affektive Selbstverständigung. Eine integrative Untersuchung über musikalische Expressivität.* Freiburg: Alber, 2016.

6

Language without Sentences
The Rhythmic Nature of Art

James Risser

In this essay I want to raise the question of art in Gadamer's hermeneutics in relation to the phenomenon of rhythm. My specific intent is not to focus on the arts of music and dance in which rhythm is prominent but to show how it displays itself in all the arts. For hermeneutics, this display of rhythm is at once tied to the articulation of meaning, a point Gadamer subtly makes in his discussion of language in "On the Way to Writing." In both speech and writing, he tells us, there is a tendency in our use of words to set them into a fixed form. The question here, especially so in the case of speaking, is how the unity and sameness of what is meant take shape in the temporal flow of an event of meaning. It is a question distinctive to Gadamer's hermeneutics in which the very being of language is tied to movement. Gadamer answers his question by appealing to his often-quoted reference to Aristotle's explanation of the formation of the unity of experience in the *Posterior Analytics*. The unity of experience, which is for Aristotle in this context the formation of the universal, is not attained by reasoning as a matter of inductive inference. According to Gadamer, it is rather a process rooted *in* experience and memory that ultimately links the formation of unity to "the secret of language and its semantic life" (Gadamer 2022, 184). Gadamer sees this same formation of unity taking place in the broader context of the search for meaning in language aimed at understanding. In this case, Gadamer adds quite remarkably, the unity of meaning is formed not from the unity of the sentence but from the unity of the phrase. What he means by a phrase is the positive sense given to it in music. It entails the shaping of notes for expression as if it constituted a musical thought, a single unit within the sequence of notes that makes complete musical sense. Gadamer points out that "in music we speak of the phrasing and recognize thereby that the musical recital includes a rhythm over and beyond the purely musical fixing through notation" (Gadamer 2022, 184). In an evident way, something similar occurs in our everyday experience with language. Besides the grammar there is something like phrasing with the formation of relative unities in the coming together of sense and sound. In a public lecture or reading with an aim at comprehending, we experience an articulating and modulating rhythm that enacts the formation of relative unity. The phrase, one might say, gives way to rhythm as a recurring sense integrated into the course of a movement.

The claim that rhythm establishes a form of unity in language beyond a merely analogous relation to music gains support from Gadamer's insistence that the unity of meaning occurring in the unfolding movement of language is never provided by the structure of logic. In a real sense, we can say that rhythm in language simply pertains to language without sentences. Such an idea is most evident in poetic verse where words resonate in meaning in a way that is incongruous with a propositional statement. In poetic verse there is an explicit intonation that shapes the words, providing something of an indication of meaning, and thus aiding the understanding of what is being said. But this is not to say that rhythm in language is only found in poetic verse. Gadamer hints at the broader scope of language without sentences even in relation to writing to suggest that it goes to the core of the event of meaning in hermeneutic experience. And if so, it is possible to say, at least in regards to the hermeneutic experience of art and not just the art of poetry, that language without sentences—the formation of meaning occurring in the movement of language—is the essential configuration in the hermeneutic experience of art. Let us see how this is so.

To start with the familiar case, it is interesting to note how Gadamer speaks about poetry in his essay "On the Truth of the Word." The poetic word has the essential feature of all art in relation to the experience of understanding, namely, it is an "assertion [*Aussage*]" that does not form an assertoric sentence.[1] This simply means that art has the capacity to say something in relation to a communicative understanding. For Gadamer, what is unique to poetry is the way in which the poetic word in its interweaving of sound and sense is a "saying" word. It is such by bearing witness to itself; it stands in its autonomy, freed from the outside intentions of both poet and reader. In its autonomy, the poetic word is self-fulling such that the meaning is "there" in the revealing capacity of language. More so, what the poetic word "says" in its autonomy has everything to do with the word attaining a linguistic identity that Gadamer calls the new ordering configuration of a text. The poetic word is to have a coherence with the whole of the poem. While acknowledging that there are different levels of coherence among poetic texts to a point at which a poem with little coherence may be untranslatable, a linguistic coherence remains inseparable from the poetic word's saying power. Such coherence cannot be governed by a rule but is self-forming. In the poem, language is bound back to its own resounding and the coherence becomes a bonding factor. It binds words together such that there can be what Gadamer calls "the truth of the word." It is here that Gadamer speaks of rhythm:

> [In the inner resounding of language] rhythm belongs to these linguistic means as a pure becoming of form by time. Rhythm is also at home in music, but in the realm of language it is subject to its own tensive relationship to the meaning that is being referred to, and thus generally cannot be restricted to precise forms of repetition. It is hard to say what it is that this poetic rhythm articulates when reading something aloud such that we notice very clearly when it falls short of its goal. One can say that basically it has to do with a balance one can feel between two motions: the movement of the meaning and the movement of the sound. Both motions, which always blend into a single motion . . . have their specific syntactical means that they employ. (Gadamer 2007, 149)

Gadamer adds that the specific syntactical means for the motion of sound extends to figurations of sound that remain below the threshold of conscious notice. Still, what comes into being in this single movement in the formation of the poetic word, he tells us, is what Hölderlin calls the *tone* (Hölderlin 1988, 62–82 and 83–88).[2] This is the enduring tone that holds together the unity of the linguistic formation [*Gebilde*] "with all the differences and degrees of difference in sensitivity to disturbance and density of coherence that are possible" (Gadamer 2007, 150). Such holding together, which effectively constitutes rhythm, *binds* the elements of the literary text to one another, joining them together in the formation so as to distinguish the poetic formation from other types of discourse [*Rede*].³

When Gadamer speaks of rhythm elsewhere he does little to develop the idea further. In "The Relevance of the Beautiful," he describes the coherence of the work of art in terms of an organic unity. It bears a center within itself as if it were a living organism with its internally structured order, and as such it "displays autonomous temporality" (Gadamer 1986, 43). The work of art is determined by its own temporal structure, not unlike the temporal character of the festival that does not dissolve into a series of separate moments but has its own fulfilled or autonomous time. While this description of autonomous temporality obviously applies to music, Gadamer thinks it applies to all the arts through the experience of rhythm.⁴ In noting how remarkable the phenomenon of rhythm is, he is quick to point out that rhythm is not be found in either the objective temporal relation between sounds or the mind of the listener alone. In relation to our experiencing, it is what is immanent within a given form that we are only able to hear when we "rhythmize" ourselves, that is to say, when we actively engage with it (Gadamer 1986, 45). Gadamer maintains that every art imposes its own temporality upon us, including that of painting, which is to say that we must learn how to dwell upon the work in a specific way. That way of dwelling Gadamer calls "tarrying [*Verweilen*]," a "taking time" outside the ordinary experience of time as the incessant flight of instances. It is a temporal experience of a repose in which one is able to abide with what is occurring and presenting itself—a releasement into a conversation of sorts with the artwork that would hold together the unity of the formation and thereby be itself rhythmic.

It is curious that Gadamer has so little to say about rhythm, given his insightful remarks on both music and poetry throughout his writings. One gets the sense, though, that he would not be far from what Plato will say about rhythm. In the *Republic*, the education of the guardians requires training in music [μουσική] so that they can be attuned to the features of beauty and order that lie within it.⁵ Rhythm and harmony are to insinuate themselves into the movement of and ultimately the disposition of the soul. The word *harmony* [ἁμονία] in Greek does not mean a simple consonance but involves a jointure as in the joints between wooden planks or a suture that stitches together. And in this context, *rhythm* [ῥυθμός] pertains to the proper measure of the formation and its order. But if we are to properly understand the meaning of the Greek ῥυθμός, we would have to trace the word even further back to its roots in a way that others have done.

Heidegger for one does just this in his Heraclitus Seminar with Eugen Fink. After Fink raises the question of language in relation to their discussion of Heraclitus's fragment 30, Heidegger appeals to the work of the Greek musicologist Thrasybulos Georgiades who makes a direct connection between language and rhythm.⁶ What we learn from Georgiades, Heidegger notes, is that the Greek ῥυθμός [Ionic ῥυσός] has little to do with the etymon ῥέω [flow]; rather, the word has to be understood as "imprint [*Gepräge*]."⁷ What is meant by imprint is not made clear by Heidegger in the discussion, and the word itself does not readily convey any immediate association with the word *rhythm*. The word is actually used by Georgiades to indicate the sense of form that is brought about by a graphic configuration—the imprint of a written letter that in effect joins and separates in the "movement" of language. Without directly saying that this is so, Heidegger notes Georgiades's appeal to Werner Jaeger's commentary on the words of the lyric poet Archilochus "Learn what rhythm holds the human" to at least give evidence that ῥυθμός cannot mean flow. If rhythm holds the human, it cannot mean flow. Jaeger suggests that we should think of rhythm in the way it is used by Aeschylus when the chained Prometheus says, "I am bound here in this rhythm" (Jaeger 1945, 126). Here "rhythm is that which imposes bonds on movement and confines the flux of things," and Heidegger affirms this interpretation: "He who is held immobile in the iron chains of confinement is 'rhythmed,' that is, joined" (Heidegger and Fink 1993, 55). In a less restricted way but still taken with its passive voice construction, we can understand Archilochus's words to say that rhythm—meaning here the natural and basic pattern in human life—is what holds the human in relations in the sense that it attunes the human to the proper measure of their existence.

Georgiades's appeal to Jaeger is to emphasize the point that humans do not make rhythm; he notes in fact that for the Greeks rhythm is to be found in the substrate of the language of the fifth century. Commenting on this remarkable statement to Fink, Heidegger makes his own remarkable statement: "This language knows no sentences" (Heidegger and Fink 1993, 55). What speaks in the archaic language—this language without sentences, language as rhythm—Heidegger insists, is not the artifice of conceptual meaning but the matter itself. Having said this, Heidegger and Fink resume their discussion of the Heraclitus fragment. We leave it to Georgiades to explain just how rhythm enters into the substrate of language. He tells us that "whenever Greek language sounded in verse, it was also a form of music" (Georgiades 1973, 52). This is not to say that verse is always sung, but that it already contains music—that is to say, rhythm—within itself.

There is a rhythmic quality that is "preformed in the peculiar quality of Greek language." Georgiades cites a passage from Plato's *Cratylus* to explain: "Those who try their ability in rhythms distinguish first the functions of the letters, then of the syllables, and in this way they come to the rhythms in order to observe then, but not before" (Georgiades 1973, 54).[8] The syllables themselves, which have a definite duration, "are the rhythmic matter from which rhythm originates" (Georgiades 1973, 55). The prototype of rhythm is to be found in the syllables. In this sense language has a linguistic rhythm given by language *itself* and not by the speaker.[9] In effect, it is language itself that takes on the task of realizing the context of meaning.

Of course, we do not speak ancient Greek today. And yet, as we learn from both Heidegger and Gadamer, language has a fundamental relation to being and with it the self-presentation of meaning. For such presentation, we are to listen to language. We speak by way of language because we have already listened to language. Certainly, for the sake of hermeneutic understanding—and this applies to the work of art in relation to what Gadamer calls "linguisticality [*Sprachlichkeit*]"—we are to let language speak. For Gadamer particularly so, language speaks in relation to the formation within the continuous movement of living language (of conversation) going into itself. In the language of conversation, unlike language structured formally by the propositional statement, "the finite possibilities of the word are oriented toward the sense intended as toward the infinite" (Gadamer 1989, 469). The word "speaks" speculatively, it does not reflect beings but expresses a relation to the whole of being. It remains to be seen how rhythm is to be understood in the context of the saying of language and foremost as the language of art.

The idea of imprint, which has the sense of form produced in the joining and separating of letters, is decisive for this understanding. If we continue to think of rhythm in relation to movement, the joining and separating occurs in relation to the pause within movement. Jaeger for one thinks that the original conception of rhythm is still evident in music and dance when we think of it as a pause, that is, "the steady limitation of movement" (Jaeger 1945, 126). In similar fashion Heidegger speaks of the rest or "repose [*Ruhende*]" that is necessarily at work in poetic verse. In his essay on the poetry of Stefan George, Heidegger notes how the poem succeeds only when the poetic word resounds in the (poetic) "song," adding that the resounding is poem's rhythmic character, which "does not mean flux and flowing but 'form [*Fügung*].' Rhythm is what lends 'repose [*Ruhende*],' what forms the movement of dance and song, and thus lets it rest within itself. Rhythm bestows 'repose [*Ruhe*]' " (Heidegger 1971b, 149, trans. modified). Elsewhere, Heidegger characterizes the work of art, and not just poetry, in terms of a unitary repose—a resting that includes movement, for only what moves can rest. The repose is "an inner concentration of motion," a tensive repose that effectively holds the movement together (Heidegger 1971a, 48). Heidegger's use of the word *Fügung* is his essay on George is noteworthy for its association with the phenomenon of rhythm. The verb form has the sense of structuring or composing, but also the specific sense of arranging and joining. *Fügung* is, as a temporal condition, a structuring movement that joins so as to make the movement intelligible. In this sense *Fügung* is not simply form but also, by virtue of its capacity for joining, an articulating configuration.[10]

But rhythm as form and formation has an even richer history. In his frequently cited essay, Benveniste points out that it was Democritus who made ῥυθμός into a technical term to indicate one of the ways that express the relationship of differences among bodies. Ῥυθμός, which Aristotle conflates with σχῆμα (schema) in reporting this, is a differentiation in form, as the letter A differs from N by form. Here the concept of ῥυθμός is unambiguous. It is always form, and distinctly so as "the characteristic arrangement of parts in a whole" (Benveniste 1971, 283). To be more precise, Benveniste distinguishes ῥυθμός from other expressions in Greek for form, such as σχῆμα, μορφή, and εἶδος. What is unique to ῥυθμός lies in the suffix -μός, which indicates a modality of accomplishment. Specifically, it indicates "the particular modality of accomplishment as it is present to the eyes," as in the difference between the act of dancing and the particular dance seen as it *takes place*. Accordingly, ῥυθμός as form is not the same as σχῆμα, which indicates a fixed form, but "designates the form in the instant that it is assumed by what is moving" (Benveniste 1971, 285). It is the pattern of a fluid element, the (rhythmic) form of things that can be found in all (meaningful) movement, and thus the term for describing all configurations without natural necessity. To the question then of how the original concept of ῥυθμός came to express what we understand by our modern notion of rhythm, Benveniste attributes the change to Plato. According to Benveniste, Plato applies ῥυθμός to the movement the body makes in dance, a form of movement that is subject to a measure. Ῥυθμός is the *order* in movement that is subject to meter and thus gains an association with the concept of harmony, as noted above. Rhythm is now more than the arrangement of the elements; it has a temporal character as well. There is the "rhythm of a dance, of a step, of a song, of a speech, of work, of everything which presupposes a continuous activity broken by meter into alternating intervals" (Benveniste 1971, 287).

Having said this, let us return to our initial consideration of the place of rhythm in the hermeneutic experience of art. We could hardly make an advance here if we held to the view that rhythm is simply a measure of periodic repetition. If we follow Benveniste, we know that rhythm is a certain kind of configuration of movement, a configuration that is formed, unlike a schema, in the manner of a "how."[11] Rhythm has a performative character such that it is instituted in the enactment of movement. Such is evidently the case for Gadamer regarding the inner resounding of the language of the poetic word and, most obviously so, the form of organization in music. It is less obviously so in the case of painting and the other plastic arts. But there is good reason to think that Gadamer would agree with Henri Maldiney, who adapts Benveniste's notion of rhythm for his phenomenology of painting, claiming that rhythm runs through a painting just as it runs through a piece of music. Like Gadamer, Maldiney regards the painted image as an event of being, that is, an event of worldly appearance. For him specifically the image exists as "a field of tensions" in which the discontinuous elements are occurrences held together by rhythm as immanent form coinciding with its own genesis (Maldiney 1993, 131). As an example, he notes Cézanne's paintings of Mont Sainte-Victoire in which the "sky, earth, and mountain are permeated with the same [rhythmic] breath which, simultaneously, is the expression of their mutual exchange."[12] The stability we see in a painting is the self-forming rhythm within the space in which it appears.[13] In this configuration of sensible appearance, the image has, as with Gadamer, a living, organic quality, as if it were an animated image not unlike the articulation of breath.

By extending the notion of rhythm to painting we are in a position to defend the view that *every* work of art is a unique rhythm.[14] Every work of art is an "imprint" forming a unity in relation to its differential elements.[15] And so too for hermeneutics. The configuration of rhythm, unlike constructions of reason and the work of concepts, constitutes a composition, which is precisely what we call a text—a work that has texture, a work in which something has been woven or fitted together as an articulation given over to interpretation. Text in this sense pertains to both word and image, and approximates Gadamer's word for the artwork, namely, *Gebilde*.[16] In *Truth and Method* Gadamer describes the movement of play becoming art as "transformation into structure [*Verwandlung ins Gebilde*]," but the English translation of *Gebilde* as structure fails to indicate what the German word is able to say, beginning with the root word *Bild*, which is an image or picture. *Gebilde* is a formed image, a creative configuration. In ordinary use, *Gebilde* can refer to patterns in textiles or the structure of a building. What is *Gebilde* has been actively formed, and Gadamer uses the word to convey the sense that an artwork has developed into its own pattern from within, which is precisely what defines rhythm.

In several essays, especially his late essay "The Artwork in Word and Image," Gadamer describes this formation in a way that affirms the rhythmic character of art. If we grant that art as creation brings something new into the world—"that whole worlds are able to rise up out of nothingness"—the formation of the new, he tells us, has little to do with the ordinary sense of making, as if the artwork were simply a product of handiwork (Gadamer 2007, 201). If such were the case, the formative activity in the formation would reside solely with the artist. While indeed the artwork is made by someone, the artwork is able to stand for itself, to exist independently of prior intentions, just as we grant authority to a text when reading for the sake of understanding what is being said in it. What is to be experienced hermeneutically in the artwork is the formation that has come to appearance in it beyond the process in which it originated. The artwork as *Gebilde* is set forth on its own as a self-sufficient creation "to present itself in its look and appearance" (Gadamer 1986, 126, trans. modified). When Gadamer then offers an account of the configuration of art's demand to be apprehended in itself as pure appearance, he does so by describing what can only be called the rhythmic nature of art. Gadamer writes:

> What this means can be grasped particularly clearly in the transitory arts. Poetry, music, and dance have none of the tangibility of things as such, yet the transitory and fluid stuff of which they are made composes itself into a fixed unity of a configured creation [*Gebilde*] that remains the same . . . [In these] reproductive arts the artwork must constantly be formed anew. What the transitory arts teach us most vividly is that presentation is required . . . for any creation that we call an artwork. It demands to be built up [*aufgebaut*] by the viewer to whom it is presented . . . It is only something that appears and displays itself when it is formed in the viewing. (Gadamer 1986, 126, trans. modified)

In the configured creation that is art, whether in performing or plastic art, the pure appearance is to be apprehended for understanding in the presentation of its viewing, which is to say, in its taking place—the very *movement* of presentation.

That all art is to be seen in relation to movement is a claim first made by Heidegger, albeit not with the same language we see here. In "The Origin of the Work of Art," Heidegger describes the work of art as a standing-in-itself and opening up a world. In its complete dynamic, the work of art exists in the strife of self-opening (world) and self-sheltering concealing (earth). Such movement is for Heidegger the way in which truth as unconcealment happens in art. Art is accordingly the "setting-to-work of truth," the setting-into-work "bringing the work character of work into movement and happening" (Heidegger 1971a, 71). In his own remarks on Heidegger's essay, Gadamer notes approvingly that this description of the artwork shows the inadequacy of the traditional categories of form and matter to account for the nature of art. He also appears to agree with Heidegger that the arising of this world in the artwork "is at the same time its entrance into a reposing form [*ruhende Gestalt*]."[17] It is the work of art in its movement coming to rest, a rhythmic movement that frames the mode of *becoming* and the issue of truth in art.

But in saying this, Gadamer does not simply follow Heidegger. In "The Artwork in Word and Image," Gadamer gives a variation of the movement of presentation in art in relation to what he considers to be art's distinctive ontological makeup. The being of art, he tells us, is akin to nature and thus is to be understood in terms of the movement that is like life itself. This is the same movement as the movement of being in Aristotle's concept of ἐνέργεια. More than an accomplished actuality [ἔργον] in which something has its existence through an already completed production, ἐνέργεια is an actualizing actuality. It is actuality being carried out in relation to "the fulfilling of its being in itself" (Gadamer 2007, 210).[18] It is literally "being-at-work" and needs two words to convey its intended sense: activity and actuality. Accordingly, art is a self-accomplishing actuality: something comes forth in the artwork in the sense that something is truly there in its appearing. Such truth is not sentence truth but refers to the superior reality that emerges in the experience of art. What came forth and how it came forth, he tells us, cannot be explained and put into words. This is not to suggest a mysticism in the experience of art. Rather, it is not unlike the experience of reading in which the design [*Formgestalt*] that has been built up, *that has taken shape*, comes forth. It comes forth "thanks to the means possessed by the language of art in poetry, sculpture and picture, which in the flow of its play builds up the design" (Gadamer 2007, 218). The articulated figuration [*Gebilde*] that presents itself for understanding lies in this performative movement: music is to be heard, poetry is to be read, painting is to be viewed. So, Gadamer claims: "Art has its being in the 'enactment [*Vollzug*],'" the living event of its appearance (Gadamer 2007, 215). We can equally say that the work of art is to come forth in its rhythm as the form of movement—the order and measure [*ratio*] of the work of art.[19]

And what then of the act of interpreting, which is itself part of the event of meaning? Would this not also have a rhythmic character? Such is indeed the case since the enactment is the interpretation. The enactment of art *is* the interpreting that is taking hold of the design in the artwork. Such taking hold is nothing less than the interpretive *shaping* occurring with intonation and phrasing. For Gadamer, this shaping is not a construction but the attempt to go along with the work so as to be present in the presentation.[20] In going along with the work, we are "taken in" by the configured sense "in the significance it radiates and which it distinguishes *as* a structure" (Gadamer 2022, 100). Equally so, it is the experience of being drawn into what the language of art in the work of art wants to say. It involves going along with it, as if in a conversation which has a movement of its own.[21] The interpreter does all this through the temporal experience of repose that Gadamer calls *tarrying*. As noted above, tarrying is a distinct way of "taking time." It is the temporal experience of "filled time," which does not simply pass away in a sequence of one after another. It is time gathered up into itself in the manner of a pause, a temporality of "at the same time." In the act of interpreting, the interpreter is taken in by the rhythm of the work in relation to which the interpreter in effect becomes rhythmed.[22]

Notes

1. The importance of the word *Aussage* for Gadamer's reflections not just on poetry but also on art in general is evidenced by its use in the full title of volume 8 of his *Gesammelte Werke: Ästhetik und Poetik I: Kunst als Aussage* [*Aesthetics and Poetics: Art as Assertion*]. *Aussage* can be translated as statement, declaration, or assertion. In its literal sense *Aussage* is a saying-forth [*Aus-sage*].

2. Hölderlin speaks of tone in "On the Difference of Poetic Modes." The different poetic modes he refers to are the lyric, epic, and tragic. While each mode

has a different tone, each tone is not a discrete genre. Each tone reflects a particular attunement with the world and functions relatively in what Hölderlin calls the "alternation [*Wechseln*]" of tones in relation to a fundamental tone.

3. Hölderlin, it seems, would want to extend Gadamer's remarks here. Purportedly in conversations with Sinclair, Hölderlin said: "When rhythm has become the sole and unique mode of thought's expression, it is then only that there is poetry. In order for mind to become poetry, it must bear in itself the mystery of an innate rhythm. It is in this rhythm alone that it can live and become visible. And every work of art is but one and the same rhythm. Everything is simply rhythm. The destiny of man is a single celestial rhythm, as every work of art is a unique rhythm" (quoted in Blanchot 1989, 225). Agamben quotes a slightly different sentence purported made by Hölderlin: "Everything is rhythm, the entire destiny of man is one heavenly rhythm, just as every work of art is one rhythm, and everything swings from the poetizing lips of the god" (quoted in Agamben 1999, 94).

4. In his essay "Music and Time" Gadamer is quite explicit about the distinctive character of the autonomous temporality of music in relation to the autonomous temporality in the other arts. In the hermeneutic experience with music, time itself comes to stand for a while. "In the other arts, too, 'understanding' will have the same temporal shape and truth will also be present 'in the performance [*im Vollzug*].' But nowhere does it pass by as this pure moving than as in music. Elsewhere, there is always something in it that stands, be it an unequivocal meaning of words or the sense of discourse that one examines . . . There is still a something even in the sequence of dance moves or in the structured sequence of the image, sculpture, or architecture. That nothing stands except the moving itself, that is the truth of performance that music is" (Gadamer 2021, 255).

5. The Greek μουσική does not simply mean music, but what pertains to the Muses. Plato uses the word here in its common meaning of sung poetry.

6. Heidegger was well acquainted with the work of Georgiades, who taught for a time at the University of Heidelberg before taking a position at the University of Munich. Gadamer knew Georgiades as a friend during his time in Heidelberg and refers to his work in several places.

7. That the word ῥυθμός is not derived from ῥέω is also a claim made by Benveniste in his *Problems in General Linguistics*. He notes that the connection between ῥυθμός and ῥέω as flow seems obvious and has been maintained by several scholars. We learn the principle of things from nature and the flowing movement of the waves readily gives rise to the idea of rhythm; but the sea does not flow and "ῥυθμός is never used for the rhythm of waves." Even in its ancient use, ῥυθμός "never refers to flowing water" (Benveniste 1971, 281–82).

8. Georgiades is citing the *Cratylus*, 424c1–2.

9. Georgiades points out that in modern language, quite unlike ancient Greek, the syllable itself is neither long or short "but is made long or short by the speaker who forms it exactly as he wishes in order to invest it with meaning" (Georgiades 1973, 57). See also Georgiades 1977, 81–86.

10. In *Introduction to Metaphysics*, Heidegger uses the word *Fug* [fittingness] to translate the Greek word δικη. "Here we understand the fittingness first in the sense of 'joint [*Fuge*]' and 'structure [*Gefüge*];' then as 'arrangement [*Fügung*],' as the direction that the overwhelming gives to its sway; finally, as the 'enjoining structure [*fügende Gefüge*],' which compels 'fitting-in [*Einfügung*]' and compliance" (Heidegger 2000, 171).

11. It is often overlooked how hermeneutic understanding is a matter of the *how* and not the *what*. In the afterword to *Truth and Method*, Gadamer notes how language functions differently in hermeneutics than it does in science. For hermeneutics, the verbal formulation does not merely refer to something that can be verified in other ways, "instead it makes something visible in the how of its meaningfulness" (Gadamer 1989, 463).

12. The complete passage reads: "A red purple at the left edge of the painting, the shiny red to the right and more red furtive ones in the middle ensure the diffuse and precise dispersion, thereby sustaining a suspension of the gaze. Departing from each of these hotbeds the gaze is braced by more trajectories, which is why equal forces would make it flicker were not suspended by the whole space. For this is one. Sky, earth and mountain are permeated by the same breath which, simultaneously, is the expression of their mutual exchange" (Maldiney 1993, 33; quoted in Thomsen 2018, 122).

13. "A rhythm does not unfold in time and space. It generates its own space-time. It cannot be explained by it; it implies it. The advent of a rhythmic space goes hand in hand with the constitutive transformation of all the elements of a work of art in the moment of formation, in the rhythmic moment" (Maldiney 2012, 20).

14. See the quotation from Hölderlin above in footnote n. 3. Among the German Romantics, Hölderlin is not unique in this view. It is also held by Schelling and others in their discussions of music and the language of art. In his *Philosophy of Art*, Schelling describes rhythm as the music within music (see Schelling 1989, 107–11).

15. It is important to recognize that the unity produced in rhythm does not displace difference. This is most obvious in music in which rhythm, as a pattern, is holding the differential notes together. That rhythm is an interruption of pure sequence and thus of itself involves difference is a point emphasized by Lacoue-Labarthe in *Typography: Mimesis Philosophy Politics* (see Lacoue-Labarthe 1989). This point is also made in a different way by Agamben. Agamben relates rhythm to the Greek ἐποχή, which has the sense of holding back and suspending. He wants to claim that the work of art in its rhythm hurls us into a more original time, which gives and holds back (see Agamben 1999, 100–102).

16. For an excellent treatment of the image as text from the point of view of Gadamer's hermeneutics, see Schmidt 2013.

17. This is Gadamer's phrase for Heidegger's description of art in "The Origin of the Work of Art," but can be applied equally to Gadamer's own account of art (see Gadamer 1994, 104).

18. In his description of ἐνέργεια, Gadamer notes the associated term ἐντελέχεια, which combines the idea of completeness [ἐντελές] with the activity in the sense of a continuing effort [ἔχειν].

19. Agamben makes a similar statement in *The Man without Content* (see Agamben 1999, 41).

20. Gadamer explains what he means by presence and being present in "Hearing–Seeing–Reading" (see Gadamer 2022, 208).

21. "Being in the mode of tarrying is like an intensive back-and-forth conversation that is not cut off but lasts until it is ended. The whole of it is a conversation in which for a time one is completely 'absorbed in conversation,' and this means one is 'completely there in it'" (Gadamer 2007, 211).

22. For Gadamer, interpretation is never a matter of adding something to what is to be understood, but of putting together again what is already there in the work. In this sense, interpreting itself involves a "pause" in the movement of interpretation that is conjoined to the work in its enactment. Rilke captures this gesture quite well in the first stanza of the first poem in the second part of *The Sonnets to Orpheus*: "Breathing: You invisible poem! Complete / interchange of our own / essence with world-space. You counterweight / in which I rhythmically happen" (Rilke 1986, 73).

Bibliography

Agamben, Giorgio. *The Man without Content*. Translated by G. Albert. Stanford: Stanford University Press, 1999.

Benveniste, Emile. *Problems in General Linguistics*. Translated by M. E. Meek. Miami: University of Miami Press, 1971.

Blanchot, Maurice. *The Space of Literature*. Translated by A. Smock. Lincoln: University of Nebraska Press, 1989.

Gadamer, Hans-Georg. *Ethics, Aesthetics, and the Historical Dimensions of Language. The Selected Writings of Hans-Georg Gadamer. Vol. 2*. Translated and edited by P. Vandevelde and A. Iyer. London: Bloomsbury, 2022.

———. *Hermeneutics between History and Philosophy. The Selected Writings of Hans-Georg Gadamer. Vol. 1*. Translated and edited by P. Vandevelde and A. Iyer. London: Bloomsbury, 2016.

———. "Music and Time." Translated by C. R. Nielsen and D. Liakos. *Epoché* 26, 1 (2021): 251–58.

———. *The Gadamer Reader: A Bouquet of the Later Writings*. Translated and edited by R. E. Palmer. Evanston: Northwestern University Press, 2007.

———. *The Relevance of the Beautiful and Other Essays*. Translated by N. Walker. Edited by R. Bernasconi. Cambridge: Cambridge University Press, 1986.

———. "The Truth of the Work of Art." In *Heidegger's Ways*. Translated by J. W. Stanley, 95–109. Albany: State University of New York Press, 1994.
———. *Truth and Method*. Revised ed. Translated by J. Weinsheimer and D. G. Marshall. New York: Continuum, 1989.
Georgiades, Thrasybulos. *Greek Music, Verse and Dance*. Translated by E. Benedikt and M. L. Martinez. New York: De Capo Press, 1973.
———. "Sprache als Rhythmus." In *Kleine Schriften*, 81–96. Tutzing: Verlegt bei Hans Schneider, 1977.
Heidegger, Martin. *Introduction to Metaphysics*. Translated by G. Fried and R. Polt. New Haven: Yale University Press, 2000.
———. "The Origin of the Work of Art." In *Poetry, Language, Thought*. Translated by A. Hofstadter, 15–88. New York: Harper & Row, 1971a.
———. "Words." In *On the Way to Language*. Translated by P. Hertz, 139–58. New York: Harper & Row, 1971b.
Heidegger, Martin, and Eugen Fink. *Heraclitus Seminar*. Translated by C. H. Seibert. Evanston: Northwestern University Press, 1993.
Hölderlin, Friedrich. *Essays and Letters on Theory*. Translated by T. Pfau. Albany: State University of New York Press, 1988.
Jaeger. Werner. *Paideia. Vol. 1*. Translated by G. Highlet. New York: Oxford University Press, 1945.
Lacoue-Labarthe, Philippe. *Typography: Mimesis Philosophy Politic*. Edited by C. Fynsk. Cambridge, MA: Harvard University Press, 1989.
Maldiney, Henri. *L'art, l'éclair de l'être*. Seyssel: Éditions Comp'Act, 1993.
———. *"Notes sur le rythme."* Henri Maldiney: penser plus avant . . . Actes du colloque de Lyon (13 et 14 novembre 2010). Edited by Jean-Pierre Charcosset, 17–22. Chatou: Editions de La Transparence., 2012.
Rilke, Rainer Maria. *The Sonnets to Orpheus*. Translated by S. Mitchell. New York: Simon & Schuster, 1986.
Schelling, Friedrich Wilhelm J. *The Philosophy of Art*. Translated by D. W. Stott. Minneapolis: University of Minnesota Press, 1989.
Schmidt, Dennis J. *Between Word and Image: Heidegger, Klee and Gadamer on Gesture and Genesis*. Albany: State University of New York Press, 2013.
Thomsen, Bodil Marie Stavning. *Lars von Trier's Renewal of Film 1984–2014*. Aarhus: Aarhus University Press, 2018.

7

Gadamer and Pareyson on Hermeneutics and Improvisation

ALESSANDRO BERTINETTO

Improvisation and Interpretation

At first glance it seems hard to argue that hermeneutics can offer fertile cultural ground for a philosophical discussion of *improvisation*. Philosophical hermeneutics is about *interpretation* as the key dimension of the human experience of the world. And a simple definition of improvisation, particularly—but not only—in the field of performing arts (music, dance, theater, performance art), cannot help but consider the *difference* not only between improvisation and composition, but also between improvisation and interpretation.

Insofar as it is characterized by the coincidence of invention and performance, improvisation differs from composition, since it is usually true for composition (paradigmatically, a musical composition) that the inventive activity is concluded before the concrete realization (e.g., the sound realization that takes place in a musical performance). Of course, the relationship between composition and improvisation is much more complex. For example, it can be argued that improvisations are also *compositions*, in the sense that—while not having the normative value of a composition as a musical work that offers instructions for its performances—every improvisation is a composition of elements: in music, a composition of sounds; in dance, a composition of gestures, figures, and movements; in theater, a composition of words, actions, and gestures. Moreover, a composition can certainly be the result of improvisational activity: even when it is not directly staged in front of an audience, artistic creativity can in fact be improvisational. Nonetheless, the fact remains that the interpretation of a composition amounts to performing an action (or series of actions) that, even in its aesthetic dimension, is different from that performed by one who improvises.

Consequently, even with respect to interpretation, it seems that the differences with improvisation are sharp and obvious (see Bertinetto 2016a, 92–99). Those who perform a musical composition have at their disposal a cultural construct,[1] often in the form of a score, which contains indications of the artistic content that the performer does not invent, but manifests to perceivers. In the case of a theatrical play, actors must perform a written story following a playwright's script and the director's directions. Finally, the dancers perform the dance steps indicated by the choreographer. Performers in these cases are interpreters, because they have the undoubtedly not easy task of communicating to an audience an artistic content already articulated by its author. In this sense, performers do not invent the artistic content experienced by the audience, but, as one might say at least following certain Platonist trends in the contemporary debate on musical ontology, *transport* it: a content is transported from the notational dimension of scores, scripts, and choreographies to the actual-concrete dimension of the musical, theatrical, or dance performances. Instead, improvisers do not merely transport or communicate an already artistically shaped content. Rather they invent what they are realizing artistically and simultaneously communicate it to an audience. Improvisers give shape on the spot to the artistic product offered to the audience.

Of course, the performance of a composition is in some way, even if unintentionally, *improvised*, since performers must respond to the specific unprecedented situation of the performance, including the expressive nuances that characterize the performances of the other performers (for example, in the case of a string quartet). However, for interpreters the contingency of the present moment is an ontologically ineradicable condition of their doing, which consists in manifesting a construct that is already formed, and that one must precisely interpret, having prepared the performance by having in mind what *must* be (see Benson 2003, 154). Instead, in improvisation as an intentional[2] practice of producing art "on the spot," the performance is prepared in relation to what it *can* be and its aim is "giving form in the instant" (Ferrari 2006, 125). In other words, the intentional and attentional relationship to the present unforeseen and contingent situation—in relation to both the specific cultural tradition of the performance at issue (baroque, jazz, rap, etc.; improv theatre, commedia dell'arte, etc.; contact improvisation, butō, etc.) as well as to the stages of the performative process in fieri—becomes a formative source of meaning.

Performers become improvisers by marking their difference not only from composers but also from interpreters. Yet, like composers, improvisers are authors of what they do; and like performers they perform an artistic content for an audience. But while composers are authors who control the production process, being able to correct what they do and revise possible mistakes, improvisers are authors exposed to the contingency of the performative situation and cannot revise the steps taken. Rather than proceeding on the basis of a blueprint model, they work retroactively, responding to moves made earlier (see Gioia 1988; Feige 2014). In this sense, their control over the creative process is more labile; their artistic making is an active-passive interaction with other performers, with the materials and tools at their disposal, with the referential artistic tradition of their practice, and, more generally, with the concrete and specific performative situation. Their creativity is a kind of distributed agency (see Clarke and Doffman 2017).

Hence, this particular way in which improvisers engage in the role of authors of artistic contents is interpretive-hermeneutic, even though, as I have just observed, improvisers are defined as such precisely because of their difference from interpreters of already realized artistic works. Or to put it even more sharply: improvisers, while realizing their specific artistic dimension as formally different from composers and interpreters, achieve a synthesis between the composer's and the performer's dimensions: a synthesis such that their composing (in the moment) is interpretive, and their performing is compositional.

Yet, the hermeneutic character of improvising, and also, note well, the improvisational character of interpretation, has a deeper dimension. To understand in what sense this is the case, Gadamer and Pareyson are crucial thinkers. As at least some important hermeneutical texts of Gadamer seem to suggest, his hermeneutic theory is rooted in the idea that interpretation, as a central quality of human experience, has an "improvisational" character. Pareyson's aesthetic theory, which, arguably, is a philosophy of art as improvisation, emphasizes the primarily interpretive character of the formativity of artistic making. Discussing these aspects of Gadamer's and Pareyson's thought not only shows that Gadamer's and Pareyson's hermeneutics are philosophically relevant to improvisational practices, but also allows an interesting light to be shed on hermeneutics from the perspective of improvisational practices.

Gadamer's Improvisational Hermeneutics

The purpose of the investigation of Gadamer's masterpiece, *Truth and Method* (1960), is to clarify the articulation of understanding, by explaining the modes of being in which interpretation is realized. Accordingly, the interpretation of cultural constructs such as texts, documents, artworks, etc., provides the model for the general experience of the world. In understanding, experiences of truth and meaning are realized that are irreducible to the method of modern scientific thought, which is incapable of grasping the most proper aspects of the human sciences. In fact, there are zones of truth and meaning, in which human beings fundamentally inhabit and that are outside of the cognitive area proper to the mathematical and natural sciences. Of these extra-methodic experiences of truth—typically, the historical, legal, philosophical and, artistic experiences—art constitutes an important paradigm both because the performance and enjoyment of an artwork pose specific hermeneutic questions of interpretation and because certain notions playing key roles for the artistic sphere—play, transformation into form [*Verwandlung ins Gebilde*], self-representation, mimesis, etc.—are also strategic for the description of the fundamental structures of human experience as such in terms of understanding, language, and truth.

First of all, the dimension of play has a special relevance to artistic experience (Gadamer 2004, 102–10). Gadamer's main point is the emphasis on the fact that players do not dominate play but are subservient to it. To play is to enter an experiential space to the rules of which one has to submit and in which participants must surrender part of their authority as individuals to the more complex process that is taking place. In short, the protagonist of the play's experience is the play itself, which presents *itself* through the players and, especially in performing arts, *for* someone: the audience (Gadamer 2004, 110). Surely, the work of art is a particular play: a play that is shaped through a "transmutation into form" in which reality acquires more defined contours than the chaotic ordinary reality and through which a fundamental experience of truth can be had (Gadamer 2004, 112). This experience is interpretive in character. Indeed, as is paradigmatically the case in the performing arts, interpretation must be activated for the work to be realized. The work is offered to the audience only through its multiple interpretations, which are not something incidental to the artwork, but are coessential to it: "The work of art cannot simply be isolated from the 'contingency' of the chance conditions in which it appears, and where this kind of isolation occurs, the result is an abstraction that reduces the actual being of the work. It itself belongs to the world to which it represents itself. A drama really exists only when it is played, and ultimately music must resound" (Gadamer 2004, 115). How should performers behave with respect to the work? Should they treat it as an object already totally in itself consistent, autonomous and well-defined that they must faithfully portray, manifest, and communicate to an audience through an activity that simply makes the work accessible to an audience without contributing anything to its artistic realization? Should interpretation simply act as a decoding device for the instructions encoded in the score or script?

Gadamer's answer is well-known. The artwork is not indifferent to its realization in performance. The performance does not merely portray the work passively, but further realizes it, contributing to its historical being. Artworks themselves stimulate the continuation of creativity through performance: "the performing arts have this special quality: that the works they deal with are explicitly left open to such re-creation and thus visibly hold the identity and continuity of the work of art open towards its future" (see Gadamer 2004, 117).

Fidelity to the work [*Werktreue*] is not a fact to be achieved through a decoding mechanism, but an aesthetic ideal that is realized in different ways. Performative interpreters *cannot* abstract from the specific historical and contextual situation in which they perform the work in such a way as to access its alleged objective structures and then communicate them to the public in a transparent way. The idea of an objective presentation of the work is unrealistic because the being of the work is affected not only by the historical context of its creation by a composer or playwright, but also by the historical context of its performative interpretation. Therefore, striving for authentic historical performances is at most an illusory ideal. Gadamer writes it explicitly: "Historicizing presentations—e.g., of music played on old instruments—are not as faithful as they seem. Rather, they are an imitation of an imitation and are thus in danger 'of standing at a third remove from the truth' (Plato)" (Gadamer 2004, 118). The correctness of a performative interpretation cannot be settled according to the imitative conformation to an alleged objective model. Rather, it is a question of merging the horizons of the performer and the work in a present contemporary to every present, embracing both the work and its interpretation (see Gadamer 2004, 119). Indeed, performative interpretations are not transparent vehicles of cultural contents, but parts of the construction of those contents. Moreover, in order to access the presumed objective content of the work and communicate it faithfully by making themselves transparent means of communication, interpreters would have to enter the authors' minds; they would have to grasp the intentions of their realizations regardless of the cultural content that they can access through their interpretation. But this is unrealistic: interpreters cannot read the authors' minds. What interpreters can do is be faithful to the concrete testimonies of the authors' activities. Accordingly, performers should turn, through their interpretation, to documents (scores, scripts, but also writings, recordings, videos, letters, etc.) in dialogue with which they can offer a faithful (or unfaithful) representation: faithful to *their* way of exposing themselves to the truth of the artwork (Bertinetto 2019).[3]

In this regard, it is well known that Eric Hirsch accused Gadamer of confusing *subtilitas intelligendi* and *subtilitas explicandi*, namely the reconsideration of the past and the understanding of the past itself (Hirsch 1967). Gadamer, according to Hirsch, simply denies the past. Instead, Hirsch defends that it is necessary to reach the objective knowledge of the past, so that it is not reabsorbed in the present perspective of the interpreter (see Hoy 1982, 11–40). But the point, for Gadamer, is precisely to deny that one can distinguish clearly—naturalistically—between the past as a fact and the way it is interpreted. To Hirsch's (and Emilio Betti's[4]) naïf objectivism, Gadamer opposes a different, one may say, *holistic*, kind of objectivism, according to which the cultural object is imbued with, and transformed through, historical processes and interpretations (and is not simply *there*): accordingly, the distinction between past (the artwork) and present (its interpretation) can only be implemented starting from the historical relationship that implies both. The artwork is not a historical fact simply because it is placed in a past time. The work is historical because of its cultural effects in which its own interpretations are co-implied. The artwork is accessible only by virtue of, and from, this co-implication with its interpretations—this co-implication is famously called "fusion of horizons" (Gadamer 2004, 305, 337, 367, 370). The hermeneutic activity, in which also a performing interpretation consists, is therefore a dialogue through which a dialectic between *question* and *answer* unfolds thanks to which interpretation is all the more effective as it recognizes its own situatedness and its belonging to the history of the effects [*Wirkungsgeschichte*] of the work that it is interpreting (Gadamer 2004, 299ff.)

Interpreting a work means recognizing the question to which the work (or text) offers the answer—beyond the conscious intentions of its author. This involves questioning the meaning of the work (or text). But this question is in turn prompted by the work (or the text) itself that interrogates the interpreter in the context of a certain tradition. In this dialectical process, the horizon of the work (text) and that of the interpreter merge and, as a consequence, the history of the effects of the work develops and the tradition, to which both work and interpreter belong, lives further.

Therefore, every understanding is rooted in a situation. A text, a speech, or an artwork is not a simple expression of their authors' subjectivity (see Gadamer 2004, 396): their truth come to expression through dialogues with the interpreters. And each time the concrete situations of the interpreters are fundamental conditions of understanding: they cannot possibly be ignored; rather, they must be valued. Performing arts highlight even more this character of dialogue and situatedness of the hermeneutical enterprise in which human existence consists: in fact, the physical reality of the work depends on its interpretative performances (see Hoy 1978, 43–72). It is not merely a matter of adapting preconceived ideas, or the image that has been made of the objectivity of a work of art, to the particular situation of the interpreter: rather, the interpreter must respond to the situation, valuing it as "affordance" (see Gibson 2013) for a response that realizes the work in and through that particular situation. Since interpretation is never a simple theoretical knowledge of an objective datum, but is a form of praxis in which the effects of a cultural construct are carried out through *application* to a specific situation, the activity of the performer who realizes a performative work of art is a paradigmatic expression of the *phronesis* (the Aristotelian "practical wisdom"), which consists in a practical exercise of sensitivity to the possibilities entailed by the specific situation of the performance and to the effective and unique ways of responding to this situation (see Gadamer 2004, 306–36). Hence, the interpreter's situation is creatively valued as an expression of the work that is actively operating through its *Wirkungsgeschichte*. Thus, interpretation is articulated not only in understanding and explanation, but also requires the application: application does not take place after the understanding has already taken place. Instead, application is the specific goal of understanding right away. Understanding always takes place as an exercise of appreciation and sensitivity towards the individual case: which is a "phronetic" exercise of taste as "reflexive judgment" (in Kantian terms) that is not limited to applying a norm to a particular case: rather, application to the particular case contributes to redefining the norm (see Gadamer 2004, 32–34). This implies that interpreters can be faithful to the artwork only through the tasteful application to the concrete and unrepeatable situation of the performance, which is part of the artwork's *Wirkungsgeschichte*.

Certainly, as Gadamer acknowledges, it is the artwork that guides the dialogue that takes place in the interpreter's situation. In order to properly apply a norm for the realization of the work (for example, the instructions of a score) to a specific situation and respond effectively to it, the interpreter must *listen* to the work: for the work to be relevant to their particular situation, interpreters must pay attention to it, since they already belong to the work's history of effects. And even when they aim to offer creative or revolutionary interpretations, they can only refer to innovative aspects of the tradition of the practice to which the work belongs.

It still remains to be seen what this brief presentation of some aspects of the Gadamerian philosophy of interpretation has to do with the issue of improvisation. Bruce Ellis Benson (2003) has already recognized that the theoretical framework of Gadamerian hermeneutics is perfectly adequate not only to provide an understanding of improvisational phenomena but also to show the paradigmatic character that improvisation has for the articulation of different musical activities (see Bertinetto 2013): activities in which a cultural product (a work) is appropriated by a performer in different ways to be revitalized in a cultural-historical process that develops as an ongoing fusion of horizons. Arrangements, variations, versions, interpretations, covers, mash-ups, etc., are all understood as forms of improvisation on a cultural construct of whose history of effects is a part and which, in turn, lives on through these effects produced by responsively and creatively applying them to novel concrete situations. As I have shown elsewhere (see Bertinetto 2022), this argument does not apply to music only. Improvisation is paradigmatic of cultural practices whereby a cultural construct, such an artwork, is realized in interaction with a situation unpredictable by its author. In this sense, the relationship between a work of dance, music, or theater and its performative interpretation is improvisational. Each interpretation is realized as a dialogue with the work and the other interpretations that constitute its history of effects (as Feige 2014 argues very clearly in reference to jazz). Artistic improvisation shows that the work's value as a norm for its performances is not factually, objectively, and abstractly fixed—as claimed, in my opinion erroneously, by the main (analytical) stream of contemporary musical ontology (Bertinetto 2016a; Bertinetto 2019). On the contrary, it is formed and transformed through its performances themselves: the identity and value of a work is configured through its *Wirkungsgeschichte*. Through its interpretations as well as within an improvisational performance, the normativity that is specific of the work as norm for its performances is (trans)formed in the course of the process itself according to the interactions between the participants (Bertram 2022; see also Bertinetto and Bertram 2020).

But in what sense is the dialogical hermeneutic logic of the relationship between work and interpretation *improvisational*? To answer this question, it is necessary to briefly explain how improvisation takes place. As it is shown by collective improvisations in the context of music or theatre, the meaning of performers' moves or contributions (in terms of sounds, gestures, actions, words, movements, etc.) is articulated in response to the previous moves and contributions. The improvisational process does not occur ex nihilo, but on the basis of a background of skills, abilities, conventions, aesthetic ideals, materials, and resources that constitute the condition of possibility of the performance (Bertinetto 2016a): the tradition Gadamer speaks of. This background, which constitutes the performers' reference practice, is brought into play within the performance. This means that the background's effectiveness, as well as its normative validity, is realized through responses to the specific situation of the performance that retroacts on the background, impacting on it in a transformative way.

Jazz musicians, for example, improvise in interaction with the musical and cultural tradition to which they belong and of which they constitute the expression. And while they express this tradition—in which they are embedded, embodying it through assiduous practice of training and exercise—they do not merely mirror it as a fixed objective model, but (trans)form it by responding to what happens hic et nunc in the performative situation. Performer follow to the tradition that supports them by applying it to their own situational contexts, thereby (trans)forming it. These situational contexts are not only the historical environments of artistic practices, but also the concrete performative situations in which performers are operating; more concretely, they are the performative processes in which the meaning of each move of an improviser is holistically shaped not only by the interaction with her/his own previous and subsequent moves, but also by the interaction with what all the other performers are doing.

Thus, the point is that the holistic, and self-forming (autopoietic), structure of the improvisational process makes explicit what happens in any performative interpretation. The meaning of the performance emerges through the (not always conflict-free) interaction among all the ingredients of the performance, including its cultural background (see Sawyer 2003; Bertinetto

2020; Bertinetto 2022): the genre of the performative practice at issue (e.g., bebop), the performers' personal styles (e.g., Miles Davis's cool tensional calm or Coltrane's mystical vigor), the possible cultural construct interpreted (e.g., a jazz tune like "Stella by Starlight" or "All the Things You Are"), the emotional climate of the performing situation, etc. All those elements, but not only them, contribute to the realization of that performative-interpretive *play* in which improvisation consists and that is produced through the *players* themselves. While the tradition of an artistic practice and the different cultural constructs that are part of it can offer the starting normative basis—in terms of conventions and rules for the development of the artistic practice itself—the development of the performance retroactively redesigns the normative outlines of the process itself in response to what happens concretely in the specific situation. As evidenced by the fact that to determine whether something that happens in the improvisational process is a mistake or not, we must wait for the concrete development of the performance (Bertinetto 2016b), an interpretation of a work particularly surprising—compared to the cultural canons that predispose the psychological system of expectations of the appreciators—it is not in itself a failure of interpretation. Instead, it may mean an interesting creative articulation of possibilities for the work: an articulation capable of making the work alive and through which the work may be given a new sense, making its history of effects developing in new directions. Importantly, as long as the performance lasts, this play in which the performers, but also the appreciators, participate leads to forms: forms in ongoing (trans)formation. Hence, the Gadamerian notion of *Verwandlung ins Gebilde* can be useful to understand how even in the case of improvisation the performer's interactive play shapes artworks: this play is the enactment of artistic (sonic, gestural, scenic, theatrical, choreographic) forms, through a process of (trans)formation in which the work itself consists. And when it comes to the performative interpretation of an already extant artwork of music, dance, or theatre, the work itself is per- and trans-formed through its interpretation, which is a process of *Verwandlung ins Gebilde* depending on the specific performative situation to which the artists respond.

I would like to emphasize that, as shown by performative interpretations of artworks, Gadamer's perspective does not only concern the application of the logical-procedural structures of interpretation to improvisation, but rather the highlighting of the *improvisational character of the hermeneutic process itself*. In fact, a distinguishing feature of artistic improvisation is that each performance of improvisation, by practicing a *phronesis* that is sensitive to the nuances of what is happening (see Benson 2022), carries on the tradition of a practice through the interaction—through which the normativity of the process is (trans)formed and its specific meaning emerges—with the specific and unrepeatable situation in which the process takes place and to which the performers must respond.[5] As we have seen, this feature characterizes the hermeneutic process in which human cultural experience—discussed by Gadamer in particular thanks to the guideline of art—consists. In short, *the Gadamerian conception of interpretation and hermeneutic experience is improvisational* in the clarified sense. Precisely for this reason, Gadamer's hermeneutic philosophy is a theoretically fertile ground for understanding improvisational practices[6]—even apart from the linguistic character that Gadamer assigns to the hermeneutic dimension of experience. As Gadamer explicitly writes, the acquisition of experience is characterized by a peculiar openness: it occurs on different occasions, suddenly, in an unpredictable way, but not without preparation (Gadamer 2004, 347). Just like in artistic improvisation. And as with improvisation, which can only be based on the acquisition of habits as repeatable behavioral patterns, capable of fostering a creative response to the unique situation of the performance, the repeatability that characterizes human experience (Gadamer 2004, 342) is not in contrast with the possibility of the new.

Pareyson's Hermeneutic Philosophy of Art as Improvisational Making

The invention of the new is one of the central aspects of the philosophy of art of the Italian philosopher Luigi Pareyson, a colleague and friend of Gadamer. In *Truth and Interpretation* (1971), Pareyson developed a hermeneutic philosophy that is in dialogue with Gadamer's thought. Pareyson emphasizes the inexhaustibility of truth as the origin of one's own interpretations, which are not simple manifestations of a fixed objectivity, but contribute to the hermeneutic productivity of truth itself. In a nutshell, truth is inexhaustible precisely because of the interpretations through which it develops creatively. Interpretation, one may say, is, according to Pareyson, an improvisation *on* truth. It is an improvisation on truth that does not betray truth. Instead, it articulates its inexhaustibility.

Some years earlier, Pareyson had already developed his own philosophy of art in his book *Estetica. Teoria della formatività* (1954). Here he argues that art is a making, an operating, an acting; an acting that is distinguished from other modes of acting because the norm (or set of norms) that the action must follow is not already constituted before the very act that applies it. It is invented when it is realized, through the very practices with which it is performed. Art is "such a making that, while it makes, invents the way of making": it is a *poietic* "form," because "in the very course of the operation invents the *modus operandi*, and defines the norm of the work while it makes it, and conceives by executing, and designs in the very act that it realizes" (Pareyson 2010, 59).

This definition of art is surprisingly similar to a definition of improvisation as a kind of making that invents its own way of proceeding as it unfolds, that is, as a coincidence of invention and performance. Improvisation is, in fact, a mode of action that, although based on a background of skills, resources, materials, conventions etc. (see §2), creates by itself the norm of its own performance and its own interpretive context in the course of its performance. Beyond the literal similarity between the Pareysonian definition of art and the formal definition of improvisation, here I am interested in the *spirit* of a proximity that is conceptual in nature. However, the examination of this conceptual link can constitute a theoretical gain only if one highlights that, differently from some currents of contemporary aesthetics, Pareyson does not conceive of improvisation as a territory foreign to art, or as a mere exception to the rule, but rather as something like the germ from which art originates as a specific kind of formative making. Improvisation, as exemplary (per)formative making, offers the paradigmatic conceptual coordinates of art making. On the basis of the idea of art as a kind of formativity that acts by inventing the norms of its own proceeding through the making itself, Pareyson reworks the whole conceptuality of aesthetics in order to account for improvisational and, in general, for performative phenomena, which seem to be paradigmatic cases of artistic formativity. Hence, philosophy of art must not accept as unquestionable the primacy of the artwork, understood in structural and objectual terms; rather, the aesthetics of the artwork must be understood as a historically and culturally conditioned field of aesthetics as a philosophy of art, where philosophy of art means first and foremost philosophy of artistic making.

In fact, Pareyson maintains that the improviser's activity condenses the specific features of the artistic procedure as such, from its preparation to its operational unfolding. The features of improvisation that are paradigmatic for art as whole are some of those discussed in contemporary studies on the aesthetics of improvisation (see Bertinetto 2016a and 2022): extemporaneity, adventure, risk, exploration, innovativeness, tensive collaboration between conventional preparation and creative acceptance of the unexpected cue, tentative character of the production process, creative functionality of the accident. In the quest for invention, the improviser "is forced to renounce at the outset the intention of wanting to foresee or somehow prevent the unexpected; rather, he must from the outset dispose himself to 'accept' it precisely so as not to have to suffer it, . . . not to be surprised by it, . . . not to lose the initiative" (Pareyson 2010, 86). And although this condition, given the extemporaneous nature of their activity as well as the risks arising from insufficient technical preparation, exposes improvisers to the danger of becoming entangled in the murk of cliché and trite convention, their task is to find a way to master the automatisms they must nonetheless make use of, which is precisely what all artists are called to do.

Thus, improvisation becomes an exemplary model of art as a formative practice. In fact, the process of improvisational making manifests the "tension of research" between desired success and possible failure, that pertains to art as such (see Bertram 2021). Improvisation shows emblematically that in art good achievements are not guaranteed. The outcome of a creative process is constitutively subjected as much to the risk of failure as to the happiness of unpredictable invention. This implies the *adventurous* nature of the artistic process. If before beginning the production process its outcome is unknown, then the possibility of failure is intrinsic to the artistic formative process.

That product whose formation requires creative invention of the manner of its own process is artistic. Unlike other activities and operations, the success of which depends on rules and predetermined purposes, in art nothing is known beforehand, "and we just have to wait for the result by operating and doing" (Pareyson 2010, 67). In this sense the work is self-referential: it establishes its own normativity, which consists in the "adaptation of the work to itself" (Pareyson 2010, 67). An artistic plan is authentically formative when it is also as such in fieri; therefore it coincides with the process of the formation of the work (see Pareyson 2010, 60, 66). Indeed, as Gadamer would have it, "there is a leap between the planning and the executing on the one hand and the successful achievement on the other" (Gadamer 1986, 33). Success emerges out of planning and cannot be reductively traced back to it. This suggests that artistic creativity is, as such, improvisational (Bertinetto 2012).

Moreover, artistic activity requires the ability to imagine multiple possibilities of action and to choose creatively the good one through experiments, tests, attempts. It is demanded to achieve not only unpredictable results, but also results that are *unthinkable* before the process by which they are achieved (Pareyson 2010, 69). It therefore requires the ability to voluntarily take *risks*: it is an exploratory process, a process whose path is dominated by uncertainty. It is the elaboration of a "grammar of contingency" (Bertinetto 2022, 33–77).

The experience of artistic making is, just like that of improvising, an *experience* in the sense of *Erfahrung*: it is about making a journey (*fahren* = to travel), whose development is not known in advance (see Gadamer 2004, 86, 341ff.). It is a searching process, which, by trial and error, looks for its own meaning, for its own normativity, and is based on what Pareyson calls "*spunti*," that is cues or affordances: environmental opportunities for interaction. *Spunti* are elements provided by the material that artists interact with in the course of the creation process: if discovered, recognized, and well interpreted, they can suggest new ways of creative construction. A cue can be an "'accident' occurring during a musical improvisation that urges its own unfolding" (Pareyson 2010, 131) or the veins of a block of marble, or a symbolic image, or a spot of color. As material elements of the formation process, these cues already contain essential aspects of art and everything that constitutes possibilities, suggestions, proposals for the creative process becomes a cue. However, the development of the cues is not in itself already channeled into the safe tracks of automatic execution devices. Instead, it coincides with the formative activity of inspired artists, who grasp in the felicitous cue that they are presented with a sudden free gift to pay respectful attention to. Therefore, true artists are those who, balancing activity and receptivity, have the ability and readiness to transform into a creative resource every accident and obstacle into which the formative process stumbles.

In particular, in improvisation the obstacles posed by the material take on the value of cues and the incident is stimulus to be turned into unprecedented creative possibilities within the process in which the improviser "on the one hand seeks to converge and regroup a chaos around the powerful and germinal poignancy of a center of organization, and on the other hand already anticipates the delineation of developments claimed by the germs felicitously discovered" (Pareyson 2010, 86).

Therefore, improvisation has an *aggressive* character to it, in the etymological sense of the Latin expression *ad gradior* [I go to meet], that means the readiness to confront oneself with the unexpected and to respond appropriately to it when it arises: which requires the subtle and fine skill of acting inventively out of events that would otherwise undermine the process itself. Indeed, the unexpected is sought and produced by good improvisers, who know that certain creative possibilities can occur solely as unforeseen. Improvisation is aggressive in the sense that it seeks to deal with the unexpected.

Hence, improvisation is exemplary of the way cues initiate the formation of an artwork (Pareyson 2010, 86), providing opportunities for its articulation. As noticed by Robert Valgenti (2022, 64), this process "takes the familiar form of a hermeneutic circle of interpretation—an ongoing process through which the understanding of the whole can only be achieved by knowing its constituent parts, and likewise, the knowledge of the parts requires some understanding of the whole." Gadamer, who conceives of human existence as an ongoing process of understanding, maintains that in the artistic realm this circle implies "the interplay of the movement of tradition and the movement of the interpreter" (Gadamer 2004, 293). Pareyson, while generally emphasizing the responsibilities and risks of any interpretations, defends that

> the artist, as a participant in a larger tradition of social institutions and artistic forms, responds to her material through the familiar and common expressions that result from dedicated practice and membership within a shared cultural history—identity through belonging to a community and the responsibilities that accompany such membership. But in another sense, there is also real risk in the material—whether it is cultural or physical—as the force of its demands, along with its potential indifference and even outright resistance to the vision of the artist, threaten to extinguish the spark of a novel idea or a revolutionary form. (Valgenti 2022, 64)

Hence, the creation of an artwork actually requires that "a physical and resistant material is taken up by the artist" (Valgenti 2022, 64) in an interpretational way (see Pareyson 2010, 44). In other words, a hermeneutical tension is in play between the artists' creative moves and the material. This may be productive but may also fail. It succeeds when the tensional encounter between the artist's personality and the otherness of the material manifests opportunities for the generation of an artwork as a self-formed whole. Artists must therefore not only impose themselves on materials, but also listen to their otherness, in an attitude that is, at the same time, active and passive. Without going into the details of Pareysonian aesthetics and his conception of improvisation (see Bertinetto 2010; Valgenti 2022), the here important point is that improvisation is once again paradigmatic of the way artists' creative activity unfolds as a performance of interpretation of the cues offered by the material.

It is the interpretive encounter—adventurous and risky—between the personality of the artist and the otherness of the material that can produce the unexpected success, that is, that offers the opportunity for the successful outcome of a process that is set in place by inventing its own procedures and norms.

Conclusion

Improvisation and interpretation, though formally distinct, express the proper character of human existence through their inextricable intertwining. Both Gadamer and Pareyson defend that to grasp this hermeneutic character of existence, artistic experience is very instructive.

In the wake of an examination of the experience of art, Gadamer examines interpretation as a fusion of the horizons of the work interpreted and the performing interpreter that takes place through the latter's ability to listen to the work, of whose *Wirkungsgeschichte* s/he is already a part, enhancing it, and further realizing it, through his/her response to the specific concrete situation in which s/he interprets it. In this sense, *interpretation has an improvisational character*, since improvisation is a performance that brings forth its own meaning from the interaction between one's response to the situation in which the performance takes place and the cultural and material background of the artistic practice at issue.

In elaborating his philosophy of art, Pareyson highlights the paradigmatic character of improvisation for artistic creativity. Art, like improvisation, is a making that invents its own way of making. It is an adventurous and risky process in which the artist is confronted with the cues offered by the material without any guarantee of success. The encounter between the artist's personality and the otherness of the material is interpretive. Thus, *improvisation is*, in this sense, *interpretive* and, at the same time, *exhibits the interpretive character of artistic creativity* as such.

Thus, looking at improvisation from the perspective of hermeneutics teaches us that although they are distinct activities, improvisation and interpretation are indispensable to each other. Improvisational creativity is not ex nihilo: it is interpretive. Interpretation is not the mirroring of the objectivity of an artifact and the subjectivity of an author's mind: it is the improvisational fusion of the horizons of the work and of the performer in the unrepeatable and unique perspective of the concrete situation in which the work is (further) realized.[7]

Notes

1. By defining texts, documents, works of art—and thus not only images, but also musical works—as "cultural constructs," I do not mean to deny the concrete materiality nor the historical objectivity of a text or of an artwork. Rather, I intend to emphasize that their meaning, which also concerns their materiality and objectivity, is historical and cultural and, it can be said, is negotiated through human practices, including the practices of understanding, interpretation, and performance.

2. "Intentional" in Beisbart's sense (2022). On intentionality and improvisation, see also Bertinetto 2016a, 81–91 and Bertinetto and Grüneberg 2023.

3. Moreover, it goes without saying that being faithful is per se not an aesthetic nor even a moral obligation. It is an obligation only if specific normative criteria of specific historical artistic practices apply. On the contrary, in some artistic practices it can be an obligation to be innovative or revolutionary.

4. See Betti 1990 and Bleicher 1980, 38–94. On Betti's notion of interpretation, explained within the framework of an interesting discussion of improvisation as a paradigm of interpretation in law and music, see Buffo 2018, 226–30.

5. In this sense I endorse Daniel M. Feige's idea that "the dynamic nature of traditions against 'traditionalist' views becomes explicit in the case of jazz improvisation" (Feige 2024, 106). I would only add that this happens also in many other kinds of artistic improvisation.

6. In this regard see, for instance, Daniel M. Feige's "hermeneutic" account of Jazz (Feige 2019 and 2024 [forthcoming]).

7. I thank Daniel M. Feige for some important comments to this text. This article has been made possible thanks to a research stay at the FU Berlin funded by the Alexander von Humboldt Foundation.

Bibliography

Beisbart, Claus. "Improvisation and Action Theory." In *The Routledge Handbook of Philosophy and Improvisation in the Arts*. Edited by A. Bertinetto and M. Ruta, 100–13. London–New York: Routledge, 2022.

Benson, Bruce E. "Improvisational Phronesis." In *The Routledge Handbook of Philosophy and Improvisation in the Arts*. Edited by A. Bertinetto and M. Ruta, 259–70. London–New York: Routledge, 2022.

———. *The Improvisation of Musical Dialogue*. Cambridge: Cambridge University Press, 2003.

Bertinetto, Alessandro. *Aesthetics of Improvisation*. Leiden–München: Brill–Fink, 2022.
———. "'Do Not Fear Mistakes—There Are None.' The Mistake as Surprising Experience of Creativity in Jazz." In *Education as Jazz*. Edited by M. Santi and E. Zorzi, 85–100. Cambridge: Cambridge Scholars Publishing, 2016b.
———. *Eseguire l'inatteso. Ontologia della musica e improvvisazione*. Roma: il Glifo, 2016a.
———. "Improvisation and the Ontology of Art." *Rivista di Estetica* 73 (2020): 10–29.
———. Improvvisazione e formatività." *Annuario filosofico* 25/2009 (2010): 145–74.
———. "Musical Authenticity as 'Being True to the Moment.'" *The Polish Journal of Aesthetics* 54, 3 (2019): 9–28.
———. "Musical Ontology. A View through Improvisation." *Cosmo* 2 (2013): 81–101.
———. "Performing the Unexpected." *Daimon* 57 (2012): 61–79.
Bertinetto, Alessandro, and Georg W. Bertram. "'We Make Up the Rules as We Go Along.'—Improvisation as Essential Aspect of Human Practices?" *Open Philosophy* 3, no. 1 (2020): 202–21.
Bertinetto, Alessandro, and Patrick Grüneberg. "Action as Abductive Performance: An Improvisational Model." *International Journal of Philosophical Studies* 31 (2023): 25–53.
Bertram, Georg W. "Art and the Possibility of Failure." *Studi di Estetica* 19 (2021): 26–39.
———. "Improvisation as Normative Practice." In *The Routledge Handbook of Philosophy and Improvisation in the Arts*. Edited by A. Bertinetto and M. Ruta, 21–32. London–New York: Routledge, 2022.
Betti, Emilio. *Teoria generale dell'interpretazione*. Milano: Giuffré, 1990.
Bleicher, Joseph. *Contemporary Hermeneutics*. London: Routledge, 1980.
Buffo, Angelo Pio. "Interpretation and Improvisation. The Judge and the Musician between Text and Context." *International Journal of the Semiotic of Law* 31 (2018): 215–39.
Clarke, Erik F., and Mark Doffman, eds. *Distributed Creativity: Collaboration and Improvisation in Contemporary Music*. New York: Oxford University Press, 2017.
Feige, Daniel M. "Kleine Hermeneutik des Jazz." *Musik&Ästhetik* 23, no. 91 (2019): 9–29.
———. *Philosophie des Jazz*. Berlin: Suhrkamp, 2014.
———. "Living Tradition: Jazz Improvisation in the Light of Gadamer's Hermeneutics." In *Gadamer, Music & Philosophical Hermeneutics*. Edited by S. McAuliffe, 97–110. Cham: Springer, 2024.
Ferrari, Emanuele. "Esecuzione musicale e improvvisazione." In *Il senso dell'istante. Improvvisazione e formazione*. Edited by F. Cappa and C. Negro, 119–36. Milano: Guerini, 2006.
Gadamer, Hans-Georg. *The Relevance of the Beautiful and Other Essays*. Translated by N. Walker. Edited by R. Bernasconi. Cambridge: Cambridge University Press, 1986.

———. *Truth and Method*. Revised ed. Translated by J. Weinsheimer and D. G. Marshall. London: Continuum, 2004.
Gibson, John. *The Ecological Approach to Visual Perception*. Brighton: Psychology Press, 2013.
Gioia, Ted. *The Imperfect Art. Reflections on Jazz and Modern Culture*. Oxford: Oxford University Press, 1988.
Hirsch, Eric D. *Validity in Interpretation*. New Haven, CT: Yale University Press, 1967.
Hoy, David C. *The Critical Circle*. Berkeley–Los Angeles–London: University of California Press, 1982.
Mazzoni, Augusto. *La musica nell'ermeneutica contemporanea*. Milano: Mimesis, 2005.
Pareyson, Luigi. *Estetica. Teoria della formatività*. Milano: Bompiani, 2010.
———. *Truth and Interpretation*. Translated by R. T. Valgenti. Edited and revised by S. Benso. Albany: State University of New York Press, 2014.
Sawyer, Richard K. *Group Creativity*. Mahwah: Lawrence Erlbaum, 2003.
Valgenti, Robert T. "Material and Improvisation in the Formative Process." In *The Routledge Handbook of Philosophy and Improvisation in the Arts*. Edited by A. Bertinetto and M. Ruta, 60–72. London–New York: Routledge, 2022.

8

Playing and Reading
The Performative Paradigm in Gadamer's Aesthetics

Elena Romagnoli

Reframing Gadamer's Aesthetics Nowadays

What we may call postmodern or post-metaphysical readings of Gadamer's philosophy have played a prominent role in the recent tradition of studies on hermeneutics. This has led, among other things, to emphasize the anti-foundationalist basis of hermeneutics and to try to formalize its break with the question of "truth" in a strong sense. This interpretive tendency can be seen in Richard Rorty's and Gianni Vattimo's pioneering readings of Gadamer's thought.[1] In brief, both authors, although in different ways, have focused on language as the human being's unsurpassable horizon and as the expression of an anti-foundationalist conception.[2] On the one hand, such interpretations have been decisive in disseminating and further developing Gadamer's thought; on the other hand, however, they result in a relativistic and in a sort of nihilistic conception that has little to do with it. In response to such approach, other scholars, inspired by Jean Grondin's seminal works, have developed what we may call a metaphysical reading of hermeneutics, which stresses, in particular, the deep roots of Gadamer's philosophy in the Greek and medieval traditions,[3] thus reinforcing the centrality of the concepts of truth and tradition. At the same time, despite recalling a fundamental legacy of Gadamer's philosophy, while answering the dismissive criticism of authors like Jürgen Habermas (1973) and John D. Caputo (1987), such a line of inquiry based on the ontological paradigm of hermeneutics can be problematic in accounting for contemporary phenomena that elude the traditional categories of metaphysical origin, as in the case of contemporary artistic phenomena.

Notwithstanding the merits of both approaches (the post-metaphysical and the metaphysical), in the present contribution I will follow a *third way*, which is based on a reading of Gadamer's aesthetics as *performative*, aiming both to distance it from postmodern readings and their relativist outcomes, alien to Gadamer's philosophy, and to emphasize its "a-metaphysical" aspect (see Di Cesare 2013, 52). In contrast to the strand that seeks to reconcile hermeneutics with metaphysics, I will rather attempt to emphasize the anthropological dimension in Gadamer's philosophy (consistent with Romagnoli 2023 and Romagnoli 2024): this does not imply denying the presence of metaphysical themes or repudiating the centrality of tradition in the development of Gadamer's thought. Rather, my aim is to show the presence of an alternative paradigm in Gadamer's philosophy, though scarcely emphasized in standard readings; according to this paradigm, art is conceived as a dynamic and processual event, and is characterized by the interaction among the audience, the author, and the work of art. The aim is to bring out some implicit elements of Gadamer's philosophy, in order to develop them in a direction that may also go beyond Gadamer himself, prefiguring potential new paths in contemporary hermeneutics.

Referring to a performative paradigm in Gadamer's philosophy could appear to contrast with that strand of performative aesthetics, originated in the 1990s, which constituted itself as a direct antithesis to hermeneutics, as in Walburga Hülk's research.[4] This opposition derived from a textualist reading of Gadamer's thought, which considered it as incompatible with performance as a dynamic event that is free from any reference to the text. Recently, performative aesthetics has been developed in a systematic way by Erika Fischer-Lichte (2008), who, despite weakening the contrast with hermeneutics and speaking of a complementarity between the two strands, has credited anyway Gadamer with a conception of art that is still flattened on the artistic object. In agreement with what Marcello Ruta has claimed, my thesis is that there is neither an opposition nor a complementarity between hermeneutics and performative aesthetics. Rather, hermeneutics has an *underlying* performative potential in itself (see Ruta 2017). In this sense, I will therefore speak of a performative character of the work of art at the very basis of Gadamer's conception, an aspect that Cynthia R. Nielsen and James Risser have recently drawn attention to (see Nielsen 2022, 63–67 and Risser 2017, 49–60).[5]

My aim is to show how, in Gadamer's conception, the work of art is essentially considered in terms of movement and interaction, namely as a performance. My interpretation is grounded on the concept of play as *Darstellung*, which can also be extended to the figurative and literary arts, by leveraging the idea of reading as performing the work itself, a topic that Gadamer especially developed in some of his essays published after *Truth and Method*. I will proceed by recalling how the first part of *Truth and Method* builds on the concept of play by leveraging the twofold meaning of game and presentation, which has its paradigmatic manifestation in the performing arts of music and drama. Subsequently, I will highlight the presence of a paradigm reversal where, after this emphasis on the centrality of play, it is instead the ontological concept of picture that becomes the main thread of Gadamer's argument in the following pages of *Truth and Method*. In the face of such an inner tension that is present in *Truth and Method*, I will finally move on to show how Gadamer's intention to question "aesthetic differentiation" can find an adequate development by stressing the concept of reading as performing, in a way that can be applied as much to the literary as to the figurative arts.

The Twofold Meaning of Play and the Performative Arts

As we run through the first part of *Truth and Method*, which deals entirely with art and aesthetic experience, we can highlight Gadamer's fundamental reference to the concept of "play [*Spiel*]." This concept is understood by Gadamer in connection with the notion of "presentation [*Darstellung*]," which, in turn, can be meant as enactment, as a performative event that has its emblematic reference in the arts of reproduction, namely drama and music (despite the latter being less explicit in Gadamerian texts[6]). Indeed, the critique against the subjectivism of aesthetic consciousness and its outcomes (the isolation and musealization of art) has a fundamental cornerstone in play as an element that focuses on the *activity* of playing, not on the individual players.

Gadamer clearly stresses that the aesthetic experience should not be understood as a subject-object relation (a point he reproaches in the concept of *Erlebnis*), being rather a sort of transformative, processual experience, namely *Erfahrung*.⁷ In this sense, Gadamer goes in a similar direction to Georg W. Bertram's recent definition of "art as human praxis" (see Bertram 2019), especially considering that Gadamer identifies "movement [*Bewegung*]" as the fundamental feature of play:

> If we examine how the word "play" is used and concentrate on its so-called metaphorical senses, we find talk of the play of light, the play of the waves, the play of gears or parts of machinery, the interplay of limbs, the play of forces, the play of gnats, even a play on words. In each case what is intended is to-and-fro movement that is not tied to any goal that would bring it to an end. (GW 1, 109; Gadamer 2013, 108)

Movement is thus understood in the broadest possible sense and then specified by Gadamer in the etymological form of the art of dance: "Correlatively, the word '*Spiel*' originally meant '*Tanz*,' and is still found in many word forms (e.g., in *Spielmann*)" (GW 1, 109; Gadamer 2013, 108). In addition to this anti-subjectivist aspect expressed by play, the emphasis on its character of self-presentation stresses a performative conception: "One can say that performing a task successfully 'presents it [*stellt sie dar*].' This phrasing especially suggests itself in the case of a game, for here fulfilling the task does not point to any purposive context" (GW 1, 113; Gadamer 2013, 112).

Although the title of this section of *Truth and Method* is "Play as the Clue to Ontological Explanation," in the initial development of the argumentation play seems to have more an *anthropological* basis than a strictly *ontological* one: "The fact that the mode of being of play is so close to the mobile form of *nature* permits us to draw an important methodological conclusion. It is obviously not correct to say that animals *too* play, nor is it correct to say that, metaphorically speaking, water and light play as well. Rather, on the contrary, we can say that man *too* plays" (GW 1, 110–11; Gadamer 2013, 109, emphasis added). Emblematically, Gadamer goes so far as to claim that human's "playing too is a *natural process* [*Naturvorgang*]" (GW 1, 110–11; Gadamer 2013, 109, emphasis added). This naturalistic and anthropological dimension of the play is further developed in later essays such as "The Play of Art" (1973) and "The Relevance of the Beautiful. Art as Play, Symbol and Festival" (1974), where play is defined as "an elementary phenomenon that pervades the whole of the animal world and, as is obvious, it determines man as a natural being as well" (GW 8, 86; Gadamer 1998, 123).

It is precisely "the medial sense of play" (GW 1, 111; Gadamer 2013, 110) that enables Gadamer to relate it to the mode of being of the work of art, since in German *Spiel* indicates the *game* as well as the artistic presentation in the sense of *drama* (as in the English *play*). This concept is then extended to art, where the self-presentation of play does not remain isolated but opens up to an "audience [*Zuschauer*]": "All presentation is potentially a representation for someone. That this possibility is intended is the characteristic feature of art as play. The closed world of play *lets down one of its walls*, as it were" (GW 1, 114; Gadamer 2013, 113, emphasis added).

From this point of view, the *relational* character of the work of art comes to light. Art is always conceived for someone, and it is itself only insofar as it is *enacted*, *presented*, or *performed*. All these English words are aimed to render the two different terms used by Gadamer, namely *Aufführung* and *Vollzug*—the latter becoming central especially in his later essays, as I will stress later. When play is presented to someone, it acquires its own perfection: play becomes a "presentation for an audience" (GW 1, 115; Gadamer 2013, 114). As mentioned before, Gadamer specifically refers to dance in order to explain the etymology of play as movement: play is itself only when it is played, just as a musical or theatrical work cannot be reduced to the score or the script, as it is itself only when it is performed or staged. Artistic performance therefore involves an opening, the fact that one is addressing someone, namely the audience: "But however much a religious or profane play represents a world wholly closed within itself, it is as if open toward the spectator, in whom it achieves its whole significance" (GW 1, 115; Gadamer 2013, 114).

Indeed, the audience is not merely conceived of as the passive recipient of a precast product. Rather, it actively contributes to the very presentation of the work—an aspect that is fundamental to all arts, as we will see. As a consequence, it clearly emerges that Gadamer's aesthetics contrasts with what he calls "aesthetic differentiation," which results in detaching art from the other spheres of life and in the spectators' passivity. The presentation of the work is connected to the cultural act, where "the relation to the community is obvious" (GW 1, 121; Gadamer 2013, 120).

From this point of view, we see how in those initial pages of *Truth and Method* Gadamer's criterion is rooted in the model of the arts of reproduction or, more precisely, the performative arts, particularly drama and music, as the expression "letting down of one wall" testifies. Gadamer indeed claims that "the same is true for drama generally, even considered as literature" (GW 1, 121; Gadamer 2013, 120). In fact, the focus on the dynamical character of art also allows Gadamer to show the social character of the work of art: "The performance [*Aufführung*] of a play, like that of a ritual, cannot simply be detached from the play itself, as if it were something that is not part of its essential being, but is as subjective and fluid as the aesthetic experiences in which it is experienced" (GW 1, 121; Gadamer 2013, 120).

The essential character of the work of art thus coincides with "performance." This occurs, as Gadamer points out, even in the "liminal case" of the *Hausmusik*, which seeks to be more authentic music-making by being performed for the players themselves, not for an audience (GW 1, 114; Gadamer 2013, 115). Even in that circumstance, the musicians strive to provide a "good performance," as if for an imaginary spectator or for themselves, who become both spectator and performer. Indeed, Gadamer's claim is to explain what a work of art consists in, "given that it exists only in being played and in its presentation as a play [*in der Darstellung, als Schauspiel*], though it is nevertheless its own being that is thereby presented" (GW 1, 122; Gadamer 2013, 121).

Thus, the value of play emerges together with its semantic link to "spectacle [*Schauspiel*]," which, as such, can only exist in presentation. Presentation is based on interaction: it characterizes both play and art, which can be itself only in being represented for someone, in its interaction with the viewers. This paradigm of art as interaction can explain in which sense art belongs to, and cannot be isolated from, its world, as in the case of aesthetic consciousness. Indeed, Gadamer explicitly points out that "the presentation [*Dartsellung*] or performance [*Aufführung*] of a work of literature or music is something *essential*, and not incidental to it, for it merely completes what the works of art already are" (GW 1, 139; Gadamer 2013, 135, emphasis added). That the work exists only in its enactment implies that it is constituted each time by its interaction with that particular audience and situation.

The fact that the work exists only in its being presented relates to the question of its temporality: Gadamer engages on such analysis on the concept of "festival [*Fest*]," the essence of which is to be repeated differently yet identically every time (see GW 1, 128; Gadamer 2013, 126). The reference to the festival has a powerful social (and also political, i.e., democratic) entailment, in the sense that "the festival is for everyone,"[8] evidence of the centrality of the spectators' contribution: "To be present means to participate. If someone was present at something, he knows all about how it really was" (GW 1, 129; Gadamer 2013, 127). This paradigm is explicated in the example of tragedy, Greek tragedy in particular, highlighting the continuist and social basis of Gadamer's philosophy, rooted in the emblem of the festival as a shared event. In fact, the very conception of the Greek tragedy, where the spectator was transformed by the performance, contrasts with the idea of aesthetic consciousness, which aims at a suspension of everyday life through art.

Here, the *anti-exceptionalist* element of Gadamer's conception comes to the fore, criticizing the aesthetics of "genius" and its outcomes, as well as contrasting the distance of aesthetic consciousness with participation "in the communion of being Present" (GW 1, 137; Gadamer 2013, 134), as shown in classical tragedy. This explicitly emerges in the claim that "however much the tragic play performed solemnly in the theatre presents an exceptional situation in everyone's life, it is not an experience of an adventure producing a temporary intoxication from which one *reawakens* to one's true being" (GW 1, 137; Gadamer 2013, 134, emphasis added). Against this isolation of art in everyday life, "the elevation and strong emotion that seize the spectator in fact *deepen his continuity with himself*" (GW 1, 137; Gadamer 2013, 134, emphasis added).

Picture versus Performance?

What has emerged so far shows the essential elements of the work of art, namely its presentation as enactment, its inherent relationality, and its social nature. The point is to show whether these characters can apply even to arts that are not strictly performative. Gadamer's intent in the following pages of *Truth and Method* takes inspiration from the figurative arts: "Let us first ask this question of the plastic arts. We will find that the most plastic of the arts, architecture, is especially instructive" (GW 1, 139; Gadamer 2013, 135).

Gadamer focuses on the concept of "picture [*Bild*]," which, by leveraging the etymological meaning of German, can explain the aesthetics of the "figurative arts [*bildende*]" that include sculpture. In particular, Gadamer contrasts the Platonic concept of picture with its modern variation: the modern picture emblematically represents the procedure of aesthetic consciousness. Indeed, it appears to be immediately "usable," in a manner that is totally disconnected from its context, as happens when a picture is placed in art galleries. "Such pictures," Gadamer observes, "apparently have nothing about them of the objective dependence on mediation that we emphasized in the case of drama and music . . . The 'picture' thus appears to confirm the immediacy of aesthetic consciousness and its claim to universality" (GW 1, 139–40; Gadamer 2013, 136). At first sight, picture could apparently act as the confirmation of "aesthetic differentiation," and for this reason it represents a fundamental challenge in Gadamer's theory.

It is at this point that Gadamer develops a long analysis of picture, pointing out that "the intention of the present conceptual analysis, however, has to do not with theory of art but with ontology" (GW 1, 138; Gadamer 2013, 141). In fact, the analysis of the pictorial work is based on the relationship between the "original [*Ur-bild*]" and the "picture [*Bild*]" of that original—which is different from a mere "copy [*Ab-Bild*]"—with a view to showing the ontological primacy of the picture as well as conveying the rootedness of painting in its world, as opposed to aesthetic differentiation. However, as I will try to show, it is possible to respond to the so-called separatist notion of art without referring to its potential ontological bearing and picking instead the thread of play from its anthropological foundation.

To sum up, according to Gadamer, the picture does not constitute a diminution of what it represents; on the contrary, it makes the original true to the highest degree: "Every such presentation is an ontological event and occupies the same ontological level as what is represented" (GW 1, 145; Gadamer 2013, 141). On this basis, Gadamer upholds the well-known theory of picture as "an increase in being" of the original. By explicitly referring to the Neoplatonic tradition, he states that "the content of the picture itself is ontologically defined as an emanation of the original." This is a point that, after being thematized in the first part of *Truth and Method*, also reappears in the final pages of the book, where Gadamer refers to beauty as the "idea of 'shining [*scheinen*]' . . . Beauty has the mode of being of light" (GW 1, 486; Gadamer 2013, 489). According to him, the sacred image can aptly explain the essence of art: "But, as we know, only the religious picture (*Bild*: also, image) displays the full ontological power of the picture" (GW 1, 147; Gadamer 2013, 143). Gadamer thus goes so far as to claim that "a work of art always has something sacred about it" (GW 1, 155; Gadamer 2013, 150), for the sacred always has a connection to the profane, the latter being inevitably defined in opposition to the sacred.

It is at this point that Gadamer's argumentation shows a reversal in the interpretive paradigm he had employed thus far. In fact, previously he had aimed to show how the concept of play also fits the figurative arts, while now the ontological concept of picture is used as a new criterion, to be extended to the other arts as well.[9] In other words, the picture, which at first glance might appear to be the least suitable notion for a reading of "aesthetic non-differentiation," instead becomes the preferred paradigm, especially when it comes to the representation of religious subjects, where the ontological scope would be brought into sharper focus. So, a contrast seems to exist between a modern reading of the picture, as uprooted from its context, and the resurgence of a Neoplatonic tradition, based on the ontological bearing of the picture. Indeed, in those pages Gadamer can state that "the work of art is conceived as an event of being [*Seinsvorgang*], and the abstraction performed by aesthetic differentiation is dissolved" (GW 1, 156; Gadamer 2013, 151).

Truth and Method thus seems to display two different paradigms of art: a *performative* one, based on the model of play, and an *ontological* one, centered on the model of picture. In this regard, an expert interpreter of Gadamer like Günter Figal has focused on the centrality and irreducibility of the concept of image-picture with respect to that of play: the former has the merit of recalling the "objectivity" of art, as well as the difference existing among the different forms of art. Indeed, according to Figal, "contemplating a picture is different from performing a piece of music or a theatre play. Whereas a play or a piece of music, indeed, finds its actuality in performance, a picture has 'actuality' on its own terms" (Figal 2022, 175). In Figal's view, the concept of *Bild* runs contrary to the subjectivism that, for him, underlies the term *Vollzug*, understood as enactment, which involves the action of a subject who enacts or represents precisely that work of art: "The term is not felicitous, because *Vollzug* indicates a subjective activity rather than an actuality readers of pictures and poems would take part in; the meaning of the verb *vollziehen* is 'to carry out' or 'to execute,' and Gadamer certainly does not want to say that the actuality of pictures and poems is 'carried out' or 'executed.' Moreover, one can doubt whether Gadamer's view is convincing at all, and especially so in regard to pictures" (Figal 2022, 175). The answer to such objection is decisive in properly understanding what is meant by performative character: the painting or the literary text, as well as the properly performing arts, are not enacted, or represented *by* a subject. On the contrary, a performative reading that focuses on the concept of *Vollzug* stresses that it is in the *interaction* with the viewpoint of the observers or readers that art is such, that it becomes a work of art. To correctly understand the concept of performance, one has to focus on the relational essence of the artistic experience, where, if either pole is missing, the whole process, and thus the representation of the work, fails. This perfectly emerges in the prerogative of play: as stressed by Nielsen, "phenomenologically and hermeneutically, the play-movement is central to the game and to the work of art, as both are presented or come forth only through being played, performed, or enacted" (Nielsen 2022, 144). The presentation is essential to the work of art to such a point that "without the ongoing movement of play, the game ceases, and the artwork falls silent" (Nielsen 2022, 144).

Along these lines, it is possible to answer the question of the isolation and musealization of art in the modern world—which in the section of *Truth and Method* on the concept of picture is resolved by recalling the ontological matrix of the image and its sacred function—by referring instead to an alternative paradigm of art. Gadamer himself indeed stated: "Here it becomes clear why starting from the concept of play is methodologically advantageous" (GW 1, 139; Gadamer 2013, 120). In fact, the concept of play is capable of explaining that "the work of art cannot simply be isolated from the 'contingency' of the chance conditions in which it appears . . . It itself belongs to the world to which it represents itself" (GW 1, 139; Gadamer 2013, 120).

Reading as Performing

As I said before, Gadamer leverages the ontological concept of picture to overcome the aesthetics of *Erlebnis* and to recall the truthful, transformative, and continuist character of art. However, it should be noted that the same goal can be achieved by disregarding the ontological bearing and by focusing instead on the concept of play as the performative character of art in relation to the concept of reading. In *Truth and Method*, literature still plays a marginal role compared to the subsequent writings, where the tackling of poetic and literary texts becomes central, as highlighted by Gadamer's reading of Celan and Rilke, among others (see Gadamer 1997). This does not imply a *textualist* turn in Gadamerian texts, but rather seems to open Gadamer's philosophy towards a *performative* vision.[10]

Gadamer speaks of the performance as an inseparable aspect of the work itself: "It is in the performance [*Aufführung*] and only in it—as we see most clearly in the case of music—that we encounter the work itself" (GW 1, 121; Gadamer 1998, 120). In *Truth and Method*, Gadamer indeed already claimed that "the same is true for drama generally, *even considered as literature*" (GW 1, 121; Gadamer 2013, 120, emphasis added). As "a drama really exists only when it is played, and ultimately music must resound" (GW 1, 139; Gadamer 2013, 120), in the same way this applies to poetry as well: namely, even in the silent reading of poetry we hear the verses resonate and so poetry is "presented." This is a fundamental claim that Gadamer develops in various essays following *Truth and Method*, including the relevant writing "Music and Time. A Philosophical Postscript" (1988), where Gadamer explicitly draws a connection between music and literature by saying that "it is essential to let a text speak [*einen Text sprechen zu lassen*], perhaps even in front of others, the audience. To let a text speak—to be able to do that—we call interpretation. What one making music does and what the reader does in reading with understanding seems the same" (GW 8, 364; Gadamer 2021, 474). From this point of view, just as the performance of a musical piece is always an unrepeatable moment, similarly one who reads a poem multiple times will never understand the text identically, since with each new reading he or she will glimpse facets of it that he or she had never noticed before: this is the iterability of art that the concept of festival brought out.

In "Music and Time," the centrality of the concept of *performance* emerges as emblematic of the work of art. Indeed, Gadamer refers to the concept of *Vollzug* that, as the English translators of the essay have suggested, "is a central concept in Gadamer's writings on art and poses certain challenges for translation owing to its polysemic character, among them it can be translated as 'performance'" (Gadamer 2021, 472). Indeed, in that essay Gadamer explicitly maintains: "The word 'performance [*Vollzug*]' in this sense did not come to me randomly—a wonderful word, full of dialectical tension" (GW 8, 364; Gadamer 2013, 475).

Moreover, Gadamer claims that "as it is in poetry, so also in the prose of thought. There is still a something even in the sequence of dance moves or in the structured sequence of the image, sculpture, or architecture. That nothing stands except the moving itself that is the truth of performance [*Vollzug*] that music is" (GW 8, 365; Gadamer 2021, 475–76). Namely, every art is rooted in performance, something that music (or, we can say, performative arts) more emblematically expresses. It is no coincidence that the ninth volume of Gadamer's *Gesammelte Werke*, entirely dedicated to his interpretations of various poets, is entitled *Hermeneutik im Vollzug*; moreover, the centrality of this term also emerges in an important late essay such as "The Artwork in Word and Image: 'So True, So Full of Being!'" (1992),[11] where Gadamer declares *Vollzug* to be a fundamental characteristic of art along with *Zeitlichkeit*: "Art has its 'being' in the performance [*Die Kunst ist im Vollzug*]" (GW 8, 319; Gadamer 2007, 215).

Here, we can see how in the works after *Truth and Method* a performative paradigm unfolds, based on the consideration of reading (including silent reading) as the enactment of the prose or poetic text.[12] The work must be read, that is, it must become *speaking*: this makes it possible to show how literary works can also be elucidated by the performative paradigm. However, even in the pages of *Truth and Method*, the central role that reading plays in literature had already emerged apropos of the relation between reading and literature: "Literature—say in its proper art form, the novel—has its original existence in *being read*, as that the epic has it in being declaimed by the rhapsodist or the picture in being looked at by the spectator" (GW 1, 166; Gadamer 2013, 160, emphasis added). Moreover, Gadamer claimed that "like a recitation [*der Vortrag*] or performance [*die Aufführung*], be read [*die Lektüre*] belongs to literature by its nature. They are stages of what is generally called 'reproduction' but that in fact is the *original* mode of being of all performing arts, and that mode of being has proved exemplary for defining the mode of being of *all art*" (GW 1, 166; Gadamer 2013, 160–61, trans. modified). In that vein, Risser has drawn attention to the concept of *Vollzug* (along with the notions of mimesis and transformation) as an element that is common to all the arts, to explain the dynamism and openness of the work of art, with special reference to poetry. According to Risser, "Gadamer describes the mode of being of the work of art in yet a third way as *Vollzug*. The German word does not easily translate into a single equivalent word in English. *Vollzug* conveys the sense of executing, performing, enacting in relation to a fulfilling accomplishment" (Risser 2022, 53).[13] In particular, Risser shows how this concept can also be deployed for poetry: "Music is to be heard, poetry is to be read, painting is to be viewed. The *Vollzug* is at once the interpretation that the interpreter attempts to follow along" (Risser 2022, 54).

Along these lines, Gadamer expresses himself in the epilogue to his book *Who Am I and Who Are You?* (1969), which can be considered a kind of programmatic statement of intent on the relationship between hermeneutics and the literary arts. Far from being a method of interpreting poems, hermeneutics focuses on the reader's point of view. Indeed, Gadamer emphasizes that, to truly understand a poem, one does not need a specialist understanding of the specific situation that gave rise to the work. Rather, the reader "need not to be scholarly, or especially learned. He or she must simply try to keep listening" (GW 9, 383; Gadamer 1997, 67), namely listening to the voice of the text through continuous reading. This is a point that Gadamer stresses in Celan's footsteps: "In response to inquiries, Celan often gave a single piece of advice: simply keep reading the poems again and again" (GW 9, 444; Gadamer 1997, 149).

On this basis, a fundamental hermeneutical criterion is introduced: "An interpretation is correct only when it is finally able to disappear completely, having entered completely into a new experience of the poem" (GW 9, 451; Gadamer 1997, 165). That is, the reading of the work, its performance, allows it to give rise to a new artistic creation, which changes according to the different readings provided. The work, understood as an "object," obviously remains the same, for example *that* text written by Celan: what changes, however, is the work of art, understood as an activity, which by *interacting with* the readers is modified and expanded every time.

This also shows the participatory nature of the work of art, to which both authors and readers contribute. The work is constructed through interaction with readers, and "we must trace the form out as we see it because we must construct it actively—something required by every composition, graphic or musical, in drama or in reading" (GW 8, 118; Gadamer 1998, 27). In this sense, in "The Relevance of the Beautiful" Gadamer makes the example of the famous staircase described in *The Brothers Karamazov*: everyone has the impression of seeing it clearly, but everyone will imagine the staircase differently (see GW 8, 118; Gadamer 1998, 27). In fact, what is told by the novel unfolds the space of freedom left by the work of art, which the reader is called to fill, giving rise to a new artistic creation each time.

Reading Pictures and Buildings: Against the Aesthetic Differentiation

That being said, the criterion of reading as performance can also be transferred to the figurative arts. Indeed, Gadamer states that "similarly in the visual arts. A synthetic act is required in which we must unite and bring together many different aspects. We 'read' a picture, as we say, like a text. We start to 'decipher' a picture like a text" (GW 8, 118; Gadamer 1998, 27). In his later essays, indeed, Gadamer specifically focuses on the concept of reading, not as "the mere sequencing of word after word after word. This is spelling out or repeating after" (GW 8, 276; Gadamer 2022, 207). Rather, reading is reassessed as "a quiet way of letting something speak again, and this presupposes the anticipations of the understanding" (GW 8, 276; Gadamer 2022, 207). Reading thus acquires a universal value to such an extent that Gadamer emphatically claims: "All our experience is reading. It is a reading out [*Auslesen*] of that to which we are directed and reading oneself [*Einlesen*] in the whole that is so articulated. Thus, reading too, which makes us familiar with poetry, helps existence become livable" (GW, 8, 278; Gadamer 2022, 209).

The criterion applied here to explain the figurative arts is not the ontological criterion of the work of art as emanation, but rather that of the reading of the work of art, understood as its enactment. Gadamer explicitly took position on the connection between the concepts of *Vollzug* and reading: "I have focused on the concept of reading in order to distinguish clearly between the externality of what merely exists—for example, the colours or words or letters—and what the concept of *Vollzug* has to show us" (GW 8, 393; Gadamer 2007, 218). An unplayed score or an unread novel would not be a work of art. Reading the literary work constitutes its representation, which changes according to the reader's perspective: similarly, for painting or in general for the figurative arts.[14]

This is not, however, as Figal claimed, a relapse into a subjectivist dimension whereby the painting, or the work in general, would subsist only thanks to a subject who enacts it. The painting or the literary text, as well as the properly performing arts, are not enacted, or represented by a subject; rather, it is their interaction with the viewpoint of the viewer or reader that makes them proper works of art. The point is that the painting, as well as literature, becomes a work of art only in the interaction with the viewer's point of view. Only by drawing attention to the processual aspect of the work can we avoid falling into a subjectivist reading, criticized by Gadamer in the first place.

According to Gadamer, the same can be said of architecture, and consequently we can learn to read buildings as artistic works. In his essay "On the Reading of Buildings and Paintings" (1979), he explicitly declares that

> it is also true of the work of the plastic arts that one must learn to see it and that it is not in the naïve gaze at the visible whole which stands before us that the work is readily understood, that is to say: experienced as an answer to a question. We will have to "read" it; we will have indeed to spell it until we are able to read it. The same is true for architecture: we must "read" it. (GW 8, 334; Gadamer 2022, 97)

In this sense, "we must take advantage of these analogies between a work of literature and the creations of the plastic arts" (GW 8, 334; Gadamer 2022, 334). The concept of reading can account for the anti-subjectivist, relational, and societal character of the concept of play as *Darstellung*, hinting at the ineradicable relationship of a work of art with its world. A work of art, whether literary or figurative, cannot be art without a relationship with the spectators. As Di Cesare pointed out, reading becomes emblematic of understanding in its dialogical sense: "For the later Gadamer, reading, that is, giving voice, expands until it coincides with hermeneutics itself" (Di Cesare 2013, 65).

The focus on reading thus does not imply a process of flat appropriation, but rather an interaction between different points of view: reading often also implies going back through the reading to better understand a particular passage. As we read, we perceive that "a horizon of anticipation has not been fulfilled. This is like a shock. We go back. We read one more time, we rectify, we change the emphasis and all of those things that we all know bring something written or printed again to speech" (GW 8, 336; Gadamer 2022, 99). It is the shock of understanding that characterizes the relationship with the works of art as well as with every otherness in general. On the spur of that shock, we go back and reread the work and we learn new aspects of it, giving it a new form, constituting an inexhaustible process.

It is via this concept of reading that the literary and figurative arts can also be thought of as performative. Reading is neither a mere deciphering of texts (a kind of philological methodology) nor an appropriation of a final meaning of a work of art. It is instead the infinite process of presentation and understanding of art that has its counterparts in philosophical dialogues as a performance of philosophy itself. The performative reading makes it possible to rethink the work of art, not as a definite object that can be isolated from everyday experience, but as movement and interaction involving the audience, opening up important and promising paths for stressing the democratic relevance of Gadamerian aesthetics and its social implications, as a horizontal praxis involving the audience in an anti-elitist way.

Notes

1. See Vattimo 1997. Vattimo places the tradition of Nietzsche and Heidegger at the centre of hermeneutics, providing an interpretation of Gadamer's philosophy through the lens of "weak thought," to which Gadamer has often been erroneously assimilated.

2. See their speeches on the occasion of the celebration of Gadamer's one hundredth anniversary in Heidelberg: Rorty 2004, 21–29, and Vattimo 2001, 60–67.

3. See Grondin 2013; Grondin 2018; Grondin 2019. See also the volume Grondin 2020.

4. The concept of "performative" originated in analytical circles from the work of Austin 1962. It has since been transposed to numerous areas: the "performative turn" in aesthetics, in particular, refers to a conception that spread at the end of the twentieth century with respect to art as opposed to hermeneutics, in which the latter was conceived, however, as based on an idea of art that reduces the artwork to the text and to the mere artistic "object." In particular, Hülk 2004 openly stated that the "performative" paradigm was to be understood as opposed to deconstructive and hermeneutic conceptions.

5. A similar *desideratum* also emerged in the introduction to Malpas and Zabala 2010, XVIII: "Understood as indeed a mode of philosophical 'praxis,' one of the consequences of hermeneutics is that it becomes real only in its 'performance'—only in the hermeneutic 'act' or 'event.'"

6. On the role of music in hermeneutics, see Benson 2003; Bertinetto 2022; McAuliffe 2023.

7. "Instead, the work of art has its true being in the fact that it becomes an experience that changes the person who experiences it [*die den Erfahrenden verwandelt*]" (GW 1, 108; Gadamer 2013, 107). A reflection on the concepts of *Erlebnis-Erfahrung* was already central in Heidegger's works on art (see Heidegger 1971 and 1979) and was later developed by Gadamer. On this topic, see Davey 2016.

8. The social and democratic character of the festival in Gadamer's thought has also been stressed by an author from a different background, the pragmatist philosopher Richard Shusterman, according to whom "[t]he aspect of art as festival reinforces art's value as a unifying medium which 'unites us in its communicative dimension.' Here, Gadamer tries to overcome the Marxist allegation of art as an oppressive enemy of the people, dividing society by appealing to (and serving) only the cultural elite" (Shusterman 1988, 752). On this point, see also Grondin 2001, 43–50 and Walhof 2017. For a reassessment of Gadamer's thought against a conservative reading and its opening to social and political questions (in dialogue with Arendt, McDowell, and Rorty), see Marino 2011 and 2015.

9. For a reading that developed the concept of *Bild*, see Boehm 1987.

10. Differently, according to Figal, "introducing the paradigm of theatre play Gadamer had marginalized this product character of artworks, pictures included, already in *Truth and Method*. He could apply this paradigm to pictures only with the assumption that pictures, albeit produced, mainly are self-manifestations of someone so that in contemplating a picture one would take part in this self-manifestation. However, in abandoning this idea, Gadamer conceives the actuality of pictures only as that of their 'reading,' to which the essence of pictures is reduced" (Figal 2022, 175).

11. This text has been regarded as a watershed in Gadamer's concept. However, in a different way, Tate 2012 argues, as I do, that the conception of art as *Vollzug* already features in embryo in *Truth and Method* and is then explored in later writings.

12. This peculiar notion of reading as a sort of performance was partly developed by the so-called Konstanz School of reception aesthetics, as it features in authors such as Iser 1984 and Jauss 1991. For an anthropological reading of Jauss, see Dreon 2012.

13. On the polyvalence of this word, Risser recalls Heidegger's influence and the connection with that of *energeia*: "In 'The Artwork in Word and Image,' Gadamer tells us that *Vollzug* captures the meaning of the Greek *energeia*. In the philosophical tradition *energeia* is usually translated in English as actuality, but in Aristotle's use of the term, *energeia* does not mean simply an accomplished reality, but a reality in relation to an end [*telos*] within itself. A better English translation of this word, as we see in the translations of Joe Sachs, would be (reality) being-at-work, an actualizing actuality, so to speak" (Risser 2022, 53). On this topic, see also Tate 2001.

14. On the role of the contemporary pictures in Gadamer's aesthetics, see Tate 2001, 56–68.

Bibliography

Austin, John L. *How to Do Things with Words*. Oxford: Oxford University Press, 1962.
Benson, Bruce E. *The Improvisation of Musical Dialogue: A Phenomenology of Music*. Cambridge: Cambridge University Press, 2003.
Bertinetto, Alessandro. *Aesthetics of Improvisation*. Leiden–München: Brill–Fink, 2022.
———. "Performing the Unexpected. Improvisation and Artistic Creativity." *Daimon* 57 (2012): 61–79.
Bertram, Georg W. *Art as Human Praxis. An Aesthetics*. Translated by N. Ross. New York: Bloomsbury, 2019.
Boehm, Gottfried. "Zu einer Hermeneutik des Bildes." In *Seminar: Die Hermeneutik und die Wissenschaften*. Edited by H.-G. Gadamer and G. Boehm. Frankfurt a.M.: Suhrkamp, 1978.
Caputo, John D. *Radical Hermeneutics. Repetition, Deconstruction, and the Hermeneutic Project*. Bloomington: Indiana University Press, 1987.
Cull Ó Maoilearca, Laura, and Alice Lagaay, eds. *The Routledge Companion to Performance Philosophy*. London–New York: Routledge, 2020.
Davey, Nicholas. "Lived Experience Erlebnis and Erfahrung." In *The Blackwell Companion to Hermeneutics*. Edited by N. Keane and C. Lawn, 326–32. Chichester, West Sussex: Wiley, 2016.
Di Cesare, Donatella. *Gadamer. A Philosophical Portrait*. Bloomington–Indianapolis: Indiana University Press, 2013.

Dreon, Roberta. "Leggere, comunicare, fare: Wolfgang Iser dalla teoria della letteratura all'antropologia." *Ermeneutica letteraria* VIII (2012): 105–114.

Figal, Günter. "Image (Picture)." In *The Gadamerian Mind*. Edited by T. George and G.-J. van der Heiden, 165–76. New York: Routledge, 2022.

Fischer-Lichte, Erika. *The Transformative Power of Performance. A New Aesthetics*. Translated by S. I. Jain. New York: Routledge, 2008.

Gadamer, Hans-Georg. *Ethics and Aesthetics in History. The Selected Writings of Hans-Georg Gadamer. Vol. 2*. Translated and edited by P. Vandevelde and A. Iyer. Bloomsbury: London, 2022.

———. *Gadamer on Celan. "Who Am I and Who Are You?" and Other Essays*. Translated by R. Heinemann and B. Krajewski. Albany: State University of New York Press, 1997.

———. *Gesammelte Werke* [GW]. 10 vols. Tübingen: Mohr Siebeck, 1985–1995.

———. *Literature and Philosophy in Dialogue. Essays in German Literary Theory*. Translated by R. H. Paslick. Albany: State University of New York Press, 1994.

———. "Music and Time. A Philosophical Postscript (1988)." Translated by C. R. Nielsen and D. Liakos. *Epoché: A Journal for the History of Philosophy* 26, no. 1 (2021): 251–58.

———. "The Eminent Text and Its Truth." Translated by G. Waite. *The Bulletin of the Midwest Modern Language Association* 13, no. 1 (1980): 3–10.

———. *The Gadamer Reader: A Bouquet of the Later Writings*. Translated and edited by R. E. Palmer. Evanston: Northwestern University Press, 2007.

———. *The Relevance of the Beautiful and Other Essays*. Translated by N. Walker. Edited by R. Bernasconi. Cambridge: Cambridge University Press, 1998.

———. *Truth and Method*. Revised ed. Translated by J. Weinsheimer and D. G. Marshall. New York: Bloomsbury, 2013.

Grondin, Jean. *Du sens de choses. L'idée de la métaphysique*. Paris: PUF, 2013.

———. "Gadamer's Basic Understanding of Understanding." In *The Cambridge Companion to Gadamer*. Edited by R. J. Dostal, 36–51. Cambridge–New York: Cambridge University Press, 2002.

———, ed. "Herméneutique et métaphysique. Une articulation renouvelée." *Le cercle Herméneutique* 34–35 (2020): 9–134.

———. *La beauté de la métaphysique. Essais sur ses piliers herméneutiques*. Paris: PUF, 2019.

———. "The Metaphysical Dimension of Hermeneutics." In *Hermeneutics and Phenomenology*. Edited by P. Fairfield, 125–37. Bloomsbury: London, 2018.

———. "Play, Festival, and Ritual in Gadamer. On the Theme of the Immemorial in His Later Works." In *Language and Linguisticality in Gadamer's Hermeneutics*. Edited by L. K. Schmidt, 43–50. Lanham. Lexington Books, 2001.

Habermas, Jürgen. "Der Universalitätsanspruch der Hermeneutik." In *Hermeneutik und Ideologiekritik*. Edited by K. O. Apel, 121–59. Frankfurt a.M.: Suhrkamp, 1973.

Heidegger, Martin. *Nietzsche I: The Will to Power as Art*. Translated by D. F. Krell. New York: Harper & Row, 1979.

———. *Poetry, Language, Thought*. Translated by A. Hofstadter. New York: Harper & Row, 1971.

Hülk, Walburga. "Paradigma Performativität?" In *Avantgarde, Medien, Performativität. Inszenierungs- und Wahrnehmungsmuster zu Beginn des 20. Jahrhundert*. Edited by M. Erstić, G. Schuhen, and T. Schwan, 9–26. Bielefeld: Transcript, 2004.

Iser, Wolfgang. *Der Akt des Lesens*. Paderborn: Wilhelm Fink, 1976.

Jauss, Hans Robert. *Ästhetische Erfahrung und literarische Hermeneutik*. Frankfurt a.M.: Suhrkamp, 1991.

Malpas, Jeff, and Santiago Zabala, eds. *Consequences of Hermeneutics. Fifty Years after Gadamer's Truth and Method*. Evanston: Northwestern University Press, 2010.

Marino, Stefano. *Aesthetics, Metaphysics, Language: Essays on Heidegger and Gadamer*. Newcastle: Cambridge Scholar Publishing, 2015.

———. *Gadamer and the Limits of the Modern Techno-Scientific Civilization*. Bern–Berlin–Bruxelles–Frankfurt a.M.–New York–Oxford–Wien: Peter Lang, 2011.

McAuliffe, Sam. *Improvisation in Music and Philosophical Hermeneutics*. London: Bloomsbury, 2023.

Nielsen, Cynthia R. *Gadamer's Hermeneutical Aesthetics. Art as a Performative, Dynamic, Communal Event*. New York: Routledge, 2023.

———. "Gadamer on Play and the Play of Art." In *The Gadamerian Mind*. Edited by T. George and G.-J. van der Heiden, 139–54. New York: Routledge, 2022.

Risser, James. "The Poetic Word, Art, and the Arts." In *The Gadamerian Mind*. Edited by T. George, and G.-J. van der Heiden, 49–60. New York: Routledge, 2022.

Romagnoli, Elena. "The Hermeneutics of Performance and the Performance of Hermeneutics. Music as a Paradigm for Gadamer's Conception of Art." In *Gadamer, Music & Philosophical Hermeneutics*. Edited by S. McAuliffe, 257–72. Cham: Springer, 2024.

———. *Oltre l'opera d'arte. L'estetica performativa di Gadamer tra idealismo e pragmatismo*. Pisa: ETS, 2023.

Rorty, Richard. "Being That Can Be Understood Is Language." In *Gadamer's Repercussions: Reconsidering Philosophical Hermeneutics*. Edited by B. Krajewski, 21–29. Berkeley: University of California Press, 2004.

Ruta, Marcello. "Hermeneutics and the Performative Turn: The Unfruitfulness of a Complementary Characterisation." *Proceedings of the European Society for Aesthetics* 10 (2018): 557–97.

Shusterman, Richard. "'Review' of Hans-Georg Gadamer." *The Relevance of the Beautiful and Other Essays*. *History of European Ideas* 9, no. 6 (1988): 751–52.

Tate, Daniel L. "In the Fullness of Time: Gadamer and the Temporal Dimension of the Work of Art." *Research in Phenomenology* 42, no. 1 (2012): 92–113.

———. "The Speechless Image. Gadamer and the Claim of Modern Painting." *Philosophy Today* 45 (2001): 56–68.

Vattimo, Gianni. *Beyond Interpretation: The Meaning of Hermeneutics for Philosophy*. Translated by D. Webb. Stanford: Stanford University Press, 1997.

———. "Interpretare il mondo è cambiare il mondo." In *"L'essere, che può essere compreso, è linguaggio." Omaggio a Hans-Georg Gadamer*. Edited by D. Di Cesare, 60–67. Genova: Il melangolo, 2001.

Walhof, Darren. *The Democratic Theory of Hans-Georg Gadamer*. London: Palgrave Macmillan, 2017.

9

On the Challenge of Poetry to Thought
A Gadamerian Perspective

Gert-Jan van der Heiden

Poetry poses a particular challenge to thought. Gadamer's reflections on the poetic word in several essays included in the eighth and ninth volumes of his *Gesammelte Werke* (respectively, *Ästhetik und Poetik I* and *II*) attest to this challenge. In this contribution, I aim to examine in some detail how Gadamer understands the relation between poetics and philosophical hermeneutics and explicate the implied challenge of poetry for thought. As an avid reader of the modern lyrical poem, Gadamer often suggests that this challenge finds its culmination point in this form of poetry and the modern experience of world and language of which this poetry attests. The question of how and why the lyrical poem intensifies this challenge and at the same time exemplifies the philosophical hermeneutic conception of the poem, can only be addressed after a detour in which we first establish the contours of Gadamer's account of the relationship of philosophy and poetry and offer an explication of the nature of the poem and the poetic word.

These ideas are developed in two steps. First, I discuss in general terms the particular ambiguity that Gadamer discerns in the relationship of poetry and philosophy and show how he aims to account for it. Second, I discuss what I call the *inventio* of the poem. *Inventio* is a particular fertile notion, coined in classical rhetoric, and has the double, ambivalent sense of both discovery and invention. Under the heading of discovery, I discuss the particular claim to truth of the poem and of the poetic word. Gadamer's account of this truth is complicated but essential to capture the philosophical relevance of the poem. Under the heading of invention, I discuss the poem as a configuration or composition and I do so especially in terms of the notion of order [*Ordnung*]: as a composition, the poem is an order and attests itself to the order that it is. Especially this notion of order enables a proper analysis of the particular challenge posed by the lyrical poem. I conclude with that analysis.

Profound Difference and Close Proximity: On the Relation of Poetry and Philosophy

Hölderlin's famous description, as recalled by Heidegger (1976, 312), portrays thinking and poeticizing, *Denken* and *Dichten*, as neighbors in the realm of language; they live in close proximity but also dwell on the most separate mountains. Gadamer's account of the relationship between poetry and philosophy emphasizes a similar ambivalence and offers a concrete and clear interpretation of what this proximity and difference exactly consist in.[1] For him, the linguistic form that poetry and philosophy adopt as poem and dialogue, respectively, position them as two "extreme cases within the large domain of linguistic forms" (GW 9, 336, my translation). Yet, the poetic word also includes an interpretive moment, and this moment brings poetry and thought closer together than one might have anticipated (GW 8, 22). These short observations provide us with the two basic questions guiding this first section: What exactly is the difference in linguistic form between the poem and the dialogue? What is the interpretative moment of the poem, bringing it close to thought?

The Movement and the Standing of Language

In an image borrowed from Paul Valéry, to which Gadamer (e.g., GW 8, 19, 59, 233; GW 9, 362) often returns, apophantic language, whether in an everyday, scientific, or philosophic context, erases and withdraws itself when showing the particular subject matter [*Sache*] about which it speaks. Apophantic language is thus like a coin that represents a particular value of gold but is not the gold itself. For Gadamer, this image is not meant to evoke the suggestion that apophantic language is a mere sign system. By contrast, it means for him that what is shown and what is understood in apophantic language, is not simply this word or that linguistic expression, but rather the subject matter about which is spoken. The very being and essence of apophantic language consists in the showing and presenting of that which is spoken about to a listener or reader. In fact, as soon as these linguistic utterances draw the attention to themselves rather than to the subject matter they are supposed to disclose, language falls prey to its *Unwesen*, its non-essence and untruth. This happens, for instance, when people repeat linguistic utterances without understanding the subject matter they are supposed to disclose. In such instances, as Heidegger (1977a, §44b) already suggested, the utterance is dealt with as a being *separate* from the subject matter it is supposed to show in its discoveredness. This separation of word from subject matter makes it possible to conceive of language as a mere sign system in the first place. In this conception, the word is understood as a separate being only arbitrarily linked as a sign to another being. Yet, for Gadamer, this separation is the very moment in which the inner spiritual relation of the word to the subject matter is lost and forgotten (GW 1, 409–10): the very essence of the word consists in the presentation [*Darstellung*] of its subject matter. Consequently, apophantic language has its truth in its disclosive nature. Thus, the forgetfulness or withdrawal of language is productive here, since it allows a particular subject matter to show itself, to preserve its disclosedness, and to be shared. By contrast, when the word or linguistic utterance insists on itself or is dealt with as a being in itself, separate from its subject matter, language deteriorates in its non-essence.

In poetic language, however, the word is present in a different way. In the poem, it is the word itself that matters; the poetic word is Valéry's gold itself. This means in particular that the poetic word should not fade away, but should rather hold out, insist on itself, and *stand*: "The poem does not stand before us as a thing that someone employs to tell us something. It stands there equally independent of both reader and poet. Detached from all intending, the word is complete in itself [*Das Gedicht steht vor uns nicht als etwas da, womit jemand etwas sagen möchte. Es steht in sich da. Dem Dichtenden wie dem Aufnehmenden steht es in gleicher Weise gegenüber. Abgelöst von allem Meinen ist es ganz, ganz Wort!*]" (GW 8, 72; Gadamer 1986, 107).[2] Yet, what does it exactly mean that the poetic word stands and that it shows and insists on itself? In light of the possibility of decline that inhabits apophantic language, it might be helpful to emphasize that, for Gadamer, the poetic word stands and shows itself *as word* and *not as (linguistic) sign*. Unlike a sign, a word is marked by an inner unity with the subject matter and, unlike a sign, which only refers or signifies in one way or another, the essence of a word affirms this unity being the presentation [*Darstellung*] of the subject matter [*Sache*]. Differently put, the linguistic utterance and the word in general concern the very appearance of the subject matter; yet, this appearance does not supplement, as another, separate being, the subject matter; rather, the linguistic appearance is itself *of* the subject matter and is a modality of its very being.[3] From these preliminary remarks, one could derive a first formal determination of what it means that the poetic word stands as word: it does not erase itself to present its subject matter *because the nature and essence of the word itself is the subject matter of the poetic word*. The poetic word speaks of the word and of its unity with the subject matter as such and in general.

Yet, let us take a step back to get a better sense of this particular expression to characterize the poetic word, quite dear to Gadamer and often repeated by him: *das Wort steht*. The verb *stehen*, just as the English "to stand," has a vast semantic field, so in order to grasp the semantic subfield to which Gadamer alludes when using it for the linguistic nature of a text or a poetic word, one should note that, in its most elementary sense, the expression *it stands* concerns the specific ground that a word may offer. For example, when someone gives their word, this word is the ground of the promise and the one who receives such a promise will hold the other to their word. The written word—and being part of literature, the poetic word belongs to the realm of the written word—offers another example: it provides a specific ground to which we may always return when reading and interpreting a text. In English, one would say: "But this is what the text says." In German, however, one can use the verb *stehen*, as Gadamer for instance writes in one of his interpretations of Celan: "So aber steht es im Text" (GW 9, 446). The word that is used—in German one could again say: *das Wort daß da steht*—or the expression that is written is the ultimate ground of appeal that offers the interpreter a particular hold.[4] The same sense resounds in the famous Lutheran phrase used in reference to the Bible: "It is written"; or, rather: "Es steht geschrieben." The script, the word of Scripture is ultimately prescription, *Vorschrift* (see also GW 9, 373–75), on which the reader must and can rely as the ultimate ground of appeal.

It is in this sense that Gadamer considers the poem [*Gedicht*] and the dialogue [*Gespräch*] to be two extreme cases among the plurality of linguistic forms (GW 9, 335–39). To think is to be moved by what one encounters and this movement is a striving to understand, which is nothing less than the life of understanding (Risser 2012, 63–65). Dialogue is the linguistic form and appearance of thought's movement, namely the to-and-fro of *Wort* and *Antwort*, word and response (GW 9, 338). Similarly, in the hermeneutic dialogue with a text and in the hermeneutic experience of tradition, the text is understood as a partner in conversation who has something to say to me that I did not anticipate. In this sense, interpretation and understanding themselves are marked by this lively to-and-fro movement. However, as soon as one shifts one's attention from how the interpreter is moved when striving to understand toward the way in which the word in its most true or eminent sense addresses us, the focus changes from interpreting and the to-and-fro movement of language to saying [*sagen*], which is the verb Gadamer uses to distinguish how the word addresses and to characterize the very mode of being of the word: "Wort sein heißt sagend sein" (GW 8, 40), "To be a word means to be a word that speaks, a *telling* word" (Gadamer 2002, 118; note that the verb *sagen* is not rendered here as "to say," but rather paraphrased as "to speak" and "to be telling").

What does Gadamer exactly have in mind when he uses the everyday verb *sagen*, "to say," to capture the essence of the word and why is the standing poetic word "saying" in an eminent sense? The somewhat complex linguistic and etymological connections may offer a first orientation to these questions. First, the German noun *Sage* translates the Greek *muthos*. When Heidegger and Gadamer both characterize the essence of poetry in terms of *Sage*, they mean to connect the particular power of expression of this German word to the sense and role of *muthos* in ancient Greek thought and culture. Second, the German *Dichtung*—poetry, poetics, or even literature—is etymologically derived from *dictare*, to prescribe, but unlike the German *Vorschrift* or the English *prescription*, the Latin verb does not refer to writing; instead, it is derived from *dicere*, to say (Heidegger 1999, 29; Nancy 2015, 209–10).

These connections elucidate how, for Gadamer, the saying of an eminent word is binding and compelling up to the point of being a prescription. This is why the word that stands is saying in this eminent sense. The poetic word is not up for negotiation. In the to-and-fro movement of dialogue, other words can be chosen and found to be more adequate and up to the task to present the subject matter under discussion. The poetic word, by contrast, stands and cannot be substituted or supplemented by any other word. It is in this sense that poetic saying dictates and binds; and it can maintain this character because the poetic word is fixed and, hence, strictly repeatable (GW 9, 339).

This intrinsic connection of saying to standing in the eminent word allows us to draw out two more characteristics of what it means "to be saying." The poetic word stands on its own, it is *selbstständig*: independent, autonomous, and self-reliant; and it is *vollständig*: complete and whole without needing anything outside itself to either verify or supplement it, as Gadamer (GW 8, 74–75) insists. *Selbstständigkeit* and *Vollständigkeit*, notions that vary on *stehen*, thus further explicate the sense of saying [*Sage*] that Gadamer awards to the poetic word and that marks for him the very sense of the adjective "true" in the expression "the true word": "It is a saying that says so completely what it is that we do not need to add anything beyond what is said in order to accept it in its reality as language . . . The poetic word is thus a statement [*Aussage*] in that it [*diese Sage*] bears witness to itself and does not admit anything that might verify it" (GW 8, 75; Gadamer 1986, 110). Gadamer's suggestion that the poetic word is complete and self-sufficient and attests only to itself and to nothing else has important implications for the attitude of the listener. Elsewhere, Gadamer (GW 1, 344–45) notes that historians try to go back behind the texts because these texts express something beyond that which they are saying—they are the expression [*Ausdruck*], for instance, of an ideology or of the spirit of the times. This surplus of expression can only be accounted for and deciphered by a critical interpreter, by a master of suspicion who is hardly interested in what the text attests itself but only in what it expresses despite itself. Such interpreters, however, no longer approach the text *as a word* but only *as a sign or symptom* pointing towards something else. Much of what Gadamer writes here in relation to the poetic word, to how it stands and says, can be read as a rejection of the claim that this mode of suspicious critical interpretation can do justice to what the word itself *is*. This mode of interpretation is only possible when it is taken for granted that language is made up of signs. For Gadamer, however, the poem that stands and insists on itself, is the locus in language where the mode of being of the word is preserved most purely. The word *as word* requires not the attitude of the critic but rather that of the listeners who place themselves in the horizon opened up by what the word says. Perhaps, despite the impact of critical thought on literary theory in the last decades, the recent post-critical turn is capable of teaching us again what Gadamer has always defended, namely that the word in its most eminent sense is independent and complete, attests only to itself, and needs nothing beyond itself.

ORIENTATION AND PLURIVOCITY

The Dutch poet Martinus Nijhoff, the grandson of the founder of the publishing house with the same name, wrote the famous lines: "Lees maar, er staat niet wat er staat," which I would translate, perhaps somewhat unpoetically, as: "Just read, it does not say what it says," while adding that in the Dutch, as in the German, the verb that is rendered as "to say" is again "to stand [*staan* or *stehen*]." The poetic word stands since it is written. Yet, it is impossible to simply identify what the word says—"er staat niet wat er staat [it does not say what it says]." This simple phrase from Nijhoff's *Awater* allows us to point to a basic similarity between poeticizing and interpreting, despite the profound difference between the linguistic forms of the poem and the philosophical dialogue.

This similarity can be brought to light once we discern that philosophical thinking cannot be reduced to the goal of reaching a concept. For a philosophy that aims to arrive at a univocal concept and that can only move within the realm of univocity, every ambiguity or plurivocity is confusing and needs to be overcome. However, when confronted with the excess of sense or meaning in a poem, we do not confront an *arbitrary* surplus over what can be determined univocally. Perceived in light of the goal to reach a concept with one, univocal sense, the poem might be experienced as *disorienting* and as *non-sense* to the extent that it resists identification, that is, as long as it insists on not saying what it says. However, as Gadamer notes, the poem is the exact opposite of disorientation and non-sense. The poem does disclose a particular *orientation* and it does point in a particular direction [*Richtungssinn*] (GW 8, 20). In fact, this is *exactly* what it does and is. To orient is not to identify or pinpoint, but it is to open up a plurality of sense, a *Vieldeutigkeit*.

The poem thus invents—in the original sense of the Latin *inventio*: discovers and creates—a new orientation for sense and opens a particular plurality of sense. Here, the insistence on sense rather than non-sense is crucial. Because it concerns sense, the poem can be understood. Yet, understanding here is not being oriented towards the explication of a univocal meaning. Therefore, Gadamer would never agree with one of Ricoeur's somewhat remarkable characterizations of interpretation, namely: "Interpretation is the work of the concept" (Ricoeur 1975, 383). Instead, Gadamer notes that *deuten*, to interpret, is a particular mode of thinking that strives to attune to the orientation and direction invented by the poem: "We may well ask whether we can interpret such ambiguity except by revealing that ambiguity [*ob man das Vieldeutige im Grunde überhaupt anders deuten kann, als indem man es in seiner Vieldeutigkeit offenbar macht*]" (GW 8, 20; Gadamer 1986, 69). Although phrased in a modest, questioning way, this citation offers a crucial determination of interpretation as a mode of the human capacity to think. The task of thinking when interpreting a poem is not to overcome ambiguity, but to manifest and elucidate it as orientation and plurality of sense. Thinking does not aim to reduce the poem to a concept that identifies univocally its linguistic images and figures, but rather aims to place the reader in the orientation the poem evokes and to point in its direction of meaning. Interpretation is thus neither conceptual nor in the service of the concept, but its task is rather to make the reader responsive to the poem's address and to allow the reader to share in the open orientation of sense the poem invented. Thus, a remarkable parallel exists with Gadamer's account of experience. Against a whole philosophical tradition, he maintains that the completion of experience is not found in the concept; rather, it is found in an attitude of openness and receptivity for other sense (GW 1, 361; van der Heiden 2021, 198–202); similarly, *Deuten* or interpreting (GW 8, 18–24) is not striving towards the concept, but is concerned with manifesting the poetic plurivocity of sense and thus with placing the reader in the open orientation to sense that the poem is.

The *Inventio* of the Poem: On Truth and Order

Looking back on our reflections on how Gadamer sees the relation between philosophy and poetry, one might be inclined to take a step back and wonder: "This is all very well, but *why* should we be interested in the multiplicity of meaning and sense the poem has to offer? Does the univocity of the concept not offer thinking a much more solid grasp and ground? So why this concern with poetic plurivocity?" It seems to me that Gadamer's response is characteristic for his approach to art in general and poetry in particular: "The ambiguity of the poetic word answers to the ambiguity of human life in general, and therein lies its unique value" (GW 8, 23; Gadamer 1986, 71, translation modified). There is thus a truth claim in the poem. The plurivocity of the poem is not simply a merely linguistic phenomenon, but rather mirrors the ambiguity of human existence and presents it. Our existence is marked by openness and orientation as well as by the tendency to get entangled, trapped, and perhaps even lost in the ambiguity that goes hand in hand with this openness and orientation. By answering to this plurivocity, "the poetic word . . . bears witness to our own being" (GW 8, 79; Gadamer 1986, 115). The poetic answer is thus an *inventio*, both a discovery and an invention. In this section, I want to develop these two aspects in more detail and show, in the course of the somewhat longer reflection on the second aspect, how and in which sense the modern lyrical poem both poses a challenge and exemplifies Gadamer's understanding of the poem.

THE TRUTH OF THE POEM

At various occasions, when Gadamer speaks of the truth of the word, he first and foremost means it in the sense of *a true word*, where *true* is meant in the sense of *real* or *genuine* as in the expression *true gold*. As discussed before, for him, to be a word means to be saying. Thus, the true word is the word that says and speaks eminently. If every word is a word because it is *sagend*, the eminent, true word must have an exceptional *Sagkraft*, that is, capacity to say or power of expression; this means that the true word must be *vielsagend*, that is, telling, revealing, and significant. The German *vielsagend* literally states: saying much or saying many things at once, and in this sense the eminent word is not only *vielsagend*, but also *vieldeutig*, it gives much to interpret and gives rise to many interpretations; it is plurivocal. Therefore, it is the poetic word that is saying in this eminent way.

Moreover, as is clear from our previous considerations, the poetic word also counts as an eminent word because it stands. One could ask, somewhat naïvely, why and in which sense Gadamer thinks that a word that stands is saying in a more eminent way. Are the words in a dialogue, fleeting as they may be, not also capable of being revealing and telling? Probably, what is crucial here for Gadamer, is the focus on the word itself. One can say many things with words, but there is a certain eminence to the word that is capable of showing the word itself. The poem shows what and how a word is. In order to be able to hear and understand a word as *vielsagend* and *vieldeutig*, as revealing and plurivocal, it is necessary to dwell upon it. In German, one would express this with the verbs *verweilen*, to stay or abide with the word, or *stillstehen*, literally: to stand still with or at the word. This duality of the standing word and the reader standing by the word characterizes the true word: "that *it stands* and that one *stands by it*" (GW 8, 40; Gadamer 2002, 118). When the word itself is fleeting and moving and when it erases itself in favor of the subject matter it makes manifest, one cannot abide with that word.

This leads us to another important expression that Gadamer introduces to further elucidate the truth claim of the poem. We can only stay close to a word that abides, stands, and remains there; inversely, it is only the word that abides and stands that can be and hold itself in our nearness. This mutual "holding in nearness [*in die Nähe halten*]," is not a formal or external character of the poetic word but rather marks the very truth of poetry, as Gadamer writes: "The truth of poetry is that it accomplishes [*zustande bringt*] such 'holding or keeping of nearness [*Halten der Nähe*]'" (GW 8, 78; Gadamer 1986, 113, translation modified).

To understand this latter expression, one needs to be attentive of the specific place of the poetic word within language as a whole. In his beautiful essay "Vergänglichkeit" (GW 9, 171–79), Gadamer notes that humans do not simply submit to the basic experience that all that exists is transitory; rather, by speaking they transform the mere fleetingness of all that is. In fact, to speak about something, also in everyday language, is to commemorate and to bear witness to what is not or what is no more: "For what is language other than the creation of memory and memorials as well as the bringing to mind and the making present of what is not?" (GW 9, 171, my translation). That which is absent, that which has disappeared, that which has departed from existence is made present and manifest by language and thus kept close to us: "what is common to all speech [is] that that which the word evokes is there" (GW 8, 78; Gadamer 1986, 113, translation modified). That which has faded away as well as all those whom we have we lost on the way are somehow held in nearness by language. Language thus preserves and safeguards what is lost, what is not or no longer. This testimonial essence of language is marked by the particular sense of truth to which also the later Heidegger (1977b, 348) has drawn our attention: *Wahrheit*, he suggests, may perhaps be rethought based on its relation to *wahren* and *bewahren*, that is, to preserve, to protect, or to safeguard. Amidst the transience of all that is, the word is capable of bringing something to a stand, allowing it to abide with us in the word, allowing us to hold on to it.

While this testimonial nature pervades all language, it is most eminently there in the poem, not in the sense that the poem is better in preserving this or that lost being but rather in the sense that the poem, by its very standing, manifests the very capacity of language to hold in close proximity. In a beautiful passage, Gadamer writes the following on the relation between the finitude and transitory nature of existence and the human capacity of language: "In fact, our fundamental experience as beings subject to time is that all things escape us, that all the events of our lives fade more and more, so that at best they glow with an almost unreal shimmer in the most distant recollection. But the poem does not fade, for the poetic word brings the transience of time to a standstill" (GW 8, 78; Gadamer 1986, 114). Everything fades away and eventually escapes us, everything we experience fades out and disappears in the mist of forgetting. Yet, language and in an eminent sense the poem oppose this tendency of time and of all that exists temporally to fade away.

Language is the house of being, as Gadamer (GW 8, 78–79) repeats after Heidegger, because it is by means of language that we preserve, draw close, and familiarize ourselves with the world and what we encounter in it. By growing into a language [*einhausen*] whether it is everyday language or the language of a particular discipline or field, we familiarize ourselves with how the world appears, we preserve what fades away and is lost in the course of time, and in this way keep our singular nearness to this world. The task of poetry, as Gadamer notes, is not to extend this process of familiarization and preservation. Rather, poetry places the everyday familiar words in a constellation and order that alienates and foreignizes them from their familiar usage. In this way, poetry makes something else manifest, namely that language is for human existence the very *element* of worldly proximity, familiarity, and preservation (see also Tate 2016, 157). Thus, poetry brings language itself to language and manifests how language as our element carries our existence: it is the element in which we dwell for a while, in which we understand whatever we encounter, and in which this world and whatever is in it, is expressed, preserved, and held close. To capture in more detail how the poem can live up to this truth claim and how the word can be alienated or foreignized poetically, we turn to the question of the order and the composition of the poem.

THE ORDER AND COMPOSITION OF THE POEM

If we want to understand how and why the everyday word becomes a true word when it becomes an element in a poem, we need to consider the specific role and nature of the composition that a poem is. When turning our attention to this compositional and configurative dimension of the poem, the specific challenge of *lyrical* poetry comes into view more directly.

To be a word, Gadamer insists, is to have the capacity to say or the power of expression [*Sagkraft*]. In everyday language, many of our words seem to have lost this capacity. Yet, the poem somehow returns the potentiality to say to the word: "The word 'emerges' [*herauskommt*] in the poem with a new power of saying [*einer neuen Sagkraft*]" (GW 8, 54; Gadamer 2002, 130, translation modified). In the composition of the poem, the word is taken up in a such a way that it begins to speak. when emphasizing the *new* in the previous citation, one might be inclined to think that the poem generates another, new sense of the word, as if using it metaphorically rather than in an everyday way or literally. However, Gadamer continues by saying that the word, when integrated in the poetic composition, remains the very same everyday word but, at one and the same time, regains "its original power of saying [*seine ursprüngliche Sagkraft*]." Thus, the word once more becomes what it originally was, namely significant and revealing [*vielsagend*]. This characterization of the poetic word brings into play many of the elements discussed so far and portrays the poetic word as vivid and the poem as revivifying. The poem quickens the everyday word, and the new life of the word is not another life, but rather its original life and its original potentiality to speak regained.

The exuberance of the poem following from this Gadamerian description, seems to be at odds with the experience offered by modern lyrical poetry. In his reflections on the lyrical poem, Gadamer is struck by the "indescribable discretion" (GW 9, 363) of the poetic word, which speaks softly and quietly, even up to the point of falling silent [*Verstummen*] (GW 9, 362). This tendency seems to go in a completely different direction than the poetic quickening of the word. This is not the only challenge the lyrical poem poses to Gadamer's account. Poetry, as discussed above, is marked by plurivocity, but the plurivocal sense of the poetic word offers orientation and direction, which, in turn, the interpreter aims to make manifest. What, however, happens when the poetic word falls apart in mere "fragments of meaning" (GW 9, 380) and explodes into "word splinters" (GW 9, 372)? What does this mean, formally, for the unity of the poem? Does it not mean, in contrast to Gadamer's conception, that the lyrical poem confronts us with a plurality of meaning that is alienating *up to the point of disorienting* us and that it thus disseminates rather than directs (GW 9, 339)? Finally, to formulate one more challenge, what exactly happens to the relation between poetry and philosophy, between poeticizing and interpreting, when the poem resists translation to the degree that the lyrical poem does? After all, translating is itself interpreting. The lyrical poem seems to resist interpretation and to discard every translation as a profound betrayal and distortion of itself.

To gain access to Gadamer's responses to these severe challenges, it seems to me that it is of crucial importance to turn our attention to the notion of composition and configuration and, more precisely, to that of the order [*Ordnung*], invented by the poem. In the English literature on Gadamer's account of art, there seems to be a keen interest in his expression *Verwandlung ins Gebilde*, probably due to the fact that it tends to resist translation. *Gebilde* means *structure*, but Gadamer's attention to art is not structuralist in any sense. The German term *Gebilde* refers to *Bild* [image], and *Bildung* [formation]. As soon as the notion of *Bild* is mentioned, Gadamer's particular account of the Greek sense of *mimesis* as *Darstellung* is brought into play, and with the notion of *Bildung*, the sense of tradition as that which forms our understanding resounds. Yet, modern lyrical poetry challenges all of these notions. Interestingly, as I aim to show in a few steps, Gadamer's reflections on the notion of *Ordnung* offer an important reinterpretation of these notions.

First, the poetic word is characterized in terms of saying. Up to a point, this repeats an ancient gesture. *Sage* translates *muthos*, as was already noted. Yet, *muthos* is not only the composition or configuration of a poem. Rather, in the ancient world, *muthos* also concerns "a shared saying [*eine gemeinsame Sage*]" (GW 8, 22; Gadamer 1986, 70; see also GW 9, 339). On the one hand, *muthos* is autonomous and complete: the *muthoi* have their existence in their being said and their being handed down. On the other hand, as shared and communal, they refer to a shared horizon of interpretation, a tradition, from which also new poems speak and to which these new poems add their new variations and interpretations of the actions of gods and mortals (GW 8, 22).[5] Such a shared tradition, however, has collapsed in modernity and the lyrical poem no longer speaks from such a communal horizon of interpretation, as Gadamer emphasizes: "We live in the epoch of semantic poetry. We no longer live in a world in which a shared saying, whether it be in the form of *muthos*, salvation history, or grown tradition, surrounds our horizon as a collective memory with images that we recognize in the word" (GW 9, 339). This quote is telling because it brings into play each of the notions mentioned above. It speaks of the Greek sense of *mimesis* in the arts when it refers to "recognize," and it speaks of the shared images and of collective memory shaping our tradition, thus forming our frame of reference. Each of these elements is under pressure in the modern age and the lyrical poem reflects and expresses that *in its form*. Because it is no longer capable of speaking from a shared frame of reference, this form of poetry must pose a bigger challenge to the interpretation. Yet, the fact that the poem is more complicated to interpret might be a mere difference in degree. Gadamer seems to suggest as much when he argues that even with a particular frame of reference present, the poetic word maintains its "open indeterminateness" (GW 8, 22). This particular alienation, openness, and plurivocity, is what makes a poem a poem in general. However, unlike the poem that presupposes a shared frame of reference, the lyrical poem is confronted with an additional, different task. Its goal is not only to return the *Sagkraft* to the everyday word, but also to *invent a shared word in the first place*. As Gadamer writes in his interpretation of Celan's poetry: "At any rate, it is the word common to all [*das allen gemeinsame Wort*] that he was looking for" (GW 9, 450). This, then, is what characterizes the modern predicament and condition of lyrical poetry: a common word, a collective memory, and a shared horizon of interpretation can no longer be presupposed; instead, a common word *needs to be invented*, that is, discovered and created, opened up and made receptive to. Hence, the commonality of the word as such has not simply disappeared. Rather, this commonality can no longer be presupposed, can no longer be the point of departure for the poetic word, but instead needs to be found and created by it in the first place.[6] No longer *gegeben*, it is *aufgegeben*.

Second, a similar emphasis on creation [*poiesis*], can be found in the subtle shift from *mimesis* to order that Gadamer proposes (see GW 8, 25–36). The retrieval of the Aristotelian concept of *mimesis* in the sense of *Darstellung* [presentation], is important for his conception of art. In the recognition that *mimesis* offers, Gadamer insists (GW 8, 31–32), one does not encounter a mere derivative as Plato sometimes suggests; rather, as Aristotle has seen, the very essence of a subject matter is presented in the artwork. Yet, confronted with modern art, this emphasis on *mimesis* and recognition to account for what the artwork is and does, has become problematic. If there is recognition, it is only of "fragmentary gestures . . . a last remainder of familiarity and . . . a partial recognition"; in other instances, modern art even confronts us with the sheer breaking down of this ancient model: "imitation and recognition fail and we remain desperate" (GW 8, 33).

Yet, as Gadamer insists, this is not the last word on the ancient model and its significance for modern art. He notes that it is crucial to be aware that, for the ancients, *mimesis* originally concerned the presentation and recognition of *order*. For the ancients, order is first and foremost *kosmos*. *Mimesis* is in the first place the presentation of this cosmic order and the attunement of the human being to this order through the subsequent orders of music and the soul (GW 8, 34–35). Clearly, the modern predicament is that such an encompassing order of all that is, can no longer be presupposed. In this sense, the modern artwork, whether image, picture, or word, can no longer be understood as the imitation or presentation of *kosmos*. Yet, as Gadamer insists, the sense of order remains, and the artwork is and remains presentation of and "attestation to order" (GW 8, 36).

Hence, also here, the modern predicament implies that no given order can be presupposed. Therefore, it is the artwork that needs to invent order. Consequently, the order borne witness to by the artwork is not that of a *kosmos* in which everything has its assigned place. Rather, the artwork attests to the human "spiritual capacity to order [*geistige Ordnungskraft*]," the spiritual capacity to create and discover order; this capacity "makes our life what it is" (GW 8, 36; Gadamer 1986, 103). The artwork invents a composition and a specific configuration of elements. In a world of decay and falling apart—an experience that is intensified in the modern world in which a "shared saying" and a shared horizon of interpretation can no longer be presupposed—the artwork does not simply repeat this transience, but rather and instead orders it. Exactly in this way, it attests to the human "capacity to preserve and maintain" (GW 8, 36; Gadamer 1986, 104) that which falls away and falls apart: by giving order poetically, the word preserves what disappears.

Third, this more general consideration regarding the artwork as such and the subtle shift from *mimesis* to order, has important implications for Gadamer's understanding of the modern poem. Poetry is concerned with returning the original capacity and power to say [*Sagkraft*] to the word. The word regains this capacity only in the specific poetic order in which it is taken up. In modern lyrical poetry, the experience of a world that has become fragmented and in which no shared horizon of interpretation can be presupposed, is mirrored in its composition. Let me mention two ways in which this is done.

(1) The lyrical poem seems to discard or even reject the presentation of sense, presenting only fragments of sense and splinters of meaning thus leaving the reader desperate and frustrated in its quest for sense. Yet, this frustration is not the end of interpretation. In fact, it is building up tension, by placing the word at the center where these fragments are brought together in the unity of a new, *tense* composition in which the word comes to a stand and regains its original capacity to speak. Modern lyrical poetry departs from the experience that, in terms of Gadamer's interpretation of Celan's *Vom Ungeträumten geätzt*, language is a "mountain of words [also called 'breadland' in the poem], deposited over the entire experience of life like a covering burden" (GW 9, 391; Gadamer 1997, 78). Language seems to have lost its capacity to speak; this is the destitution from which the modern

poet departs; such a destitution rather than "eine gemeinsame Sage" is the modern predicament. Yet, as the poem notes, crumbs of language remain; these crumbs can be gathered and kneaded into something that offers nutrition. Thus, the poem describes a profound hunger for the poetic word in the context of a destitute language belonging to a world that has fallen apart, but it also speaks quietly of a discrete hope when it points to the crumbs in this destitute language that offer elements that can be brought together in a new poetic composition that revivifies and quickens the word, returning to it its capacity to speak and to address. Once we discern the destitution from which the poet departs, we understand why it is inevitable that the poem appears to be falling silent and that it is indescribably discrete and quiet: the retrieval of the original capacity to say requires that one begins by tearing down the destitute language "syllable by syllable," as Celan's *In die Rillen* prescribes. Consequently, the fragments of sense and the word splinters are the *elements* of the poem; and the reader is dictated to endure these fragments as fragments and not to suture them in an encompassing whole of which they are like the pieces of one mosaic. Yet, as fragments they are the elements that are gathered in a new composition that maintains their tension and irreconcilability. Only in this way, the poem bears witness to an invented order in which the words begin to speak again.

(2) Poetry is never fully translatable because of the intrinsic connection between the sounds and the meanings of the words gathered in the poem. Yet, in the modern lyrical poem, as Gadamer suggests, the intrinsic connection of sound [*Lautgestalt*] and meaning [*Bedeutung*], seems to be deepened up to the point of rendering the poem untranslatable, also because the composition of the poem itself is marked by tone and rhythm that attune and temporalize the words' sounds and meanings and that need to be respected if we want to be capable of hearing the word as element of the poem (GW 8, 235).

Because translation is a form of interpretation, the untranslatability of the lyrical poem poses an additional challenge to the understanding. Is understanding not general or at least shareable beyond particular linguistic boundaries? And is, consequently, meaning or sense as that which is understood not always supposed to be shareable between different linguistic communities? What order does the modern lyrical poem create when maximizing its "linguistic coherence" (GW 8, 51; Gadamer 2002, 127) and thus showing "in the clearest possible way the inseparability of the linguistic work of art and its original manifestation as language" (GW 8, 235; Gadamer 1986, 134)? Interestingly, in the context of this linguistic coherence, the poetic word apparently does not aim to create a common word for all languages but rather strives to insist on the idiomatic nature of the language in which it is composed. This particular challenge to the universality of the word is not meant as prioritizing either a structuralist or materialist account of language at the expense of meaning. Rather, what the poem aims to show by insisting on linguistic singularity is that the *Sagkraft* is preserved, sheltered, and secured (in German: *geborgen*) in an element of language that remains hidden (in German: *verborgen*) from the perspective of a universal, uprooted understanding. The word can neither be reduced to a universally shareable meaning nor to a sheer, conventional sign the structure of which can be studied. Rather, the word is marked by an intrinsic unity of sound and sense belonging to a singular language, which houses, holds, and hides the poetic word's capacity to say: "The limit of translatability designates exactly how far the sheltering in the word [*die Bergung im Wort*] stretches. In its ultimate concealedness it is the sheltering [*In seiner letzten Verborgenheit ist es das Bergende*]" (GW 8, 56; Gadamer 2002, 132). The particular order of the modern lyrical poem thus discloses more pertinently than ever how the capacity of language to preserve and to hold in nearness is profoundly connected to and rooted in the very singularity of every language. As long as we are surrounded by a common saying, this rootedness in the singularity of a tradition or a language may easily escape us. Yet, the modern predicament and its uprootedness is the poetic condition in which this connection between the particular truth claim and the singularity of poetic language can be brought out in an exemplary way.

Notes

1. This extends and deepens van der Heiden 2022b, 318–19.

2. When necessary, I also quote the German original; here, the translation misses Gadamer's emphasis on "*Es steht in sich da*" and does not account for the fact that *ganz* is not adjective here, but rather adverb: by not intending and pointing away from itself, the poetic word is completely and fully *word*.

3. Gadamer's conception of language here continues Heidegger's account of the co-belonging of being and appearing and his criticism of how these two tend to draw apart in Plato's conception of the Idea (Heidegger 1983, §§37–44); see van der Heiden 2021, 139–44. Gadamer's continuation concerns the fundamental role of language and the form of appearance of beings in the *logos*.

4. Hence, "the instability of the 'word'" (Davey 2006, XV; see also 142, 224) needs to be qualified in relation to the poetic word, because the poetic word stands and is in this sense stable.

5. The essay "Prometheus and the Tragedy of Culture" (GW 9, 150–61) offers a telling example: the shared figure of Prometheus is taken up in new poetic variations and interpretations.

6. The relation between I and You in Celan's poetry is a characteristic example for Gadamer in this respect, see also van der Heiden 2019 and 2022b.

Bibliography

Davey, Nicholas. *Unquiet Understanding: Gadamer's Hermeneutical Philosophy*. Albany: State University of New York Press, 2006.

Gadamer, Hans-Georg. *Gadamer on Celan: "Who Am I and Who Are You?" and Other Essays*. Edited by R. Heinemann and B. Krajewski. Albany: State University of New York Press, 1997.

———. *Gesammelte Werke* [GW]. 10 vols. Tübingen: Mohr Siebeck, 1985–1995.

———. "On the Truth of the Word." Translated by R. E. Palmer. *Symposium* 6, no. 2 (2002): 115–34.

———. *The Relevance of the Beautiful and Other Essays*. Translated by N. Walker. Edited by R. Bernasconi. Cambridge: Cambridge University Press, 1986.

———. *Truth and Method*. Revised edition. Translated by J. Weinsheimer and D. G. Marshall. London: Bloomsbury, 2013.

Heidegger, Martin. *Einführung in die Metaphysik. Gesamtausgabe*. Vol. 40. Frankfurt a.M.: Klostermann, 1983.

———. *"Hölderlins Hymnen 'Germanien' und 'Der Rhein.'" Gesamtausgabe*. Vol. 39. Frankfurt a.M.: Klostermann, 1999.

———. *Holzwege. Gesamtausgabe*. Vol. 5. Frankfurt a.M.: Klostermann, 1977b.

———. *Sein und Zeit. Gesamtausgabe*. Vol. 2. Frankfurt a.M.: Klostermann, 1977a.

———. *Wegmarken. Gesamtausgabe*. Vol. 9. Frankfurt a.M.: Klostermann, 1976.

Nancy, Jean-Luc. *Demande: Philosophie, littérature*. Paris: Galilée, 2015.

Ricoeur, Paul. *La métaphore vive*. Paris: Seuil, 1975.

Risser, James. *The Life of Understanding: A Contemporary Hermeneutics*. Bloomington: Indiana University Press, 2012.

Tate, Daniel L. "Hermeneutics and Poetics: Gadamer on the Poetic Word." *The Polish Journal of Aesthetics* 43, no. 4 (2016): 155–85.

van der Heiden, Gert-Jan. "An 'Almost Imperceptible Breathturn': Gadamer on Celan." In *Philosophers and Their Poets: Reflections on the Poetic Turn in Philosophy since Kant*. Edited by C. Bambach and T. George, 215–37. Albany: State University of New York Press, 2019.

———. "Gadamer and the Concept of Language." In *Gadamer's Truth and Method: A Polyphonic Commentary*. Edited by G. Lynch and C. R. Nielsen, 227–44. Lanham: Rowman & Littlefield, 2022a.

———. *Metafysica: Van orde naar ontvankelijkheid.* Amsterdam: Boom, 2021.
———. "Poem, Dialogue and Witness: Gadamer's Reading of Paul Celan." In *The Gadamerian Mind*. Edited by T. George and G.-J. van der Heiden, 318–22. New York: Routledge, 2022b.

10

Gadamerian Reflections on Celan and the Witness and Wounding of the Poetic Word

Cynthia R. Nielsen

Perhaps a poetry of fragmentation is a poetry especially suitable to or resonant with extreme sociopolitical events such as war, famine, genocide, slavery, death camps, and the like. Such experiences of terror, subjugation, and prolonged pain and torture are themselves fragmenting and destabilizing experiences. These types of experiences that destroy and permanently wound human lives have no rational justification and can never be made fully intelligible or understandable. The poet of such fragmenting experiences suffers this wound, carries this wound, and seeks through the remaining "crumbs" or fragmentary poetic words to breathe life back into words that have become malnourished, bled-out, corroding, barbed, empty, and meaningless. The poet of catastrophe seeks to make new sense from the non-sense that both language and reality have become—to find in and through language an open space of reorientation and reconnection. To do so, however, requires a receptive, responsive reader, who is willing to receive the wound that comes with the testimony of the poetic word, which witnesses to lives lost, voices silenced, and breath smothered. Both the poet and the reader who receive these word-wounds receive the poetic word as a testimony or witness to the senselessness of such events—events that shatter our solidarity (riffing on Jan Patočka) and whose shattering character we must learn to linger with so as neither to forget nor repeat, as, unfortunately, we are prone to both.

Our forgetfulness, carelessness with language, and inability or refusal to receive this testimony may pave the way not only for a rhyming with past historical atrocities but also something more like a repetition of the same.[1]

The term *wound* appears throughout my chapter and covers of a wide range of meanings and experiences—everything from physical harm to emotional, psychological, spiritual, communal, and social injury, affliction, and pain. Serious wounds, whether physical or otherwise, leave scars; they *stay with* an individual or community and shape their present and future even when such wounds are considered to be, to some degree, healed (of course, there are some wounds that never fully heal). For a *reader* to be "wounded" by Celan's late poems—that is, poems shaped by the event of the Shoah—requires that she, on the one hand, as Gadamer would say, comport herself with an openness to what the poem has to say and to allow it to make a claim on her. On the other hand—and going beyond these Gadamerian hermeneutical virtues and comportments or at least making the ethical aspect more explicit—to be wounded as a reader of Celan's poems is to be brought into a deeper ethical relationship with the subject matter of the poem than one was prior to having lingered with it. This deeper ethical relationship involves dis-comfort and a sense of dis-composure that stays with one like a wound that never fully heals but whose presence makes possible a newfound recognition of the fragility, vulnerability, and tragedy of the human condition. One comes away, as it were, not just positively transformed or enriched but also burdened, un-settled—in a word, wounded.

In what follows, I read with and against Gadamer's reflections and interpretations of poems from Celan's later work, *Breathturn* [*Atemwende*], which consists in a sequence of eighty poems composed between September 1963 and September 1965 and is organized into six cycles. *Atemkristall* is the first cycle and the sequence upon which Gadamer concentrates (Joris 2014, 460). The chapter will focus on select poems from this first cycle so that I might enter into a dialogue both with Celan's poems and Gadamer's commentary on them. Although I find Gadamer's reflections on Celan's poems insightful, I also interrogate and challenge his interpretations and am especially critical of his near silence regarding the historical context that shaped Celan's later poetry—namely, the event of the Shoah. I have chosen four poems from *Atemkristall*—*Du darfst*, *Vom Ungeträumten*, *In die Rillen*, and *Weggebeizt* because they embody tensions, longings, and struggles fundamental to our human condition. Such constitutive elements include the power, misuse, and limits of language; the experience of suffering and violence; a longing for a sense of home and genuine connection with others;

and an open or free space in which to flourish. And yet these shared *topoi* of our human condition to which Celan's poems witness, nonetheless, are shaped by a singular, historical limit experience—the event of the Shoah.

Gadamer begins with Celan's poem *Du darfst* [*You May*], which he calls the "proem to the entire sequence" and ultimately interprets it as expressing a readiness for or acceptance of death (Gadamer 1997, 73).

> CONSOLED YOU may
> welcome me with snow:
> whenever I strode through the summer
> shoulder to shoulder with the mulberry tree,
> its youngest leaf
> screamed.
> (Celan, *Du darfst,* as translated in Gadamer 1997, 70).²

In this opening poem, Gadamer highlights the play between "summer and winter," "scream and stillness," "desire and renunciation," and ultimately "life and death" (Gadamer 1997, 73).

Here at the very beginning of the sequence of poems, the theme of death is present in an interplay of contrasts. As this poem is the prelude or opening movement of the cycle entitled *Atemkristal* [*Breath-crystal*], Gadamer points to the connection between breath and language. As he observes, "[t]he poems in this sequence are, in fact, as quiet and barely perceptible as the breath-turn. They offer witness to a last constriction of life and, simultaneously, represent anew its recurring resolution, or better, not its resolution, but its elevation to a secure linguistic form [*Sprachgestalt*]. One hears it the way one hears the deep stillness of winter that blankets everything. Something ever so quiet crystallizes, something ever so small, so light, and yet so precise: the true word" (Gadamer 1997, 73–74). On the one hand, one can understand Gadamer's point about the poem crystallizing into a linguistic form and how the true word emerges from a stillness. On the other hand, one wonders whether this poem underscores the *struggle* of life and death rather than, as Gadamer claims, an acceptance or readiness for death. The poem ends not in quiet stillness but with a shriek, a scream. Is this an instance of young life from the very beginning thrown into a life-struggle and intuitively sensing death's cold wintry presence? Other than noting that death is a constant theme in Celan's poetry, Gadamer's comments on the proem (and the entire cycle of poems) mentions nothing of the historical context—for example, the death camps—that give rise to death as a theme in Celan's poetry. This absence is in my reading of Celan foregrounded. That is, my reflections, in stark contrast with Gadamer's, thematize the historical "space of catastrophe" from which Celan's poetry emerges.[3] In other words, the emphasis in my reading of Celan's poems resonates with Luitgard N. Wundheiler's claim that "Celan's poetry is dedicated to memorializing the dead of the Holocaust." While, as Wundheiler remarks, one should avoid an "overly narrow understanding" of Celan's poetry, so too should one be wary of readings that "deny or ignore any relationship to the Holocaust" (Wundheiler 1976, 36). Stated otherwise, my reading is perhaps a transgressive (Gadamerian) hermeneutical reading in that it sees the limit experience that Celan endured—the event of the Shoah and its direct and traumatic impact on Celan's life—as having a formative role in his late poetry.[4] In other words, the two are inextricably linked. Celan's trauma, losses, and experience of a (personal and collective) catastrophe that defies all rational justification gives rise to poems that stammer, scream, and embody the tension and interplay of saying something and being on the verge of silence, of playing within the limits of German language and pushing those limits. As Charles Bambach elegantly puts it, Celan's poems

> attempt to bring language to the limits of the unsayable, pushing against the boundaries of speech in an effort to mourn the numberless dead in the name of what Derrida would call a "justice of the impossible." These poems bring the German language to the strange and uncanny [*unheimlich*] limit that denies the proper relation to the homeland—or perhaps to the propriety of such a limit in the face of both the destruction of the homeland as an *Eigenes* and the homeland's destruction of the other as a *Fremdes*. (Bambach 2013, 21)

Despite reading against Gadamer on this point, I also read with him on several other points and find his reflections on Celan's poetry and the poetic word in a wider sense wonderfully insightful. For example, I agree with Gadamer's claim that the poetic word that stammers and stutters, nonetheless, communicates. Although, as Daniel Tate observes, Gadamer readily acknowledges the difficulty and challenge of Celan's poems, he rejects the view that the "singularity of a poem" could "render it incommunicable, no poem, not even Celan's, can ever be purely idiomatic. For the poetic word is a communicative event; it wants to say something, even if it struggles with saying nothing" (Tate 2019, 165).

Anyone who has dwelt with the catastrophe of the Shoah can at once understand how words fall short when trying to grapple with such inhumane cruelty. Even more so when the poet's language is the same language as the Nazi propagandists and SS guards. As Gert-Jan van der Heiden remarks, "[t]his catastrophe [of the Shoah] is also a catastrophe and bankruptcy of the only language that the poet has at his disposal" (van der Heiden 2022, 320). For Celan, this struggle with language occurs on multiple levels. On the most basic level is the question of whether the German language is appropriate for poetry that gives testimony to the thousands upon thousands of Jewish lives lost, including the lives of Celan's parents.[5] And yet, despite the death, destruction, and calculated cruelty of Nazi death camps, Celan asserts that language remained, and remained "reachable, near, and unlost" (van der Heiden 2022, 320).[6] While language is not lost, it is, nonetheless, painful, burdensome, and its capacity to harm and destroy must be acknowledged in light of the role that language played in Nazi propaganda and its impact as the language of the aggressor and of those who remained silent. In his *Bremen Address*, Celan describes this "unlost" language that remains as having passed through "the thousand darknesses of death-dealing speech [*hindurchgehen durch die tausend Finsternisse todbringender Rede*]," and yet it "offered no words for what happened [*gab keine Worte her für das, was geschah*]" in this "event [*Geschehen*]" (Celan 2000, vol. 3, 186, my translation). Somehow the poet must find a way to un-silence this speech that made itself known as "devastating speechlessness" or "appalling silence [*furchtbares Verstummen*]" (Celan 2000, vol. 3, 186, my translation). The poet must find a way to live (again) in and with this (German) language.

This idea of language having become tainted, hardened, stale, and burdensome is palpable in Celan's next poem in the sequence, *Vom Ungeträumten [By the Undreamed* (Gadamer) / *By the Undreamt* (P. Joris)].

CORRODED BY the undreamed,
the sleeplessly traveled bread-land
digs up the life-mountain.
From its soil
you knead anew our names,
with an eye
like yours
on each of my fingers,
I probe them for
a place, through which I

can wake onto you,
the bright
Hunger-candle in my mouth.
(Celan, *Vom Ungeträumten* as translated in Gadamer 1997, 74).

The poem speaks of a "bread-land [*Brotland*]" and a "life-mountain [*Lebensberg*]." These two neologisms play off one another. Bread and life go together as do land and mountain. Bread is one of the most basic sources of food and is typically accessible to even the poorest lands and peoples. In normal times—that is, times of non-famine—bread feeds families and nations; it nourishes and often brings people together for a shared meal. Language, too, is a most basic or fundamental element in human life and experience; it, too, can nourish and strengthen communities. But bread can spoil and become putrid. When such bread is eaten, it brings sickness not health. Instead of cultivating life and opening a space where one can rest and move unburdened in the open, this bread-land has hardened and become an obstacle—a mountain that blocks and hinders movement. Language, too, can rigidify. When language is co-opted by ideologies and propaganda, it hardens and becomes stale. Immovable and stonelike, this language-burden weighs one down; such language loses its freedom, its movement, its habit-ability, and, in some cases, its breath. But a sliver of hope is possible for the poetic word, which can shatter the stones of dead language and find nourishment from the crumbs of stale language-bread. From the "crumbs [*Krume*]" of this "life-mountain"—that is, what remains of language, albeit fragmentary and in need of re-configuring—"new names" can be, as Celan puts it, kneaded together.[7] This kneading activity is a collaborative ongoing effort involving the poem and engaged interpreters. That is, the poetic word calls out to those, who, through lingering and listening to the fractured, "word-splinters [*Wortsplitter*],"[8] are willing to rebuild not only some semblance of meaning but also some semblance of solidarity with those who have been so violently harmed and, in some cases, utterly destroyed. Kneading is laborious; it is an intimate action involving one's own hands and requires time, energy, and care. What emerges from this labor in the linguistic realm, or so one hopes, is the re-creation and renewal of "our names." The phrase *our names* is pregnant with possible meaning. Perhaps it refers to those murdered in the death camps. Perhaps it recalls hearing one's Jewish name intentionally or indifferently mispronounced by a German SS officer in the camp's daily roll call.[9] Or perhaps it indicates a need to recognize how words were used in a systematic way to dehumanize Jewish people; hence, there is a call to recognize, honor, and dignify the humanity and individual lives of those who were disrespected, violated, and murdered during the Nazi regime. To remember and pronounce their names with care. More broadly, *our names* might also speak of the task of cocreating a shared language from these remaining crumbs—that is, a language that is no longer a burden, obstacle, or shroud, but that facilitates understanding and solidarity, a language that allows the truth to shine into the darkness created in part by abuses and perversions of language, which, in turn, incited violent actions—that is, actions that bring about death rather than promote life and communal connection, as is the case with language grounded in truth, or what we might call in the spirit of Celan, language as life-giving bread.

The "bread-land [*Brotland*]" is depicted as having been "sleeplessly [*schlaflos*]" traveled or "wandered through [*durchwanderte*]." Rather than nourishing and giving rise to rest after eating one's share, this bread-land or stale-language facilitates neither sleep nor a sense of being satiated. Instead, one is deprived of sleep, being unable to rest or dream of a better future. The idea of propaganda as a stale petrified language can be easily connected with discourses that violently impose false names or concepts meant to dehumanize those it wishes to silence, starve, and even eradicate. Celan's image of the "hunger-candle [*Hungerkerze*]"[10] in one's mouth signals a longing not only for nourishment (and perhaps genuine rest, in which one sleeps deeply, dreams, and hopes for a future), but also a longing for a new language-path through which to connect with a "you"—that is, an engaged and open reader or listener receptive to the poetic word's gesture, desire, and testimony. The longing that the "hunger-candle" evokes conjures notions of separation, homelessness, and isolation, all of which go hand in hand with the linguistic petrification of discourses crafted to destroy solidaristic ties among people groups.

The third poem in the sequence *In die Rillen* [*Into the Grooves*] describes an experience of being shut out (or nearly so) and estranged. The poem reads as follows:

INTO THE GROOVES

of heaven's coin in the door-crack
you press the word,
from which I unrolled,
when with trembling fists
I dismantled the roof over us,

slate by slate,
syllable by syllable,
for the sake of the copper-
shimmer of the beggar's-
pan up there.
(Celan, *In die Rillen* as translated in Gadamer 1997, 78).[11]

Although we are not told why, somehow a coin has found itself stuck in a door-crack. Given the references to "heaven's coin" and "up there," the door can be understood as heaven's door. Whatever word has been "unrolled" from the coin's grooves, it did not comfort the I who sought it but rather enraged him; hence, the "trembling fists" ready to destroy and tear down the structure that has been built. That is, the I has "dismantled" the roof, whose purpose was to shelter the I and the You. Given the movement from slate to syllable, the sheltering roof is a figure for language or a linguistic structure—perhaps an understanding of scripture, a theological narrative, or a metanarrative of how the world and humans should be. The You here seems to include the divine, and the word that has been passed down or perhaps passed off as a divine word in no way comforts or shelters. The I and the You are disconnected, and the words of this supposed linguistic sanctuary have become intertwined with an exchange system—with "heaven's coins" that appear to crack open heaven's door but leave one a beggar.

Gadamer underscores the separation and estrangement between the I and You and interprets these lines as evoking "a theology of the *Deus absconditus*" (Gadamer 1997, 80). He continues with a theological interpretation of the term *word*, which has several scriptural resonances. For example, the Word in Hebrew Scripture and the New Testament is associated with God's creative power. Thus, Gadamer asks whether the I "unrolled" from the word. That is, did the I come from the Word and then become estranged from it? (Gadamer 1997, 80). Are the trembling fists symbols of the fall and the consequent estrangements from God, others, and the natural world, as recorded in the Genesis account? Yet, the poem's tone is not one of penitence; whatever language-roof or house that had been constructed—whether from an interpretation of scripture or scripture co-opted for ideological purposes or political propaganda—has been meticulously deconstructed, "slate by slate, syllable by syllable." Moving somewhat away from a theological reading, Gadamer returns to the poet's task to "seek the true word, not the word which comes from the usual, protective roof of every day, but the one which arrives from beyond as if it were his true home. Therefore, the poet must dismantle the scaffolding of every day words syllable by syllable. He must fight against the ordinary, customary, obscuring, and levelling function of language in order to lay open a view of the glimmer above. That is poetry" (Gadamer 1997, 82).

Here we turn to Celan's last poem of the *Atemkristall* cycle, *Weggebeizt*, which in English has been translated as *Etched Away* (Gadamer) and *Eroded* (P. Joris).

> ETCHED AWAY by the
> ray-wind of your language
> the garish chatter of the commonly-
> experienced—the hundred-
> tongued my—
> poem, the noem.
> Un-
> drifted,
> free
> the path through the human-
> shaped snow,
> the penitents' snow, to
> the hospitable
> glacier-rooms and -tables.
> Deep
> in the time-crevice
> by the
> honeycomb-ice
> waits, a breath-crystal,
> your irrefutable
> witness.
> (Celan, *Weggebeizt* as translated in Gadamer 1997, 123).

In this poem, we have an account of what happens to the I when language that has *not* been dialogically formed—such as ideologically rigid and harmful language—inscribes itself on or in the I. The I experiences this inscribing as a pre-scribing, which gradually erodes and corrodes its own identity, uniqueness, and solidarity with others. The I is, as Celan puts it, "etched away [*weggebeizt*]" by forces and powers from the outside, which are depicted with another neologism "raywind [*Strahlenwind*]"—more precisely, the "raywind of your language."[12] Just as exposure to the external forces of nature such as blistering sunrays and assaulting wind can burn, sear, and harm our bodies, marking our skin with their impact, so too the "garish chatter" harms through creating a false reality by way of its "hundred-tongued my-poem [*Mein-gedicht*]." Gadamer explains that *Mein-gedicht* alludes to an archaic German word *Meinneid*, which means oath and in this context signals false speech or false witness. "These false creations of language speak with a hundred tongues because they are so capricious, and this means that, in reality, they bear witness to nothing—they offer, so to speak, false witness" (Gadamer 1997, 124).[13] This false witness, the *Mein-gedicht* that performs a *das Genicht* marks out, negates, or nihil-ates the voice and testimony of the I. The poet speaks here of language or better pseudo-language that separates and divides; it erodes solidaristic bonds through its "hundred-tongued perjury-poem" and unthinking "garish chatter" that remains at the level of the "pseudo-experienced" (in Lloyd 2018, 180), those who in their unthinkingness refuse to be, as it were, wounded by reality.

As in the proem, we again encounter snow, indicating death, which, as we noted earlier, is a recurrent theme in Celan's late poetry. Thus, the path described as a "path through the human-shaped snow" appears to be a path that leads to death—a place for the discarded ones, who, perhaps, refused the corroding language-violence of degrading discourses and now lie frozen in the ice. The witness of these lost lives—an "irrefutable witness"—is the "breath-crystal," an image of the poetic word as a vestige of a human life, etched, as it were, in the ice, witnessing, along with the *human*-shaped outline in the snow, to lost humanity and individuality. This "irrefutable witness," is, as it were, re-animated and unfrozen when a responsive You receives the poetic word, which bears witness to the truth. As David Lloyd remarks, "[t]his image of the poem as a crystal of breath frozen in ice . . . peculiarly condenses the concerns of Celan's later poetry. It locates the poetic utterance deep in the narrow space of the 'time-crevasse,' as if it awaits the moment in which that to which it bears witness might be received" (Lloyd 2018, 182).

Just as no two breath-crystals are alike and each bears "irrefutable witness" to the signature singularity of an individual, the poetic word as witness, is a unique, singular breath-crystal, and yet, the poet holds out hope that this witness can be received by those willing to linger and listen. Our shared vulnerability and fragility create the conditions for an openness that allows us to attain some degree of understanding and empathy even of those experiences of extreme human suffering that most have not endured. Undoubtedly, the poetic word that Celan presents to us underscores its uniqueness and individuality not only in the complexity of its multilayered and at times impenetrable meanings but also through its neologisms and unconventional structures and syntax. To listen and receive this testimony—to be wounded by it—requires what Gadamer calls lingering or "tarrying [*verweilen*]," which describes the comportment of an engaged and receptive reader or listener. To linger or tarry with a poem is to become absorbed in and fully there with it such that we forget ourselves.[14] We simply cannot dialogue with or genuinely listen to the poem in a distracted, detached mode that all too often characterizes everyday linguistic exchanges. Along similar lines but from the side of the poet and poetic utterance, Celan says that "the poem attempts to pay careful attention to everything it encounters . . . it is a concentration which remains aware of our dates" (Celan 2005, 182). He goes on to liken poetry to "paths on which language acquires a voice; these are encounters, a voice's paths to a perceiving thou" (Celan 2005, 184). Such poetry requires, even demands a similarly attentive and attuned reader. Emphasizing this point, Gadamer states that poetry—especially Celan's poetry—requires a "patient reader," one who is "not hurried" and is willing to return to the poem again and again to *listen* to what it has to say (Gadamer 1997, 67). Listening to a poem does not mean that one will fully understand it; however, it does necessitate a willingness to dwell and *be fully present* with it, and in the case of Celan's poems, to be wounded by it.[15]

Celan's neologisms call us to a contemplative reading, to a reading, as it were, willing to receive and give testimony to the dead. Take, for example, the term *weggebeitzt,* which invokes a constellation of possible meanings and associations. The verb *beizen* can be translated into English as "to stain," "to corrode," "to strip," "to chafe," "to etch," and the list goes on. The prefix *weg-* often carries the meaning of "away" as in the verb *wegwerfen,* which means "to throw away" or the verb *weglaufen,* which means "to run away." Given the violence that ideological language is capable of, we can grasp how many of the meanings of *wegbeizen* might aptly apply to the experience of the I who suffers from this linguistic violence (Here the I is not simply the poet but *all* who have suffered from such violence, including the dead, whose breath was suffocated and whose voice silenced. Yet, the breath and voice of the poetic word gives testimony to these lives, allowing us to feel, hear, recognize, and dignify their lives). The nihil-ating force of "garish chatter" could easily chafe away, strip away, or "corrode [*wegbeitzt*]" the humanity and individuality of the I—that is, both that which the I shares in common with other humans and that which makes the I a unique individual. The poem gifts us with both aspects: on the one side, we have the human-shaped outline in the snow, which underscores commonality with other humans and, on the other, the breath-crystal, which underscores the uniqueness and singularity of the individual person. Both aspects—what is shared and what is unique—call out to be recognized and respected as both are essential for human flourishing.

We recall that in his *Bremen Address,* Celan says that in the midst of so many losses the one thing that remained was language. Although Celan knew several languages, he chose to write his poetry in his mother tongue, German, the language of his childhood and formative education. Yet, this same German language that he held so dear, this language of the poetry of "Hölderlin, Büchner, and Rilke, all of whom Celan admired," was also, as Wundheiler remarks, "the language in which the words *Endlösung* [final solution], *Sonderbehandlung* [special treatment], and *judenrein* [cleansed of Jews] were coined. It was perhaps the embodiment of these extremes in the German language that led Celan to choose it" (Wundheiler 1976, 24).[16]

Celan himself describes the challenge, burden, and wounding of German language. For this German language, which though unlost, nonetheless had been characterized by an "unresponsiveness [*Antwortlosigkeiten*]," "dreadful silence [*furchtbares Verstummen*]," and "offered no words for what happened"—even though, as Celan states, "it [*die Sprache*] went through this event [*Sie ging hindurch und gab keine Worte her für das, was geschah; aber sie ging durch dieses Geschehen*]" (Celan 2000, vol. 7, 186, my translation). Having paved the path for and then passed through the event of the Shoah, German language remained and yet is "unlost [*unverloren*]" for Celan, a neologism that underscores Celan's post-Holocaust agonistic, yet vital relation with German language. Again, turning to his *Bremen Address,* Celan further elaborates some of what he hoped to achieve through writing his poetry, and I would emphasize writing it *in German.* "In this language, in those years, and in the years after, I tried to write poems in order to speak, orient myself, explore where I was and where it wanted to go with me, in order to project [*entwerfen*] a reality for myself" (Celan 2000, vol. 7, 186, my translation).[17] It is unclear what the "it" refers to, although the German makes clear that "it" does not refer to "language" because *die Sprache* is grammatically a feminine noun and would require the pronoun "*sie*" rather than the neuter pronoun "*es.*" The term "this event [*dieses Geschehen*]" is mentioned two sentences earlier and is a neuter noun. Perhaps "it" refers to "this event." If so, the idea seems to be that writing poetry in German offered him a way to reorient himself vis-à-vis German language, history, culture, and to see, in light of what had been carried out, what place, dwelling, and future exist for him.[18] His poetry and the process and act of writing his poems were not ways of escaping reality or becoming detached from the world, but rather were attempts to find some sense of orientation, some semblance of grounding, connection, and understanding. As Carolyn Culbertson remarks, "for Celan, the demand to write issued from a distinctly interpersonal need that linguistic beings possess. This is the need to *bear witness* to loss, to find an empathetic other that will listen, and as part of this listening, engage in the process of interpretative understanding" (Culbertson 2019, 55, emphasis in original). In taking up this unlost German language and with it testifying to the humanity and individuality of thousands of murdered Jews (including his own parents), Celan nihil-ates the false perjurious speech that prepared the way for genocide (and that remained silent afterwards). The perverted language whose goal was to dehumanize and turn individuals into an anonymous mass and finally to exterminate them. "No trace of their lives was supposed to remain, they were given no graves or tombstones, and death came to them as a final confirmation of that nothingness that had been inflicted upon them while still alive" (Wundheiler 1976, 24). Celan's poetry nihil-ates that anonymity and gives witness and testimony to each individual breath-crystal, each human life lost. His poetry communes with the dead; it calls every You willing to linger, listen, and enter this "landscape of death" to receive this testimony, this witness, this breath of the true poetic word. Here Celan and Gadamer meet in that both understand poetry as dialogical, "on the way [*unterwegs*]," and calling out to an Other. As Celan poignantly states in his Meridian speech: "The poem is alone. It is alone and underway . . . The poem wants to reach the Other, it needs this Other, it needs a *vis-à-vis*. It searches it out and addresses it" (Celan 2005, 181).[19]

Along similar lines, in his *Bremen Address* Celan likens a poem to a message in a bottle, awaiting, even if only with a sliver of hope, a responsive receiver. "Because it is a manifestation of language and thus dialogical in its essence, the poem can be a message in a bottle, sent out in the belief—certainly not always intensely hopeful—that it could wash up somewhere and sometime on land, perhaps on the heartland [*Herzland*]. In this sense, poems are also on the way [*unterwegs*]: they are heading for something" (Celan 2000, vol. 7, 186, my translation). Perhaps *heartland* has a double meaning, alluding, on the one hand, to a physical place such as Germany, which must come to terms with what it has done. On the other, heartland moves beyond a physical place, pointing to a more intimate "space" in which to rest; that is—the poem must find its way into the "land of the heart" or "a responsive You [*ein ansprechbares Du*]," a You that has intended to be *fully there* and attentive to the testimony of the poetic word; a You open to the poetic word's wounding. Having posed the question: Towards what are poems on their way? Celan answers, "Towards something open, something that can be inhabited [*Besetzbares*], towards a responsive you [*auf ein ansprechbares Du*], perhaps, towards a responsive reality" (Celan 2000, vol. 7, 186, my translation). The poet, having been wounded by language and reality, nonetheless, returns to language—to the poetic word—in search of a responsive You. A responsive You that in receiving the testimony of the poetic word takes a step toward the estranged I and in so doing contributes to the possibility of rebuilding together an inhabitable world for the wounded.

Notes

1. Russia's invasion of Ukraine is one such repetition of the same in which "never again" has, unfortunately, become "again and again and again . . ." See, for example, Snyder 2022.

2. All of Celan's poems from *Atemwende* are citations from Gadamer's text unless otherwise noted.

3. Even so, I in no way mean to rule out Gadamer's reading of Celan. Rather, my reading is *one* possible reading that, like Gadamer's, emerges from dwelling with Celan's poetry, and is, as Derrida puts it also "an ethics or a politics of reading" ("The Truth That Wounds," in Derrida 2005, 166).

4. That is, Gadamer's commentary on Celan's poems in this sequence seems to *overemphasize* attaining meaning only from the poems themselves and ignores or remains too silent vis-à-vis the historical context and hermeneutical fields of meaning that shaped the poems and the trace of that world (or better, world-shattering event) that remains with them.

5. In his 1990 essay "In the Shadow of Nihilism" Gadamer comments on Celan's choice to write his poetry in German and the struggle that that involved. Having introduced Celan as a "Jewish poet of German speaking origin [*jüdischer Dichter deutscher Zunge*]," who married a French woman (and who no doubt knew French), Gadamer points out as a "very peculiar fact" that Celan "wrote poetry almost exclusively in German." He goes on to say that "Celan was more deeply bound to the German linguistic homeland [*deutsche Sprachheimat*], which offered him no home [*die ihm keine Heimat bot*], than were those other poets who occasionally still dabbled in another language" (GW 9, 371, my translation).

6. Here I quote van der Heiden's translation of a passage from Celan's *Bremen Lecture*, in which he speaks of language as the "one thing" that remained amidst everything that has been lost. The full passage in German is as follows:

"*Erreichbar, nah und unverloren blieb inmitten der Verluste dies eine: die Sprache*" (Celan 2000, 185).

7. In the English translation cited in Gadamer's text, the German word *Krume* is translated into English as "soil." My reading employs a more literal translation of the German term *Krume* as "crumbs."

8. The term "word-splinters [*Wortsplitter*]" comes from Gadamer's essay, "In the Shadows of Nihilism." Discussing modern poetics, Gadamer writes: "What appears to be a word, as it were, shatters, and in its shattering into meaning-differentiated word splinters, evokes a new cohesion of meaning [*Etwas, was ein Wort scheint, zerspringt gleichsam und evoziert in seinem Zersprungensein in bedeutungsdifferente Wortsplitter eine neue Bedeutungseinheit*]" (GW 9, 372, my translation).

9. Culbertson cites a passage from Robert Antelme in which he recounts "linguistic alienation" (Culbertson's term) during the daily roll call at Dachau. See Culbertson 2019, 52–53.

10. For Gadamer's interpretation of the "hunger-candle," see Gadamer 1997, 76–77.

11. Gadamer points out that the first line of the published edition contains a mistake in that it translated "*der Himmelsmünze*" as "heaven's acid" instead of "heaven's coin" (Gadamer 1997, 79).

12. On the term "*weggebeizt*," Joris highlights another meaning that would have been quite familiar to Celan, given the artwork of his wife, Gisèle L'Estrange. "Besides the geological reference, the word *wegbeizen* also refers to the vocabulary of art, where acid is used to create patterns on metal. GCL. Used such techniques in her etchings" (Joris 2014, 473).

13. See also the explanatory footnote at the bottom of Gadamer 1997, 124.

14. For a detailed discussion of Gadamer's notion of *verweilen* and *die Weile*, see Nielsen 2023, 63–66.

15. In his article "Dialogical Memory and Immemorial Poetics" Blake goes further and emphasizes in a Lévinasian key an ethical imperative placed upon the reader of Holocaust literature. My notion of wounding in relation to Celan's poetry resonates with the ethical dimension that Blake explores.

16. Although my chapter thematizes the violent and propagandistic abuses of German language, which played a significant role in Celan's struggles with it, Celan's relationship with German language is complex, as German was the language through which he connected, in particular, with his mother in the shared reading of German fairy tales and the German classics. Celan was not willing to let go of German language; it remained to him as "unlost" amidst all the losses, including the loss of his mother. Perhaps his choice to continue writing poetry in German was a way that he could keep his memories of his mother close—on the one hand, an act of thankfulness for her insistence that he receive a traditional German-Austrian education and the fruit that it bore and, on the other, an act of resistance in not allowing German as he knew it prior to the catastrophe to be taken from him. For

an excellent discussion of Celan's complex relationship with German language—both the positives and negatives—and his wrestling with his "German-Jewish existence in Central Europe in the middle of the last century," see Bambach 2013, chap. 3. Felstiner (2001) likewise provides a rich account of Celan's poetry, his life as a German-Jew, his suffering vis-à-vis the Holocaust, and the role of his poetry and German language in his struggle to survive.

17. The German text reads: "*In dieser Sprache habe ich, in jenen Jahren und in den Jahren nachher, Gedichte zu schreiben versucht: um zu sprechen, um mich zu orientieren, um zu erkunden, wo ich mich befand und wohin es mit mir wollte, um mir Wirklichkeit zu entwerfen*" (Celan 2000, vol. 7, 186). That Celan uses *dieser* [this] to modify *Sprache* [language] suggests that he had a particular language in mind—namely, German.

18. Bruns offers an insightful reflection on how Celan, in contrast with a Heideggerian idea of language overtaking us, might think of language itself undergoing an event. As Bruns states, "language for Celan is something that can undergo an experience with history and be overwhelmed and transformed just in the sense that it can never go back to the way it was; it is always marked by the events it lives through. Celan helps to show the marks, and perhaps that is what poets are for in a destitute time" (Bruns 1997, 43). There is a certain overlap with my use of the term *wound* in this essay and what Bruns highlights here with respect to "marking" and "being marked."

19. See also Remington's discussion of the "relation between the merely memorial and the ethically immemorial"—the latter in the Lévinasian sense. Celan's poetry, Remington goes on to say, preserves the "excess of the Shoah" as "that which cannot be narrated, nor remembered," and hence cannot be reduced to the *merely* memorial. "If we read Celan's poetry as a gesture of commemoration of the dead, we must also acknowledge that Celan gives no relief to his readers. As Celan says, the poem 'searches' for and 'addresses' its Other in the hopes of an encounter. Such an encounter, as a shattering of the self, should offer no succor" (Remington 2021, 15).

Bibliography

Bambach, Charles. *Thinking the Poetic Measure of Justice. Hölderlin–Heidegger–Celan.* Albany: State University of New York Press, 2013.

Bruns, Gerald L. "The Remembrance of Language: An Introduction to Gadamer's Poetics." In *Gadamer on Celan: "Who Am I and Who Are You?" and Other Essays.* Edited by R. Heinemann and B. Krajewski, 1–51. Albany: SUNY Press, 1997.

Celan, Paul. "Appendix: The Meridian." In *Sovereignties in Question: The Poetics of Paul Celan.* Translated by J. Glenn. Edited by T. Dutoit and O. Pasanen, 173–85. New York: Fordham University Press, 2005.

———. *Gesammelte Werke.* 7 vols. Frankfurt a.M.: Suhrkamp, 2000.
Culbertson, Carolyn. *Words Underway. Continental Philosophy of Language.* New York: Rowman & Littlefield, 2019.
Derrida, Jacques. *Sovereignties in Question: The Poetics of Paul Celan.* Edited by T. Dutoit and O. Pasanen. New York: Fordham University Press, 2005.
Felstiner, John. *Paul Celan. Poet, Survivor, Jew.* New Haven: Yale University Press, 2001.
Gadamer, Hans-Georg. *Ästhetik und Poetik II: Hermeneutik im Vollzug. Gesammelte Werke. Vol. 9* [GW 9]. Tübingen: Mohr Siebeck, 1993.
———. *Gadamer on Celan: "Who Am I and Who Are You?" and Other Essays.* Edited by R. Heinemann and B. Krajewski. Albany: State University of New York Press, 1997.
Joris, Pierre. *Breathturn into Timestead: The Collected Later Poetry of Paul Celan.* New York: Farrar Straus Giroux, 2014.
Lloyd, David. "Breath Crystals. A Vestigial Poetics of Breath in Beckett, Celan, and Arikha." *Samuel Beckett Today/Aujourd'hui* 30 (2018): 179–95.
Nielsen, Cynthia R. *Gadamer's Hermeneutical Aesthetics. Art as a Performative, Dynamic, Communal Event.* New York: Routledge, 2023.
Remington, Blake. "Dialogical Memory and Immemorial Poetics: The Ethical Imperatives of Holocaust Literature." *Humanities* 10, 1 (2021): 42. [online] https://doi.org/10.3390/h10010042.
Snyder, Timothy. "We Should Say It: Russia Is Fascist." *New York Times* May 19, 2022. [online] https://www.nytimes.com/2022/05/19/opinion/russia-fascism-ukraine-putin.html.
Tate, Daniel L. "The Verge of Silence. Gadamer on Celan and the Poetic Word." *Research in Phenomenology* 49 (2019): 163–82.
van der Heiden, Gert-Jan. "Poem, Dialogue, and Witness: Gadamer's Reading of Celan." In *The Gadamerian Mind.* Edited by T. George and G.-J. van der Heiden, 318–32. New York: Routledge, 2022.
Wundheiler, Luitgard N. "Paul Celan, Poet of the Holocaust." *Worldview* (19 Dec 1976): 24–36.

List of Contributors

John Arthos is professor and director of the Rhetoric Program in the Department of English, and director of Public Oral Communication in the College of Liberal Arts and Sciences, at the Indiana University Bloomington. He authored the following books: *The Inner Word in Gadamer's Hermeneutics* (2009), *Speaking Hermeneutically: Understanding in the Conduct of a Life* (2011), and *Gadamer's Poetics: A Critique of Modern Aesthetics* (2013). His work concerns the relationship of hermeneutics and rhetoric, as the art of discourse in the broadest sense.

Alessandro Bertinetto is full professor of aesthetics at the University of Torino, where he also teaches philosophy of music. His research interests encompass German idealism, aesthetics, hermeneutics, philosophy of music, creativity, and improvisation. His recent publications include *Il pensiero dei suoni* (2012; French trans. *La pensée des sons. Introduction à la philosophie de la musique*, 2017), *Eseguire l'inatteso. Ontologia musicale e improvvisazione* (2016), *The Routledge Handbook of Philosophy and Improvisation in the Arts*, edited with Marcello Ruta (2021), and *Estetica dell'improvvisazione* (2021; Eng. trans. *Aesthetics of Improvisation*, 2022).

Georg W. Bertram is, since 2007, professor of theoretical philosophy with a focus on aesthetics and philosophy of language at Freie Universität Berlin. In 2004 he spent a research stay at the University of Pittsburgh (with John McDowell). He was visiting professor at the University of Wien, University of Torino, Roma Tre University, and IULM Milano. He authored, among others, the following books: *Hegels Phänomenologie des Geistes: Ein systematischer Kommentar* (2017), *Art as Human Practice: An Aesthetics* (2019), *Die Freiheit des Verstehens: Eine hermeneutisch-kritische Theorie* (2024).

List of Contributors

Mariannina Failla is full professor in history of philosophy at Roma Tre University. Her research fields include Kant's philosophy, historicism and hermeneutics, nineteenth-century German psychology (Wundt, Brentano), and Husserl's phenomenology. She published, among others, the following contributions: "The Unconscious in Husserl: Psychology, Sedimentation and Temporality. Historical and Theoretical Aspects" (in *Philosophy and Madness from Kant to Hegel and Beyond / Philosophie und Wahnsinn von Kant bis Hegel und darüber hinaus*, 2023); "Edenic Animality, Feeding, Loving, and Dying: Corporal Biological Needs as Natural Historical Community by Kant" (in *Kant on Emotions. Critical and Historical Essays*, 2022).

Jean Grondin is professor of philosophy at the University of Montréal. His books include *Introduction to Philosophical Hermeneutics* (1994), *The Philosophy of Hans-Georg Gadamer* (2002), *Hans-Georg Gadamer: A Biography* (2003), *Introduction to Metaphysics* (2004), *Paul Ricoeur* (2013), *La beauté de la métaphysique* (2019), *Comprendre Heidegger. L'espoir d'une autre compréhension de l'être* (2019), *L'esprit de l'éducation* (2022), and *Metaphysical Hermeneutics* (2024). He has also edited Gadamer's correspondence with Ricœur and Derrida and coedited his correspondence with Heidegger.

Stefano Marino is associate professor of aesthetics at the University of Bologna. He authored, among others, the following monographs: *Verità e non-verità del popular* (2021), *La filosofia dei Radiohead* (2021), *Le verità del non-vero* (2019), *Aesthetics, Metaphysics, Language* (2015), *La filosofia di Frank Zappa* (2014), *Gadamer and the Limits of the Modern Techno-Scientific Civilization* (2011). He has translated two books by Hans-Georg Gadamer and one book by Theodor W. Adorno from German into Italian, one book by Carolyn Korsmeyer and one book by Richard Shusterman from English into Italian.

Cynthia R. Nielsen is professor at the University of Dallas, where she teaches courses in the areas of hermeneutics, ethics, aesthetics, contemporary continental philosophy, and the history of philosophy. Her interest in hermeneutics applies to a broad range of topics, including aesthetics, animal studies, social and political (mis)uses of language (including disinformation and propaganda), war and trauma, and Ukrainian studies. Her most recent monograph is *Gadamer's Hermeneutical Aesthetics: On Art as a Performative, Dynamic, Communal, Event* (2022). She is currently working on a book entitled *Philosophical Reflections on War, Violence, and Responsibility: Listening to Ukrainian Voices* (forthcoming, 2025).

James Risser is currently emeritus professor of philosophy at Seattle University. His published works include *The Life of Understanding: A Contemporary Hermeneutics* (2012) and *Hermeneutics and the Voice of the Other: Re-reading Gadamer's Philosophical Hermeneutics* (SUNY Press, 1997). He is the editor of *Philosophy, Art, and the Imagination: Essays on the Work of John Sallis* (2022), *Heidegger toward the Turn: Essays on the Work of the 1930s* (SUNY Press, 1999), and coeditor with Walter Brogan of *American Continental Philosophy* (2002). He has served as coeditor of the journal *Research in Phenomenology* and has published widely in the area of contemporary continental philosophy.

Elena Romagnoli is junior assistant professor of aesthetics at the University of Pisa. After her PhD in 2020, she got two postdoctoral fellowships at the University of Freiburg i.B in 2021 and at the Freie University Berlin in 2022. She is the author of two monographs: *Oltre l'opera d'arte. L'estetica performativa di Gadamer tra idealismo e pragmatismo* (2023) and *Ermeneutica e decostruzione. Il dialogo ininterrotto tra Gadamer e Derrida* (2021). She also authored several contributions in collected books and international journals. Her main fields of research are German classical aesthetics, hermeneutics, pragmatism and, more recently, everyday aesthetics.

Gert-Jan van der Heiden is professor of metaphysics at Radboud University, Nijmegen. Among his publications are the monographs *Ontology after Ontotheology* (2014), *The Voice of Misery* (SUNY Press, 2020), and *Saint Paul and Contemporary European Philosophy* (2023). He coedited *The Gadamerian Mind* (2021) and is coeditor of the series *Studies in Contemporary Phenomenology* and of the *International Yearbook of Hermeneutics*.

Author Index

Adorno, Theodor Wiesengrund, 42, 101, 103
Aeropagite, Pseudo-Dionysius, 65–73
Aeschylus, 115
Archilochus, 115
Aristotle, 1, 43–44, 61, 64–66, 70, 79–80, 83, 111, 117, 120, 133, 180
Arnswald, Ulrich, 3
Arthos, John, 8
Augustine of Hippo, 65, 67, 69, 71

Bambach, Charles, 190
Banksy, 7
Baudrillard, Jean, 7
Beethoven, Ludwig van, 19
Benson, Bruce Ellis, 128, 134, 136
Benveniste, Emile, 117–118
Bertinetto, Alessandro, 8, 128, 132–136, 138–141
Bertram, Georg W., 8, 103, 135, 139, 150
Betti, Emilio, 132
Boehm, Karl, 19
Boethius, Severinus, 69
Bruns, Gerald L., 44
Büchner, Georg, 198

Campo, Heymericus de, 66
Caputo, John D., 148
Cassirer, Ernst, 28
Cattaneo, Francesco, 3
Celan, Paul, 7, 156, 159, 170, 181, 187–200
Cézanne, Paul, 118
Champaigne, Philippe de, 21
Chang, Ting-Kuo, 43
Cherniss, Harold, 19
Chiurazzi, Gaetano, 3
Coltrane, John, 136
Culbertson, Carolyn, 199
Cusa, Nicholas of, 62–63, 65–72

Danto, Arthur C., 7
Dastur, Françoise, 81
Davis, Miles, 136
Democritus, 117
Dewey, John, 50
Di Cesare, Donatella, 5, 40–41, 148, 151, 161
Dostal, Robert, 3
Dottori, Riccardo, 36
Dutt, Carsten, 7–8

Einstein, Albert, 20

The editors gratefully acknowledge Dr. Olmo Nicoletti for his help in preparing the Index.

Author Index

Eisenstaed, Alfred, 20

Failla, Mariannina 3, 8
Fehér, István M., 3
Feige, Daniel Martin, 129, 134
Ferrari, Emanuele, 129
Ferraris, Maurizio, 4, 38, 40–41
Ficino, Marsilio, 65, 67
Figal, Günter, 3, 42, 45, 155, 160
Fink, Eugen, 115
Fischer-Lichte, Erika, 148
Flyte, Sebastian, 78
Foucault, Michel, 5
Friedländer, Paul, 1, 44
Fruchon, Pierre, 14
Furtwängler, Wilhelm, 19

Gadamer, Hans-Georg, 1 *et passim*
Gardini, Michele, 3
Gehlen, Arnold, 7
George, Stefan, 116–117
George, Theodore, 7
Georgiades, Thrasybulos, 115–116
Gibson, John, 133
Gioia, Ted, 129
Goodman, Nelson, 106
Grondin, Jean, 1–4, 8, 37, 39, 43–44, 48, 62, 147

Habermas, Jürgen, 5, 38, 148
Hahn, Lewis E., 1, 3
Hance, Allen, 46
Hegel, Georg Wilhelm Friedrich, 41, 71–72, 80, 87, 95–96, 104–106
Heidegger, Martin, 1, 5, 14, 35–36, 41–43, 62, 73, 77–88, 104, 107, 115–117, 120, 168–169, 171, 176–177
Hirsch, Eric, 132
Hofer, Michael, 3
Hölderlin, Friedrich, 113, 168, 198
Hoy, David C., 132–133

Hülk, Walburga, 148

Jaeger, Werner, 115–116
Joris, Pierre, 188, 191, 195

Kant, Immanuel, 34–35, 48, 96, 100, 133
Karajan, Herbert von, 19
Kertscher, Jens, 3
Kierkegaard, Søren, 24, 87, 106
Krajewski, Bruce, 3
Krämer, Stephan, 19, 26

Lloyd, David, 196

Maldiney, Henri, 118
Malpas, Jeff, 3
Marino, Stefano, 3, 8, 36
Marshall, Donald G., 14
Matteucci, Giovanni, 3, 35–36
McCullers, Carson, 20
McDowell, John, 93
Moliére, 20

Natorp, Paul, 19, 26
Nielsen, Cynthia, 7–8, 149, 156
Nietzsche, Friedrich W., 25, 40–41, 62
Novalis, 78–79
Nowicki, Alexis, 78

Palmer, Richard, 36
Pareyson, Luigi, 3, 128–143
Picasso, Pablo, 20
Pico della Mirandola, 67
Plato, 1–2, 19, 26, 37, 41, 44, 61–65, 68, 114, 116–117, 128, 131, 153, 180
Plotinus, 67, 70
Pöggeler, Otto, 83
Pythagoras, 66

Ricoeur, Paul, 3, 82, 173

Rilke, Reiner Maria, 62–63, 156, 198
Risser, James, 8, 10, 44, 14, 149, 158, 171
Romagnoli, Elena, 8, 50, 148
Rorty, Richard, 147
Ruta, Marcello, 148

Schleiermacher, Friedrich, 78
Schmidt, Dennis J., 3
Schmidt, Lawrewnce K., 3
Silverman, Hugh J., 3
Simmel, Georg, 6
Sokolowski, Robert, 37
Solti, Georg, 19
Stolzenberg, Jürgen, 43
Svendsen, Lars, 6

Tate, Daniel, 6, 177, 190

Thierry of Chartres, 69

Valéry, Paul, 168–169
Valgenti, Robert, 141
van der Heiden, Gert-Jan, 7–8, 174, 191
Vattimo, Gianni, 2–3, 14, 40, 54

Wachterhauser, Brice R., 3
Waugh, Evelyn, 78
Weber, Max, 62
Weinsheimer, Joel, 14
Wischke, Mirko, 3
Wordsworth, William, 79
Wright, Kathleen, 3
Wundheiler, Luitgard N., 190, 198–199

Zabala, Santiago, 3, 162

www.ingramcontent.com/pod-product-compliance
Ingram Content Group UK Ltd.
Pitfield, Milton Keynes, MK11 3LW, UK
UKHW042001140426
5217IPUK00015B/910